The American Political Pattern

STUDIES IN GOVERNMENT
AND PUBLIC POLICY

The American Political Pattern

Stability and Change, 1932–2016

Byron E. Shafer

 University Press of Kansas

Published by the University Press of Kansas (Lawrence, Kansas 66045),
which was organized by the Kansas Board of Regents and is operated and
funded by Emporia State University, Fort Hays State University, Kansas State
University, Pittsburg State University, the University of Kansas, and Wichita
State University

Library of Congress Cataloging-in-Publication Data
Names: Shafer, Byron E., author.
Title: The American political pattern : stability and change, 1932–2016 /
   Byron E. Shafer.
Description: Lawrence : University Press of Kansas, 2016. | Series: Studies in
   government and public policy | Includes bibliographical references and
   index.
Identifiers: LCCN 2016026156| ISBN 9780700623266 (hardback :
   acid-free) | ISBN 9780700623273 (paperback : acid-free) |
   ISBN 9780700623280 (ebook)
Subjects: LCSH: United States—Politics and government—1933–1945. |
   United States—Politics and government—1945–1989. | United States—
   Politics and government—1989– | Political culture—United States. |
   BISAC: POLITICAL SCIENCE / Government / General. | POLITICAL
   SCIENCE / Political Process / Political Parties. | POLITICAL SCIENCE /
   Political Ideologies / Democracy.
Classification: LCC JK271 .S4429 2016 | DDC 320.973–dc23
LC record available at https://lccn.loc.gov/2016026156.

British Library Cataloguing-in-Publication Data is available.

Printed in the United States of America

10 9 8 7 6 5 4 3 2 1

The paper used in this publication is recycled and contains 30 percent
postconsumer waste. It is acid free and meets the minimum requirements
of the American National Standard for Permanence of Paper for Printed
Library Materials Z39.48-1992.

Unremember changes.
—Act 1, Scene 1, George Orwell's *Nineteen Eighty-Four*
Adaptation by Adam White, Lookingglass Theatre Company

For
Richard F. Fenno Jr.
Charles O. Jones
and
David R. Mayhew

Contents

Preface: An American Political Pattern?

The popular complaint about current American politics is everywhere. Politicians are polarized. Public opinion is volatile. Government is gridlocked. Journalists then add their usual bias to this contemporary complaint. What is happening in our time has never been seen before. And it is, of course, the shape of politics for all time to come. Yet no one feels compelled even to try to tell you where the modern world came from, what causes it to hang around, and, by extension, what might cause it to go. Those are the concerns that motivate this volume.

To get at them, we need a picture of the overarching structure of American politics at diverse points in time. We need a small set of key elements that repeatedly structure this politics. We need an extended period in which these key elements can interact, ideally in differing ways. And we need a process of policy-making that emerges from this interaction, a diagnostic process that can be compared—that itself evolves—across time. At any given point, the result contributes to the big picture in American politics. Across time, it tells a story of political stability and, especially, political change. Without these pictures, we cannot know where we are.

Any such picture relies heavily on previous research on American politics as it has itself evolved during the long period in question. This is the evidence that has to be organized in order to talk intelligently about where the contemporary world came from and what sustains it. So a set of concepts that organizes a search for the big picture must simultaneously organize this evidence, putting it into a relationship of greater and lesser generality and power. All political phenomena are not created equal, and even the most careful research cannot make it so. Some phenomena are epiphenomena of others. Too much political research proceeds in implicit ignorance of that fact.

To cut directly to the chase: a framework that can allow the ongoing structure of American politics to emerge, both at a given point and across time, depends on a small set of organizing concepts capable of isolating this structure. These concepts need to lead directly to—they need effectively to constitute—the main *intermediary* influences on that politics. Organizing concepts do not have to be the ultimate explanation for its outcomes. Many other factors will contribute to that; we shall attend to some of these explicitly in the concluding chapter. Yet organizing concepts do need to be powerful influences on the policy-making process that characterizes an extended political period. In that sense, they really do need to serve as the major *proximate* influences on politics.

That is the initial justification for using three key concepts to organize the analysis that follows, even as their ultimate justification has to lie in the interpretive results that proceeding in this way can contribute. In any case, the three major aspects of politics that will organize the search here are *party balance*, the comparative standing of the two major parties in American society; *ideological polarization*, the programmatic distance between the main contending forces in that politics; and *substantive conflict*, the policy content of what is at stake in each successive period. Specifying these moving pieces is the first step in moving from familiar but unsystematic complaints about the contemporary world to a systematic analysis that leads up to and sustains this world in the fashion in which it actually works. In effect, the interaction of these pieces *is* the intermediary structure of American politics.

The payoff from this framework then derives from the relationship among its key moving pieces as they come together to create a *policy-making process* peculiar to an extended period. At bottom, it is this policy process—not election results—that must demarcate political eras, the periods when politics exhibits the stable operating pattern contributed by the interaction of our three key elements. The fact that many analyses of American politics proceed in ignorance of the interplay between political structure and policy-making does not make this separation any more sensible: an ostensible political structure needs to be reflected in actual policy-making, else how consequential can it be?

That said, the intermediary structure of politics that is producing a distinctive process of policy-making ought to be (and reliably is) reflected in a diagnostic pattern of election outcomes. Each political era has its associated electoral dynamic. Indeed, a change in the nature of election outcomes is what sets off the hunt for a different intermediary structure to politics. Electoral results and political structures thus work back and forth to produce a policy-making process in the real world of American politics. They must work back and forth in the analysis of that politics as well.

Three key concepts are already a modest form of generalization about the politics of their time, being summary devices for its specifics. Said the other way around, they provide a way to organize presentation of the specifics of politics and politicking at a point in time, while adding interpretive power to this historical presentation. Yet if the challenges inherent in applying these concepts to each successive period can be met—if each of the policy-making processes that define a political era and produce its diagnostic electoral outcome can be teased out through them—they also provide a way to see the larger context to politics within its period.

So the inescapable organizing question has to be: What has been the relationship among party balance, ideological polarization, and substantive conflict at any given point in time? These three grand concepts are related in one distinctive way at the current moment, and chapter 4 will deconstruct this arrangement forcefully. Yet those concepts have not always been related in this way, and that is the other essential virtue of proceeding by way of them. This is to say: there is hope that attention to the evolution of three big moving pieces will pay intellectual dividends by unmasking some major underlying dynamics, the effective dynamics of political change.

For that to happen, we also need an extended period of time, a temporal stretch in which three major aspects of politics can be observed. This period must be sufficiently long to allow these basic building blocks of American politics to interact in differing ways. It must not be so long that the social and organizational backdrops to their operation are no longer conceivably comparable. The obvious candidate—long enough to allow substantial change, not so long as to take us back to an unrecognizable world—comes from the eighty-plus years since the New Deal.

The great challenge, then, is two-sided. It must isolate extended periods when politics can be said to have operated in a roughly stable fashion, a fashion allowing the further isolation of a small set of major factors contributing to this stability, while at the same time leaving room for the gradual cumulation of alternative influences that would eventually destroy this stability and bring on a new period, a period achieving a fresh stability built around a different mix of these major factors and a different set of influences on them. If the modern world of American politics begins in 1932, then a focus on its three main moving pieces cuts this modern world more or less insistently into four lesser periods, four distinguishable eras when our organizing concepts interacted in differing ways to produce distinctive processes of policy-making:

;h New Deal Era, 1932–1938
e New Deal Era, 1939–1968
ι of Divided Government, 1969–1992
The Era of Partisan Volatility, 1993–2016

The resulting analysis is further challenged, but also saved, by the obvious fact that all such periods eventually come to an end. Something causes one or more of the big-three moving pieces to change in ways that affect their collective relationship, leading the policy-making process as a whole to shift. In hindsight, this shift usually looks abrupt, and sometimes its driving cause is abrupt too. The clearest example arrives in the opening chapter, when the stock market crash of 1929 brings on the Great Depression, and economic catastrophe leads to a major change in party balance for the nation as a whole. More often, however, while the shift can be every bit as neatly demarcated, its main causal elements must be seen, again in hindsight, to have been building for some time. The clearest example is the process by which an older organizational form of American political parties, dominant when the Great Depression arrived, began to change in ways that achieved their full impact on ideological polarization only much later, in the contemporary period.

The four periods do generate their own peculiar challenges, each in turn, when the focus is isolating a collective relationship among three of the major moving parts to American politics and the policy-making process that follows from them. Such a relationship needs to be specific to its period and not characteristic of either its predecessor or its successor. On the other hand, by demanding a template for this enterprise that is comparative across eras, the search for this collective relationship does provide a way to proceed. Analyses of all four periods will thus unfold in precisely the same order in each historical chapter: party balance, ideological polarization, and substantive conflict, leading to a distinctive (and distinguishing) process of policy-making.

Those periods go a long way toward determining the organization of what follows. Chapter 1 opens with, and elaborates upon, the High New Deal. Chapter 2 considers the far longer but strikingly different Late New Deal. Chapter 3 moves to the Era of Divided Government, so familiar in its aftermath but so initially unsettling when viewed through the lens of previous periods. Chapter 4 addresses the current period, the Era of Partisan Volatility: this is the period that sparked the entire venture. And a concluding chapter circles back to ask how the key elements of all these periods related *across time,* while attending to some further, major, missing pieces of the story.

The book itself was impelled by a number of critical events. It began life as one of six papers for the opening plenary panel at the Policy History Conference of 2014. The six of us who cut American history into periods and applied the three organizing concerns were Michael Holt of the University of Virginia and Daniel Walker Howe of UCLA for the early period, Gareth Davies of Oxford University and Richard John of Columbia University for the middle period, and Sidney Milkis of the University of Virginia plus me—Byron Shafer of the University of Wisconsin—for the modern period. Chuck Myers of the University Press of Kansas attended that session and afterward convinced his colleague Fred Woodward to read the extended paper that lay behind my personal presentation. Jointly, those gentlemen argued that a long essay should become a short book, and that was clearly the turning point in its development. One of the virtues of working with them has been that they have been willing—unafraid—to comment and advise along the way, in effect to serve as additional readers. In my experience, there are few such genuine editors left.

They might not have succeeded, even then, if their arguments had not meshed with two intellectual frustrations of my own. In one, Richard F. Fenno Jr. was the first person that I recall describing the current study of American politics as "more and more about less and less." Translation: even good analysis still needs some larger framework that organizes major versus lesser influences on its political process. Without it, we cannot know that otherwise well-developed and richly supported explanations of how the world works are not a simple epiphenomenon of some larger context.

In the other implicit stimulus, I grow increasingly frustrated by students, and now even colleagues, who have no idea where their own contemporary work should be located intellectually. Not knowing that, they too cannot know that the same otherwise solid arguments about how the world works are not a simple reflection of prior forces that brought them into being. In particular here, most generalizations about politics need to be specified with regard to points in time because these are the point(s) when the overall structure within which they reside—their larger context—allowed them to seem "general."

In any case, the next iteration of the initial essay served as the basis for an Inaugural Lecture at Oxford University, where I had the opportunity to be John G. Winant Visiting Professor of American Government in Hilary and Trinity Terms of 2015. The lecture drew a large and ever so slightly rambunctious crowd. Especially influential were three questions asked afterward by Lawrence Jacobs of the Humphrey School of Public Policy at the University of Minnesota, John Muellbauer of Nuffield College at Oxford, and Carol Sanger of the School of Law at Columbia University. Unlike me, they will no longer remember their questions, so they must be absolved of what resulted.

The Winant Professorship was also what really allowed a long essay to become a short book. Nigel Bowles, Director of the Rothermere American Institute, surely had the largest single input to this evolving manuscript by way of a continued conversation—in private but also in public seminars and lectures—about the changing structure of American politics. Jane Rawson, Head Librarian of the Harmsworth Library, facilitated secondary research in a fashion little short of remarkable. And Gareth Davies, Professor of American History, joined Nigel in giving the manuscript a thorough and serious—aka "tough"—reading, prodding me to rethink numerous aspects.

Along the way, this manuscript was actively and reliably supported by my regular research assistant, Regina Wagner, who even made the transatlantic trek at one point to move the project forward. She was joined during the summer of 2015 by new members of the research team: graduate students Emma Frankham and Alexander Alduncin, plus undergraduate research apprentice Negassi Tesfamichael. These latter were responsible, respectively, for legislative histories, ideological ratings, and voting records, all of which remain integral to the final product. All managed to respond graciously to requests for further information, a different form of presentation, or an entirely new avenue of data collection. Elizabeth Sawyer, another graduate student, completed the index, after some initial work by Negassi.

While still in England, I benefited as I always do from a couple of extended conversations with Alan Ware, now retired from Oxford, about changing political structures generally. After my return to the United States, Paul Quirk at the University of British Columbia was willing to be poked, prodded, and queried about various generic concerns for policy-making. Two referees for the University Press of Kansas, David R. Mayhew of Yale University and Jeffrey M. Stonecash of Syracuse University, then did the kind of detailed dissection of a manuscript that will either kill or cure its author. They have allowed me to thank them by name, though I wager that anyone who read those comments could name them anyway.

And all along the way, in the beginning and at the end, Charles O. Jones of the University of Virginia constantly reinforced the original argument from my Kansas editors, about what I really ought to write and how I should write it. I do not know when he began doing this kind of thing for me, but it was well under way by the time we worked together on the national party conventions in the early 1980s.

Those late comments from Dave Mayhew do not begin to capture his contribution to my education. I do know that this began all the way back when I first read the book that had been his doctoral dissertation, well before the man himself came to serve as my model of what a knowledgeable student of American politics should know. You have to ask yourself how someone with those two remarkable advisers, Jones and Mayhew, could still manage to get things wrong.

Dick Fenno of the University of Rochester somehow escaped having to comment on this one, but he has provided so much advice for so many years that he ought to be thanked (or is that blamed?) anyway. The opportunity—nay, responsibility—to return to his book *The Power of the Purse* in order to pursue this project would almost have been enough, by itself, to sustain me in its pursuit.

Those three people know that there needs to be no tension between stiff intellectual standards, professional collegiality, and personal friendship. It gives me great pleasure to dedicate this one to them.

The American Political Pattern

1 | Birth Pangs of the Modern World

The Political Structure of the High New Deal Era, 1932–1938

Party balance: *a tectonic shift from a large and established Republican majority to an even larger Democratic advantage;* **ideological polarization:** *minimally polarized electoral politics but a hugely polarizing institutional conflict between presidency and Court;* **substantive conflict:** *a world centered on issues of economic welfare, at every point and in every institution;* **policy-making process:** *essentially presidential, to an unprecedented degree.*

The modern world of American politics—the long period from 1932 to the present—began with one of the biggest shifts of party balance in all of American history. In what became recognized as the High New Deal Era, a substantial, reliable, and recurrent Republican majority that had been in place for thirty-plus years gave way to a huge Democratic majority, one that would be in place for thirty-plus years thereafter. No one in its time could have been sure that this was a lasting change in public attachments, rather than a simple vote of no confidence in the party that had been in power when the Great Depression hit—though Democrats did hope and Republicans did fear. Eighty years later, while there are still interpretive issues that demand attention, the ultimate scope of this particular shift in party balance seems inescapable.[1]

The presidential election of 1928 had appeared to confirm an ongoing, reliable, and substantial Republican majority for the nation as a whole. First registered in its continuing form at the presidential election of 1896, this majority had been rattled by internal divisions in the years immediately before the First World War, before settling back in a dominating—indeed, a blanketing—fashion as the war drew to a close. The presidential election of 1932 then represented the greatest *shift* in partisan outcomes at the national level since the modern party system,

Democrats versus Republicans, had been stabilized in the aftermath of the Civil War. What could not have been known in its time was whether this shift should be regarded as deep-seated and potentially lasting or as idiosyncratic to particular personalities, to a single contest, or, especially, to dramatic events of the day.

Republicans would continue to make some version of the idiosyncrasy argument for a very long time. With hindsight, however, analysts have overwhelmingly agreed on a huge change of partisan balance, Republican to Democratic. Scholars did continue to argue about its dynamics, pitting those who emphasized actual shifts in party attachment against those who favored differential mobilization of those previously disengaged from the major parties.[2] Of late, scholars have also argued about *when* this new and sharply different party balance should be proclaimed, pitting those who regarded the 1932 election as pivotal against those who argued for an extended period in which the products of this election—new partisan incumbents but especially new policy programs—were gradually institutionalized.[3]

Abstractly, it is not hard to think of policy responses to the partisan outcome of the 1932 election that might not have led to a new party balance for the nation as a whole. Because these remain conditions contrary to fact, it is not obvious that an ambitious incoming administration would not have self-corrected in response to programs that were failing to institutionalize its new partisan potential. Nevertheless, in campaigning to become the initial vehicle for this change, Franklin Roosevelt had sometimes sounded as if he might try to "out-Hoover" incumbent president Herbert Hoover by raising taxes, cutting spending, and balancing the budget. Had Roosevelt actually hewed to that line—he did take some early actions consistent with it—the 1932 vote might have stood as a simple vote of no confidence, to be followed by another such vote in response to essentially the same Hooverite program.

Alternatively, Roosevelt might in principle have settled on an aggressive program whose policies proved more or less clearly and in short order not to work. To accomplish this, the president would presumably have had to dilute those aspects of the New Deal that are most often saluted by economists after the fact: rescuing the banking system, inflating the currency, and, in a development actively opposed by Franklin Roosevelt, settling substantial cash bonuses on millions of veterans. In their place, he would have had to elaborate those aspects of the program that have always drawn a more skeptical professional judgment, perhaps by further augmenting the National Recovery Administration and its aspiringly comprehensive regulatory codes, as some critics within his own party certainly preferred.[4]

Once more, even under these alternatively extreme conditions, ambition coupled with duty might well have caused the Roosevelt administration to self-correct, so that the electoral upheaval of 1932 still became a new and lasting party balance. Either way, the remainder of the High New Deal Era was to confirm, less grandly but more explicitly and directly, that the general public was fully capable of adjusting its voting behavior to take account of policy outcomes and to pass judgment on them. Thus the presidential election of 1936 would confirm that the general public could pass a solid positive judgment on the policy products of the overall New Deal, just as the midterm election of 1938 would confirm that this public could pass equally negative judgments when it felt that the program was not producing.

Accordingly, despite alternative abstract possibilities and despite actual concrete disputes among professional experts about the precise dynamics that made the election of 1932 pivotal in terms of *party balance* in the United States, most of the disputants, both active partisans and professional analysts, appear prepared to accept three overall summary judgments about the arrival of a new balance in American society after 1932:

- While scholars might continue to debate the precise point at which a new majority could be said to have been institutionalized, that is, converted into a majority of Americans who would reliably call themselves Democrats rather than Republicans, it would be hard to find any voices ready to argue that the Republicans were as strong in the thirty years after 1932 as they had been in the thirty years before, and/or that the Democrats remained as weak. A serious party rebalancing did follow in the wake of the 1932 presidential election.
- At the same time, it was events of the day rather than previously established party programs that propelled this huge partisan change. John W. Davis had offered a Democratic policy program in the presidential campaign of 1924, Alfred E. Smith had offered another in the campaign of 1928, and Franklin D. Roosevelt offered a third, however ambiguous, in the presidential campaign of 1932. Yet it would be hard to find a serious voice wanting to argue

that the promised programs of Davis, of Smith, of Roosevelt, or of all three together, were what propelled this underlying partisan change, rather than public demands for a policy response to the Great Depression.

- Finally, most analysts, opponents as well as supporters of the resulting programmatic response, are prepared to accept that it was indeed the collection of policies gathered as Franklin Roosevelt's "New Deal for the American people" that ultimately confirmed a new partisan majority in the nation as a whole. That program reached broadly across American society and deeply within it. Many of its key planks—unemployment insurance, a public retirement system—remain core elements of American public policy eighty years later.

On the other hand, the overall composition of that program and the specifics of its individual pieces were still powerfully shaped by the structure of American politics in the High New Deal Era, especially by its degree of ideological polarization, by the substantive content of its legislative conflicts, and by the nature of the policy-making process that resulted.[5] Initially, then, it is necessary to ask: How was this new party balance related to *ideological polarization*? Or, said the other way around: What level of ideological polarization infused this new party balance, and just how did it do so? Yet more than in any successor period, it is necessary to go on and ask whether during the High New Deal Era these partisan attachments captured the operative ideological polarization of its time. And there, uniquely to the High New Deal, the answer was no.

Why were the appropriate answers not as straightforward as they might abstractly seem in this opening era of modern American politics? Partly, this was because the separation of powers as a grand institutional framework always provides several different places where ideological polarization can be registered. Thus the presidency, Congress, and, in this case especially, the Supreme Court are all potentially available to reflect the operative scale of polarization. Crucially, then, answers became additionally complicated during the High New Deal because these available theaters for generating and registering polarization were to produce such different results. With the presidency, polarization was potential but nascent. With Congress, polarization was effectively absent. Yet with the Court, thanks to the separation of powers, it was intense.

The choice embodied in the presidential contest between incumbent Republican Herbert Hoover, the president seeking reelection, and challenging Democrat Franklin Roosevelt, the governor of New York, was clear enough on one level: staying the course with Hoover or opting for change with Roosevelt. Yet the ideological implications of that choice were less obvious than they would come to seem after the fact. Hoover, after all, rose to national prominence for his leadership in international humanitarian relief; he was from the Progressive rather than the Old Guard wing of the Republican Party; and he had not shied away from major actions to address the Great Depression governmentally. Roosevelt too was out of the Progressive wing of his party, the Democrats, and while he had taken some actions in New York that could with hindsight be argued to prefigure parts of what became the New Deal, he was not the candidate of those who dreamed of extensive and systematic governmental intervention in the market economy.

Moreover, Roosevelt spoke forcefully and repeatedly about the need to restore fiscal responsibility and reduce the national deficit. While he would jettison that goal as the New Deal evolved, it was still noticeable within his first collective set of policy moves. The programmatic uncertainty inherent in these candidate differences in their time was marvelously captured by Marriner S. Eccles, who would become Roosevelt's chairman of the Federal Reserve Board, when he cracked, "Given later developments, the campaign speeches often read like a giant misprint, in which Roosevelt and Hoover speak each other's lines."[6] Yet at bottom, what was at issue here was very different but equally simple. Roosevelt was running a classic referendum-type campaign: if you like the current state of the nation, vote for them; if you do not, vote for us.

Roosevelt would move a long way, both programmatically and rhetorically, by the time of his reelection campaign in 1936. By then, major pieces of what would come to be recognized as the New Deal had been passed by Congress and signed by the president, while Roosevelt was sharpening new class-based themes, attempting to draw a line between the general public and his "malefactors of great wealth." Yet his opponent, Alfred M. "Alf" Landon, Republican governor of Kansas, would again be from the Progressive rather than the Old Guard side of the Republican Party, and Landon was willing to go so far as to state his support publicly for some major aspects of the New Deal program. Moreover, Roosevelt, like many other presidents seeking reelection, was centrally concerned with framing the choice as between the situation when he came into office and the situation that obtained as he was running for reelection—another (a second) variant of the referendum argument.

So the difference between the two parties as embodied in their presidential campaigns was in the process of clarifying. But that was probably all that should be said about ideological polarization when observed through this presidential lens: clarifying but not yet indisputable. At the same time, the level of ideological polarization when observed through the other nationally elective institution of American government, through Congress, was clear. At the level of individual partisan candidacies for Congress, each of the parties retained a great deal of factional diversity, the elements of which did not align the two parties neatly against each other. Thus the Republicans still featured a long-standing tension between Progressives and the Old Guard, while Democrats featured an even more complex tension among Progressives, Southern Democrats, and a growing body of urban, working-class, labor-oriented constituencies that would come to be defined as liberals by the very process of framing the New Deal.[7]

Yet the critical point here was that legislative politics in an operative sense was only minimally polarized. Or rather, to put the same point more succinctly, legislative politics was effectively *unipolar*. To begin with, the overall Democratic margin in Congress was overwhelming. A party that had held only 37 percent of the seats in the House and 41 percent of the seats in the Senate in 1928, held 72 percent of seats in the House and 60 percent of seats in the Senate by 1932—and those numbers were to go up again in each of the next two elections, to a remarkable 77 percent in the House and 79 percent in the Senate by 1936 (figures 1.1 and 1.2).[8] The Republicans might well be, as they were, split between Progressive and Old Guard factions, but the bedrock fact was that neither was of a size to matter. And just to make matters worse from the perspective of an organized opposition, Progressive Republicans were actually attracted to major aspects of the New Deal.

Even more to the practical point, the two succeeding elections of 1934 and 1936 were to be the only ones in American history in which Northern Democrats constituted a majority of the House of Representatives all by themselves (figure 1.1). Northern Democrats in the Senate would require one further election to get to the same exalted status, arriving there only in 1936. But when they did, they were worth a full 54 percent of the Senate, again all by themselves (figure 1.2). In turn, Southern Democrats, the leading dissident faction within the Demo-

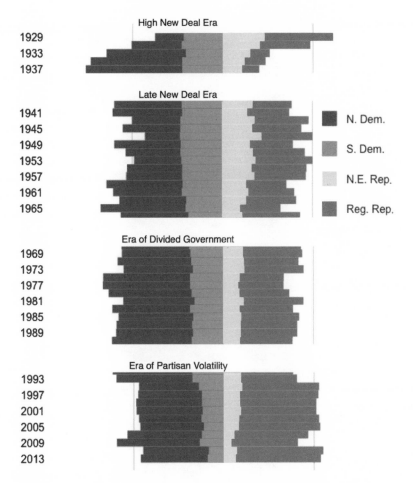

Figure 1.1. Factional Composition of the Two Parties in the
House, 1929–2014

cratic Party as the High New Deal Era began, rivaled the whole Republican Party on the numbers in 1934, before actually surpassing it in 1936. Yet Northern Democrats did not in some sense need these Southern Democrats either.

Those numbers go a long way toward explaining why the policy-making process that came to characterize the High New Deal Era was preponderantly presidential. To wit: Roosevelt was the leader of the Northern Democrats; Northern Democrats were an effective majority of Congress; party unity was never easier than when an established

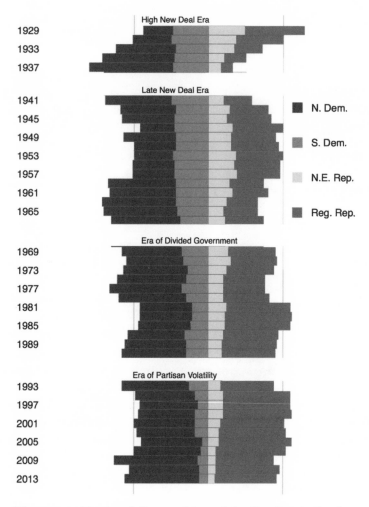

Figure 1.2. Factional Composition of the Two Parties in the Senate, 1929–2014

factional bloc could in principle act alone. For a time, then, there was not only little reason to pay attention to what the other party was doing. There was minimal reason to worry about the rest of your own party if you were President Franklin Roosevelt. Moreover, the 1934 election was the first one since the Civil War in which the party in power (that is, the party of the president) actually managed to gain seats at the midterm. That feat would not be repeated until the midterm of 1962 in the Senate and the midterm of 1998 in the House, in two succeeding electoral eras, each structured very differently.

On the other hand—and this is the key point here—the real operative polarization of the time was neither between nor within the political parties, whether observed through the presidency or by way of Congress. Instead, major operative polarization was between *institutions,* between a president attempting to introduce policies consistent with a new partisan era and a Supreme Court attempting to sustain policies consistent with an old one:

- From one side, Roosevelt as president was bringing forth that huge array of far-reaching programs that collectively constituted his New Deal. In the process, he was doing nothing less than introducing a governmental role in managing the economy and in providing social welfare that was different in kind from what went before it.
- From the other side, the Supreme Court was doing nothing more than what it had long done. It was checking to be sure that presidential programs were congruent with the Constitution of the United States. Yet it was finding that major elements within them were not, and it was perforce ruling these to be nugatory, that is, null and void.

Judged narrowly, this institutional polarization, dramatic as it was, was not strictly a reflection of partisanship.[9] Roosevelt's displeasure with the Court as an institution would be augmented by the fact that he acquired no Court nominations during his entire first term as president, where Warren Harding had gotten four and Herbert Hoover had gotten three. Yet the associated partisanship of the nine justices sitting when Roosevelt took office revealed nearly nothing about their response to his New Deal. Thus the two justices still on the Court who had been appointed by a Democratic president split reliably on New Deal cases. So did the two partisan Democrats on the Court who had been appointed by Republican presidents. Indeed, it was two of the three justices appointed by Herbert Hoover who were to be responsible for saving the New Deal when the ultimate showdown arrived.

All of that was, however, largely beside the point when the question was the relationship between party balance, ideological polarization, and substantive conflict. For the evolving partisan implications of a gathering conflict between the presidency and the Court were huge, as was the eventual policy impact of any ultimate resolution to this conflict. And it was these implications that embodied the real ideological polarization of their era. In effect, an institution embodying the ideological preferences of a new party majority was being stopped by an institution embodying the ideological preferences of an old party majority instead. Which is to say: quite apart from the explicit partisanship of the presidents appointing them or the nominal partisanship of the justices being appointed, an institution reflecting the policy preferences of the long predecessor era, when there had been a large Republican advantage in party balance, was stymieing what would become the policy preferences of the long successor era, when there was an even larger Democratic advantage.

What were they fighting about? That is, what was the *substance of policy conflict* during the High New Deal Era? The answer was overwhelmingly confined to one central policy realm, namely, domestic issues of economics and social welfare. These were close to the complete substance of the New Deal programs brought forward by President Roosevelt, with the lead exception being his contributions to repealing Prohibition. They were likewise close to all of the policy substance for the programs causing concern to the Supreme Court. (The repeal of Prohibition was not worth so much as a nod from the Court.) No subsequent political era would be anywhere near as uncomplicated, in the sense of being so unidimensional in its substantive focus.

There was a tiny hint at the very beginning of the Roosevelt administration that some international concerns—issues of foreign policy—might be added to this mix, though even these were economic welfare concerns in their essence. Thus Roosevelt did allow Cordell Hull, his secretary of state, to attend the World Economic Conference in London in June 1933, convened to consider coordination of a response to the Great Depression by the major developed nations. Yet he followed up by torpedoing that conference explicitly, and thereafter both his and the Court's agenda consisted reliably and overwhelmingly of domestic welfare matters.[10]

Moreover, the *policy-making process* associated with this unidimensional agenda was equally uncomplicated—effectively monolithic but for a small set of recognizable exceptions. In essence, the framing of public policy on economics and social welfare was an overwhelmingly presidential matter from start to finish. It was principally the president who dictated the items on which this policy-making process would focus. It was principally the president who determined the specifics of the policy that would bring these items to legislative life. It was principally the president who, with occasional exceptions, determined even the *order* in which Congress would address these specifics. No successor period would come close to being as presidentially dominated as that of the High New Deal.

The opening legislative product of the entire New Deal program, the Emergency Banking Act of 1933, would telegraph this presidential dominance in a symbolically remarkable fashion.[11] On the day after his inauguration, Roosevelt called Congress into special session. While it was assembling, his first official act as president was to declare a nationwide "bank holiday" in the face of cascading bank failures across the country. The curious basis for his authority to do so was the Trading with the Enemy Act of 1917, yet none of the other potentially major players objected. When Congress assembled, it found that its first item of business to be emergency banking legislation, intended to reopen the solvent banks, close the insolvent, and give the federal government authority to manage the transition of potentially salvageable others.

The bill for doing this went directly to the House floor under a closed rule, that is, without permission to amend. The House began consideration at 2:55 p.m., even though there were no copies available to the members, so that the bill as adopted had to be "represented" by a folded newspaper. Nevertheless, it passed by 4:05 p.m. on a shouted voice vote. The bill was taken up simultaneously by the Banking and Commerce Committee in the Senate at 1:40 p.m. By 4:10 p.m., it had been sent to the floor. At 7:23 p.m., it passed the Senate by a vote of 73–7, unamended despite an intense effort by Huey Long (D-LA). And at 8:36 p.m., six hours and fifty-six minutes after its introduction, it was signed into law. The lament by Congressman Bernard Snell of New York, minority leader of the House, was diagnostic: "The house was burning down, and the President of the United States says this is the way to put the fire out. And to me at this time, there is only one answer to that question, and that is to give the President what he demands and says is necessary to meet the situation."[12]

No other single piece of legislation would command this much deference by Congress to the president. In that sense, the symbolism of the folded newspaper is overstated. But in fact, the entire opening surge of legislation to begin creating what became the New Deal has been memorialized in a metaphor that is simultaneously a tribute to the fundamentally presidential nature of this policy-making process, namely, the "Hundred Days." In truth, Roosevelt followed passage of the Emergency Banking Act with a request for discretionary authority to slash spending, and he followed that with the Beer and Wine Revenue Act, to begin the process of dismantling Prohibition.

But then came the unprecedented parade of New Deal measures that would complete this hundred days—and remain a benchmark for presidential dominance ever since.[13] The full "grocery list" is crushing:

March 31: Civilian Conservation Corps Act

April 5: Executive order requiring the exchange of all gold for currency

April 19: Prohibition of gold shipments abroad

May 12: Agricultural Adjustment Act

May 12: Federal Emergency Relief Act

May 18: Tennessee Valley Authority Act

May 27: Federal Securities Act

June 5: Congressional resolution repealing the gold clause

June 6: National Employment System Act

June 13: Home Owners Refinancing Act

June 16: Emergency Railroad Transportation Act

June 16: Glass-Steagall Act of 1933, regulating the banks and creating the Federal Deposit Insurance Corporation (FDIC)

June 16: National Industrial Recovery Act, including creation of the Public Works Administration

On the one hand, this was a powerfully comprehensive product, involving inflation of the currency, provision of direct economic relief, commencement of economic regulation, institutionalization of public employment, rescue of home ownership, and regulation of transportation. Its individual pieces were groundbreaking, their collective impact only more so. On the other hand, a focus on the hundred days, while rightfully symbolic of the overall process of policy-making in its era, risks implying that Congress was inert in the face of these presidential initiatives, thereby ignoring a smaller set of intermittent, individualized, but still substantial initiatives that originated within Congress and not at the White House.

Most striking among these were a few major legislative acts that became part of the New Deal as a collective project but were actively opposed by the president, to the point of having to be passed over his veto. Yet there were also autonomously congressional pieces that grew out of an earlier Democratic Party program, where this president was not opposed but would not have invested time and energy on his own. And there were, bringing the analysis full circle, major legislative initiatives that came to life in Congress, were strongly opposed by the president in private, but were then successfully co-opted by way of substitutes originating in the White House.

The most substantial of the congressional initiatives that were both important to the overall program of the High New Deal and actively opposed by the president involved cash bonuses for veterans of World War I.[14] In the process of passing the Economy Act, the first major piece of New Deal legislation with lasting programmatic content, Roosevelt had actually cut augmented benefits for veterans, passed in the late days of the Hoover administration with an eye on the 1932 election. Concerned to offer economies in the face of his emergent and comprehensive program, Roosevelt viewed these bonuses, accurately, as going indiscriminately to those who had and had not been harmed by the Depression. At the same time, he did not believe—most economists would now say inaccurately—that such payments could provide an effective economic stimulus.

Congress was diverted in the initial flush of legislative action by the Roosevelt administration, but veterans were not, so Congress returned to the issue in 1934. Its Independent Offices Act repealed major parts of the Economy Act; Roosevelt vetoed the repeal, but Congress overrode him, 310–72 in the House and 63–27 in the Senate. Congress then returned to the issue in late 1935, producing an expanded bonus bill. Roosevelt took the unprecedented step of reading his veto message to a joint session of Congress, and in the short run the Senate sustained him. But Congress returned to the issue yet again as soon as it reassembled in 1936. A new bonus bill passed the House 346–59 and the Senate 74–16, suggesting a veto-proof outcome. Roosevelt vetoed it anyway, but only in a handwritten 200-word note sent directly to the Capitol without external publicity. Three days later, his veto was massively overridden in both houses.[15]

A different strand of essentially congressional initiatives, less consequential in their impact but more regular in their appearance, grew out of the inherited programmatic orthodoxy of the Democratic Party. The New Deal would ultimately shift this orthodoxy in the direction of more comprehensive management of the economy and more extensive provision of welfare benefits (the latter known during the High New Deal Era as "relief"). Yet at its inception, many Democratic members of Congress had grown up in a world stretching well back into the nineteenth century when attacks on corporate monopolies and battles over soft versus hard money had been central. Policy initiatives deriving from this history popped up intermittently in Congress during the High New Deal, energized by those refreshed Democratic majorities.

From the antimonopoly tradition, noteworthy offspring continued into the second term of the Roosevelt presidency. Thus the Robinson-Patman Act of 1936 prohibited chain stores from discounting below a certain level, while the Miller-Tydings Act of 1937 legalized contracts that stabilized the cost of brand-name goods. From the old currency wars, the most noteworthy residuals arrived earlier, within the hundred days. Thus the Thomas Amendment injected pro-silver provisions into the Agricultural Adjustment Act of 1933, while the FDIC was tacked onto the Glass-Steagall Act by those worrying more about small savers than big banks. Franklin Roosevelt had grown up within these earlier partisan traditions; he had taken care not to offend their adherents on the way to a presidential nomination; and their themes remained useful with Progressive Republicans now that he was in office. So he tended to acquiesce in their by-products, as long as they did not actively countervail related White House measures.

If Congress was largely overshadowed, then, it was hardly inert. Perhaps most diagnostic of the situation—affirming the rising place of presidential initiatives, the continuing resilience of congressional efforts at input, but the practical triumph of the presidency within this balance—came from a third body of major legislative programs. These were the ones where a substantial effort by Congress to incubate policy met with disapproval from the president and in effect "smoked out" a counterproposal, which then ultimately became law. Generically, the White House would recognize a rising congressional demand for action, but Roosevelt would respond with a counterpart version, one derailing those parts of the congressional initiative that the president disliked most.

In fact, the last major piece of legislation in the hundred days and the one most clearly defining the New Deal response to national planning and economic management was drafted under just such conditions. The National Industrial Recovery Act (NIRA), with its attempt at government-sponsored cartelization of major industries within the American economy, was to produce the largest governmental bureaucracy and the most extensive intervention in the economy of all the New Deal initiatives. Yet the administration brought it forward only at the very end of the hundred days, delaying largely because Roosevelt's advisers could not agree on an approach to the task. They brought it forward, nevertheless, because the Senate had passed a so-called thirty-hour bill, introduced by Hugo Black (D-AL) and limiting the workweek in an attempt to spread the work. Administration advisers *could* agree that this would be disastrous for their recovery efforts.

What resulted was an amalgam setting maximum hours and minimum wages for various industries, establishing the mechanisms for developing industrial codes to govern production, and creating the Public Works Administration. Introduced in the House on May 17 when the Black bill had already emerged from the House Labor Committee, this mammoth presidential alternative would nevertheless be signed into law a month later, on June 16. The White House thereby short-circuited a major autonomous congressional initiative, while giving shape to a policy realm that the president had long wanted to enter. As such, the NIRA became the outstanding example of presidential *co-optation* of congressional initiatives, as well as one of the least-loved New Deal programs, creating massive bureaucratic complexity but neither the price competition nor the increased productivity that rhetorically justified its creation.[16]

In the end, then, the overwhelming fact about the policy-making process characterizing the High New Deal remained its presidential predominance. No one would ask of the Late New Deal, the Era of Divided Government, or the Era of Partisan Volatility whether Congress remained "relevant" to the making of public policy. The question could be answered for the High New Deal Era as well, but it needed to be asked. Indeed, it would become possible to know that this era had come to a close only when presidential dominance ceased to be a simple summary description of its policy-making process. The proximate cause of its end would be the midterm elections of 1938. The contributory cause would be a major recession in 1937. But the *measure* of the resulting demise would be a change in the relationship between party balance, ideological polarization, and substantive conflict, leading to a new and different overall process of policy-making.

Well before that, however, this president had come back in 1935 with another major round of policy programs. If these could not match the consequence of the total output from the hundred days, they would still rank as hugely consequential in any era. Like the first great round of New Deal programs, they were a mix of economic management and welfare provision, though if the first round had leaned toward the former, toward economic management, this second round leaned toward the latter, toward direct social welfare. Sometimes gathered afterward as the "second New Deal," this second set of programs, like the first, was otherwise distinguished by being thoroughly presidential:[17]

- First was the Social Security Act, combining a system of old-age insurance, unemployment insurance, and aid to the indigent and dependent. This was passed essentially intact later in the year.
- The Emergency Relief Appropriations Act, with a vast mix of works projects large and small, took only a little over three months to achieve the same successful passage.
- The Holding Company Act, attempting to break up major conglomerates in the electricity sector, had to endure protracted legislative combat but passed, only modestly amended, at the end of the session.
- So did the Banking Act, creating the Open Market Committee of the Federal Reserve Board and giving it statutory authority over the discount rate, a major new power allowing it to shape the money supply and interest rates.
- A late addition was the Wealth Tax Act, with progressive taxation aimed at expanding the reach of federal taxes among the very rich. It passed easily, had very limited ultimate impact, but served to support one of the main themes of Roosevelt's reelection campaign by stigmatizing opponents as concerned mainly with the well-being of the most privileged.

The one big bill that was not initially a White House initiative but nevertheless passed early and with surprising ease was the Wagner Act, revolutionizing labor relations by guaranteeing a right to collective bargaining and creating the National Labor Relations Board to oversee that right. This bill was originated and shepherded through Congress by Senator Robert F. Wagner (D-NY). While Franklin Roosevelt was hardly opposed to its goals, he much preferred to reach them by reauthorization of the NIRA. When the Supreme Court struck down the NIRA as unconstitutional, however, Roosevelt easily shifted to support the Wagner Act.

Collectively, that was another huge tranche of lawmaking, originating mostly at the White House and driven largely by the president thereafter. More than the recovery-oriented initiatives of the hundred days, this second tranche was an attempt to institutionalize the social engineering side of the New Deal. The reach of its social welfare provisions was impressive in the American historical context and impressive in the international context of its time as well. A comprehensive welfare state had thus arrived in the United States, courtesy of the New Deal. According to Edwin Amenta:

> On the eve of the Second World War, the United States pledged more of its national product to security in the larger sense than any major industrial nation. . . . [T]hese programs accounted for more than six percent of U.S. gross domestic product and almost thirty percent of government spending. The American performance outpaced the efforts of Sweden, today's world leader in social spending. America also outdistanced the United Kingdom, which began the Depression with the world's most advanced system of public social spending.[18]

On the other hand, the development that forced the president to change course specifically on his approach to labor law and collective bargaining, namely, the canceling of the NIRA by the Supreme Court in early May 1935, was also the development that brought the central aspect of ideological polarization for the entire High New Deal Era to a head. It was this *institutional* polarization between president and Court, and not electoral combat or legislative tussling, that came to define both ideological distinctions and substantive conflict during the High New Deal. Moreover, had this institutional tension been resolved differently, the diagnostic policy-making process of the High New Deal would have come out looking very different as well.

Nearly from the start, the Court had inquired into the constitutionality of New Deal–type programs, and in two key regards.[19] At the state level, did state governments possess the authority to legislate on their own in the realms of economic recovery and social engineering, or was this an unconstitutional intervention in the private economy? Initially, the Court appeared to conclude that they did. At the national level, was programmatic implementation sufficiently guided by congressional direction, or did it delegate powers to the bureaucracy that the

Constitution gave only to Congress? The Court was more cautionary here, such that the industrial codes of the NIRA often fell afoul of this second standard. Yet Congress appeared able to respond by repassing the banned codes as legislation, thereby restoring them—while salvaging presidential supremacy.

In May 1935, all that began to change. In *Schechter Poultry Corp. v. United States*,[20] the Court found that the NIRA code regulating the poultry industry was unconstitutional, on the familiar grounds that it represented an unacceptable delegation of congressional powers. But this time, the Court went on to find the entire NIRA apparatus unconstitutional because it moved far beyond interstate and well over into intrastate commerce, where it had no constitutional remit. May 27, when the decision was published, became known as Black Monday among New Dealers.

At the time, the president was in the midst of his second major policy push, extending the New Deal to old-age retirement, labor-management relations, trust-busting, and progressive taxation. In the short run, Roosevelt would succeed in securing all of these. But for the longer run, the *Schechter* decision was a gigantic storm cloud. It had the potential to nullify not just the emergent Wagner Act, to which Roosevelt switched his support in order to rescue the labor-management parts of the NIRA, but also his new Social Security Act, and perhaps even the Agricultural Adjustment Act, the centerpiece of his farm policy in an era when one in five Americans still lived on the farm.

Two subsequent decisions appeared to make that threat a reality. In *United States v. Butler* in early 1936,[21] the Court did indeed strike the Agricultural Adjustment Act, asserting that the powers of the act were reserved to the states. Apparently, much of the New Deal agenda had to be addressed at the state and not the federal level. Yet in *Morehead v. New York ex rel. Tipaldo* in mid-1936,[22] the Court struck down the minimum wage law in the state of New York, on grounds that it was an unconstitutional restriction of the freedom of contract. Apparently, key provisions within the New Deal agenda could not be addressed at the state level either.

An implicit partisan conflict became a nascent constitutional crisis at the point when the White House responded legislatively, by attempting to bring the Court into alignment with its view of the policy wishes of the new party majority. The president had been publicly unhappy about *Schechter* in 1935. He began to take private advice on a response to evolving Court doctrine during 1936, though his principal concern in the short run remained his own reelection. When that was massively successful—he himself lost only Maine and Vermont while his party gained further seats in both the House and the Senate—he decided to move against the Court.[23]

On February 5, 1937, Roosevelt unveiled the Judicial Procedures Reform Bill, which, amid an array of housekeeping proposals, would have allowed him to appoint six new justices and subordinate the Court to what he viewed as his electoral mandate, the proper and appropriate voice of the people. The legislative battle for this bill would occupy a good deal of both presidential and congressional time during 1937. In the ultimate sense, when registered through the policy-making process that distinguishes the High New Deal Era, the presidency would triumph over the Supreme Court. Indeed, only when it had done so could the era be definitively characterized as featuring a basically presidential process of policy-making.

And the Court did begin to change its existing preferences. Scholars would differ over how much of this change was directly due to Roosevelt's "court-packing" assault, how much of it was indirect fallout from the outcome of the 1936 election, and how much was natural evolution as the justices came to grips with a changing policy world. Regardless, in March in *West Coast Hotel Co. v. Parrish*,[24] the Court reversed itself on the ability of states to do their own New Deal–type legislation, affirming the law guaranteeing a minimum wage in the state of Washington.[25] The other shoe fell in mid-April when the Court affirmed the Wagner Act as constitutional in *NLRB v. Jones & Laughlin Steel Corp.*[26] That decision was rendered on the same day as four others involving federal regulation of labor relations. All were 5–4, all were positive, and together they seemed likely to guarantee sanctity for the entire Roosevelt program.

A month after that, Willis Van Devanter, a reliable vote against the New Deal inside the Court, announced his intention to retire at the end of the term. This implied that the president could select a justice who was solidly in favor, converting his new 5–4 margin into 6–3, again presumably from there on. Nothing in those outcomes ever promised to resuscitate the NIRA—by then it lacked political and not just constitutional support—but the entire rest of the New Deal seemed secure. The disproportionately presidential system of policy-making that had produced that program was thereby also sustained, though Roosevelt would never secure the Judicial Reform Act of 1937 as drafted. The latter would remain bottled up in the Senate Judiciary Committee for 165 days before emerging as an anodyne administrative cleanup bill, sans any new appointment powers.

Roosevelt's court-packing plan had actually been only the first of three major initiatives for 1937 aimed at institutionalizing the New Deal. In these, if Roosevelt was sure that securing the New Deal required bringing the Supreme Court under presidential sway, he came to believe that institutionalization likewise required a strengthened presidency in its own right. To that end, he introduced a major effort to reorganize the federal executive, including a cadre of new administrative assistants for the president; augmented budgetary and management agencies inside the White House; a reorganized and strengthened civil service, implicitly cementing the New Dealers into the wider government; expansion of the cabinet, while moving all the independent agencies into one or another of these expanded departments; and a new general structure for fiscal management, shifting control away from Congress and toward the presidency.

On its face, that was probably always too much for Congress to stomach, even during the High New Deal, even (or perhaps especially?) within a disproportionately presidential process of policy-making. In any case, like the court-packing proposal, the reorganization project went nowhere in 1937. Also like the judicial reform proposal, while a reorganization bill was ultimately passed by Congress, it resurfaced and survived only in watered-down form. Here, the practical upshot was that major reorganization of the executive branch would have to wait for the coming of World War II, with its associated demands on the presidency, and especially for the Cold War.[27] In the meantime, Roosevelt shifted into his third big institutionalizing effort.

A combination of his sweeping victory in the 1936 election with the legislative defeats of 1937 convinced the president that the crucial third pillar of institutionalized support for the New Deal had to involve restructuring the national Democratic Party itself. Moreover, with the 1938 elections looming, Roosevelt concluded that further temporizing was neither tactically productive nor practically sensible. In anticipation, he moved to purge the most recalcitrant officeholders in his own party, mainly Southern Democrats. This too was largely to be a failure on its own terms, though the handful of specific but dramatic failures that constituted the purge proved to be just an eddy in a larger current that was going to bring the High New Deal itself to an end.

On the one hand, then, the Supreme Court had begun to cede the policy argument to Roosevelt in March 1937 with *West Coast Hotel v. Parrish*, confirming that cession in April with *NLRB v. Jones & Laughlin Steel Corp.* This secured the previously established programmatic gains from the disproportionately presidential process of policy-making that had characterized the New Deal to that point. Ultimately, however, the substantive essence of this change proved to be even larger. For the Court would never renege on this new acceptance of the power of the elected government to regulate the American economy.

On the other hand, electoral politics was about to give this salvaged process of policy-making far less time to live productively than either side must have believed at the point when key Court decisions resolved the underlying institutional polarization. For the general public itself was to bring the High New Deal to an end at the ballot box in November 1938. In that sense, this first great *correction* to a newly dominant party balance built on a newly dominant party faction came quickly. At the midterm election of 1938, the Democrats shed seventy seats in the House, a diminishment reconfirmed in 1940 (table 1.1A). The Democratic Party as a whole would never achieve those precorrection aggregates again, at least as this is being written.

Yet this initial contraction, the partisan break point between the High and the Late New Deal Eras, looks even more striking when the structure of factional conflict inside the parties is brought back to the fore (table 1.1B). This factional structure had been the truly distinctive element of partisan politics in the High New Deal Era, as embodied in the unipolar dominance of Northern Democrats. The factional story after November 1938 would look crucially different. First, inside the Democratic Party, literally all the losses were among Northern Democrats. Southern Democrats did not lose a single seat. Second, as between the parties, these same Northern Democrats—almost three times as numerous as the Republicans in 1936—actually *fell behind them* in 1938.

Slower-changing by constitutional design, with only one-third of the body up for election at any given time, the Senate was slower in reflecting these developments as well (table 1.2). Yet reflect them it did. The same constriction of Democrats and expansion of Republicans was echoed in this upper chamber (table 1.2A) and continued in linear fashion through the election of 1946 (figure 1.2). The contraction of Northern Democrats, the stability of Southern Democrats, and the rise of both Regular and Northeastern Republicans produced the same ini-

Table 1.1. The Partisan Composition of the High New Deal, the House

A. Democrats and Republicans, 1926–1940

	Democratic Seats	Republican Seats	Other Seats
1926	194	238	3
1928	164	270	1
1930	216	218	1
1932	313	117	5
1934	321	104	10
1936	334	88	13
1938	262	169	4
1940	267	162	1

B. Democratic and Republican Factions, 1926–1940

	Northern Democrats	Southern Democrats	Regular Republicans	Northeastern Republicans	All Others
1926	93	101	144	94	3
1928	72	92	171	99	1
1930	116	100	129	89	1
1932	220	93	50	67	5
1934	221	100	53	51	10
1936	234	100	43	45	13
1938	162	100	97	72	4
1940	167	100	103	59	1

tial echo as well (table 1.2B), though factionally, it was only Regular Republicans who continued to rise (and Northern Democrats who continued to fall) through 1946 (figure 1.2). In the process, the High New Deal Era met its aggregate demise.

What had happened? In the simplest terms, a substantial recession had struck the American economy and dragged the Democratic Party down with it. Perhaps inevitably, the faction of that party most connected to economic rescue and thus to the New Deal paid a disproportionate price when that rescue appeared to lose its grip. The president may have fueled this effect by proclaiming an end to the Great Depression at the beginning of 1937, bringing forward a policy program aimed at curtailing relief and balancing the budget. Yet at bottom, the most direct way to say all this is to note that where economics, in the form of the Great Depression of 1929, had generated the massive Democratic shift that created the New Deal party system, it was likewise economics,

Table 1.2. The Partisan Composition of the High New Deal, the Senate

A. Democrats and Republicans, 1926–1940

	Democratic Seats	Republican Seats	Other Seats
1926	46	48	3
1928	39	56	1
1930	47	48	1
1932	59	36	1
1934	69	25	2
1936	76	16	4
1938	69	23	4
1940	66	28	2

B. Democratic and Republican Factions, 1926–1940

	Northern Democrats	Southern Democrats	Regular Republicans	Northeastern Republicans	All Others
1926	24	22	33	15	3
1928	17	22	36	20	1
1930	25	22	30	18	1
1932	34	22	20	16	1
1934	47	22	15	10	2
1936	54	22	8	8	4
1938	48	21	12	11	4
1940	44	22	18	10	2

in the form of a major recession in 1937, that brought the High New Deal Era to an end.

Afterward, an effectively unipolar politics was gone. An essentially presidential policy-making process was gone. And so, of course, was the era characterized by both. One obvious upshot was the arrival of a new political period, unacknowledged and unnamed when it arrived, as such eras usually are, but recognizable in retrospect as the Late New Deal Era, the subject of chapter 2. Yet that development also brings the entire analysis back around to the question of how best, in closing this chapter, to treat this first putative era within the long flow of modern American politics. To wit: Was the High New Deal the first of four distinct political periods in the modern world of American politics? Or was it better viewed as the explosion, intense but inherently temporary, that demarcates this modern world, leading to the *three* extended periods that really constitute modern American politics?

For most purposes, the answer does not matter. If the politics of the period from 1932 through 1938 are accurately described—that is, accurately arrayed in terms of party balance, ideological polarization, and substantive conflict, along with the policy-making process that resulted from their interaction—and if this array is different from that of the three political periods to follow, then a historically comparative analysis is free to move on to apply the same lens to these successor periods. Yet there is an alternative perspective, one that should be noted and can be easily summarized.

In this, the High New Deal Era is distinguished not by the intermediary structure of its politics but by the breadth and intensity of public demands for governmental policy-making stemming from the Great Depression. None of the three successor periods can be categorized in anything close to that way. Simultaneously, this putative era is distinguished by being so short that it could be treated as little more than a direct reflection of the societal rupture that demarcated the modern world, perhaps akin to the Revolutionary War and the Civil War, cataclysmic events in two earlier worlds that likewise saw the introduction of a new politics in their aftermath.

Given the intellectual purposes of this volume, the first view, of a short but consequential period that can (despite its distinguishing characteristics) be treated in the same fashion as the longer periods that would succeed it, is the view that must govern the analysis here. Moreover, the breadth and depth of governmental programs implemented during this admittedly short political era argue empirically against merging it into some other period in any account purporting to examine the evolution of American politics since 1932. If it was close to being only a moment in political time, it was still a hugely productive moment. The distinctiveness of its policy-making process then caps the argument for allowing it to claim a political era all its own.

Which is not to deny that the character and shortness of the era do create interpretive problems by comparison to any of the three distinctive (and longer) periods to follow. Again, it is hard to separate out the simple effect of economic disaster *and associated demands for a policy response* from the specific structure of politics that shaped this response for so short a time. From one side, the huge partisan imbalance of the High New Deal Era seems rooted in nearly universal discontent with the Great Depression rather than in a policy program that had, after all, not yet even been enunciated when the underlying shift in party balance began. From the other side, the critical polarization of the period, between an ambitious president and a reluctant Court, was in some sense the result of a long-established institutional—indeed, constitutional—structure. In that sense, it stretched back not to 1929 but to 1789.

What was distinctive within the political structure characterizing the era from either of these influences was the degree of philosophical and hence ideological difference between branches of government. This difference was registered initially—foreshadowed—in the massive change in party balance that inaugurated the era. By extension, the resulting policy process risked producing gridlock on a grand scale, as the Supreme Court struck down major parts of the emergent New Deal and as the president recentered his policy-making focus on reforming the judiciary. A continuation of that conflict would have generated a very different summary description of the political structure of the High New Deal Era.

In its time, the resolution that avoided this gridlock scenario was double-edged for both sides. The president succeeded in ending Court obstruction of New Deal initiatives, but only at the point where these initiatives were to prove exhausted on quite other grounds. The Court succeeded in salvaging its formal policy powers, but only at the cost of altering constitutional doctrine so as to accommodate presidential wishes. The same sort of two-sided verdict must be offered for the longer run, with party balance, ideological polarization, and substantive conflict as lenses and a policy-making process distinctive to its era as their result.

On the one hand, implicit victory by the president over the Court did allow the products of what had been a basically presidential process of policy-making to be confirmed. Without that victory, we can have no idea what we might say about the place of the years between 1932 and 1938 within the longer stretch of modern American politics, though we would surely put less emphasis on the substantive content of New Deal programs that had been rejected and on presidential domination of a policy-making process that had been strikingly diminished.

What we can know is that this confirmed process was itself to disappear in an impressively short time. The Court began to surrender in April 1937, courtesy of *West Coast Hotel Co. v. Parrish*. The electorate terminated the High New Deal in November 1938, by changing the party balance in government and, even more crucially, the factional structure beneath that balance. Many of its central policies survive to this day.

Yet the process that shaped them was gone within months. In the end, either way, nothing prevents addressing the High New Deal through a framework shared with three much longer but less programmatically intense successor periods. In that sense, the specifics of an opening analysis of this first political era of modern American politics, by way of a changed party balance, a distinctive form of ideological polarization, a monolithic substantive content, and the resulting process of policy-making, can be allowed to stand as they are.

2 | The Long Arm of the New Deal

The Political Structure of the Late New Deal Era, 1939–1968

Party balance: *institutionalization of the Democratic advantage acquired in the High New Deal;* ideological polarization: *a depolarized politics built around multiple factions and crosscutting coalitions;* substantive conflict: *expansion beyond issues of economic welfare to include foreign affairs and civil rights in a largely autonomous fashion;* policy-making process: *perpetual coalition (re)building and policy (re)adjustment, best summarized as "incrementalism."*

None of the problems that bedevil an attempt to separate out party balance, ideological polarization, and substantive conflict in the intense but short High New Deal Era trouble the analysis of its long successor period, the Late New Deal. There was no cataclysmic event to inaugurate the period, and hence no stimulus so monumental that it might overwhelm the impact of a new and distinctive mix of analytic elements. Instead, a new policy-making process resulted much more from explicitly political developments. In this, a newly institutionalized party balance, an ideological polarization different in kind from its predecessor, and a far richer matrix of substantive conflicts would have plenty of time, a full thirty years, in which to demonstrate—and confirm—the diagnostic characteristics of the policy-making process that they in turn produced.

As before, this process had to be both the ultimate product of a focus on the interaction of key analytic elements and a solid means of distinguishing the Late New Deal Era from the periods that came before and after. Yet it is not just that the aggregate levels of three key indicators were different in the new period by comparison to the old, though in fact they were. Nor was it even just that these analytic elements interacted differently in one era as opposed to another, though again they did. Rather, the place where the reality of these concepts could best be captured in the new period—and thus the appropriate measure for each—was to be different as well. And the Late New Deal would be very good at demonstrating all of this.

The first and most obvious embodiment of *party balance* for the nation as a whole was the aggregate outcome of national elections, and it began to introduce elements of change from the predecessor period. Thus in the new era, Republicans obviously could capture Congress when events were propitious, as they were at the reconversion election of 1946, just as Republicans could capture the presidency when they had a particularly attractive candidate and when the issues of the day were especially beneficial, as they were with Dwight Eisenhower and foreign affairs in 1952. The High New Deal Era had not been like that. On the other hand, Eisenhower remained the lone presidential exception from 1932 until 1968, and while he pulled a Republican Congress into office with him in 1952, this was already gone by 1954, such that even he could not recapture it when he was reelected two years later.[1]

That was the story of partisan balance in the Late New Deal Era when measured by electoral outcomes for the nation as a whole, and electoral outcomes are the bedrock measure that would have been used to examine the comparative standing of the political parties in every era up to this point. Such a measure does require a further institutional choice in the American context, since presidential and congressional elections do not always tell the same story. Yet for the Late New Deal Era—and very much unlike its successor, the Era of Divided Government—they did just that, namely, tell the same overall partisan story. Accordingly, either choice, president or Congress, attested to a continuing Democratic dominance, reduced a bit but not much from its predecessor period.

Nevertheless, one of the further hallmarks of the Late New Deal Era, a hallmark not otherwise linked to partisan politics, was the arrival of survey research as a basic tool not just for market economics but for social science more generally.[2] For the first time, it became possible to ask in a systematic fashion how individual Americans *thought about* their partisan attachments—especially their self-identification with a political party—rather than imputing this from voting behavior. For the presidential election of 1952 and forever after as this is written, what became the National Election Study asked a random sample of Americans a canonical two-step question about personal partisanship:

- First came "Generally speaking, do you think of yourself as a Republican, a Democrat, an Independent, or what?"
- For those accepting a partisan self-designation, its strength was probed with "Would you call yourself a strong or a not very strong [Republican/Democrat]?"
- For those initially claiming independence, it was probed instead by "Do you think of yourself as closer to the Republican or the Democratic party?"[3]

That schema divided the public into Strong and Weak Republican or Democratic identifiers (question 2) plus Independent Republicans, Independent Democrats, and Pure Independents (question 3). This categorization, in turn, permitted two related measures of party balance. The first combined Strong, Independent, and Weak Democrats against Strong, Independent, and Weak Republicans, with a sliver of Pure Independents in between (figure 2.1A). The second retained the full seven-category array, running from Strong Democrats through Strong Republicans (figure 2.1B). For the Late New Deal Era, however—though note,

Figure 2.1. Party Identification in the Nation as a Whole: The Late New Deal Era

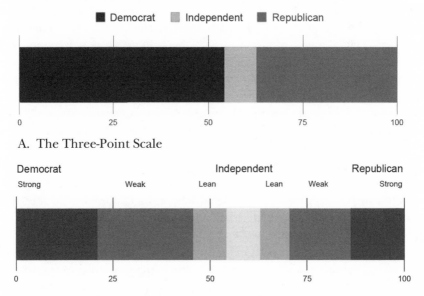

A. The Three-Point Scale

B. The Seven-Point Scale

and this is important, not for its successors—either arrangement told essentially the same story: a solid Democratic majority, with Republicans dependent on making large but always transitory inroads on it.

For the three-category picture, Democratic identifiers outnumbered Republican identifiers substantially (figure 2.1A). Indeed, assuming roughly equal turnout among these self-identified partisans, the Democratic Party could go so far as to write off not just the Republicans but also the self-described Independents and still produce a national majority. The seven-category picture inevitably offered more internal twists, yet the dominant takeaway was unchanged (figure 2.1B). Seen this way, the national Democratic Party could write off the true Independents, split the Independent Democratic identifiers, and still muster that national majority.

On the surface, then, there had been a modest aggregate change in the nationwide party balance. What had been a crushing Democratic majority was now just a statistically large one. On the one hand, it was no longer possible to believe that this evolving imbalance was a simple response to one issue, the Great Depression, so that it might dissipate as the economic crisis dissipated, much less that it was a simple response to one man, Franklin Roosevelt. The new Democratic majority of the High New Deal Era had been solidified—institutionalized—in its Late New Deal successor. On the other hand, the scope of aggregate change between the two periods in this institutionalized imbalance remained modest, hardly appearing to approach the scale of an era changer.

Yet here, that modest picture was clearly misleading, for the new nationwide aggregate in fact greatly understated the extent of partisan change. In fact, beneath this aggregated surface, the fundamental nature of an ongoing partisan majority had been transformed. It was electoral outcomes in Congress that made the transformation easiest to see. Absent these congressional changes, there might have been serious argument about whether a shift in party balance had occurred at all. Yet there had been an indisputably major shift in the *factional composition* of the two parties in Congress, and it was really change in the internal composition of an aggregated balance that heralded the appearance of—and initially distinguished—the Late New Deal Era.

Now, courtesy of this shift in factional balance, the predominance of Northern Democrats stood revealed as the crucial underpinning to the old order, an underpinning that had been destroyed by the midterm election of 1938. In its place, the crucial operative consideration for a new era would involve the shifting internal balance—that is, the shifting factional composition—of both political parties: Northern Democrats versus Southern Democrats especially, but often Regular Republicans versus Northeastern Republicans as well, and sometimes each against all. Moreover, if change in the aggregate balance nationwide had been subtle and open to interpretation, this shift in the factional composition of the two parties was evident and profound.

Change appeared at its most impressive when seen through the lower house of Congress, the House of Representatives (figure 2.2A). Northern Democrats had been an absolute majority of the House in the three Congresses of the High New Deal. They were to be an absolute majority of *none* in the fifteen Congresses of the Late New Deal Era. Indeed, with factional balance in the House as a focus, Republicans would actually outnumber Northern Democrats in thirteen of the fifteen Congresses from 1939 through 1968. The arrival of that previous dominance by Northern Democrats had been central to policy-making in the preceding era. Its departure would prove central to policy-making in its successor. And the same general story reappeared in the upper house of Congress, the Senate, fine-tuned by some structural characteristics peculiar to the body (figure 2.2B).

Throughout the Late New Deal Era, the two institutional stories were identical in terms of aggregate balance: Northern Democrats never again achieved an absolute majority in either house. Toward the end, however, they did manage to outnumber the Republicans in some Congresses in the Senate—six of fifteen for the entire period—because they did better at holding their gains after a Democratic surge in the election of 1958. Yet what this achievement emphasized simultaneously for the factional story inside the Senate was the importance of the Southern Democrats in that body, especially because its structural characteristics—the filibuster in particular, but also the general role of seniority in creating committee chairs and even the Senate norm of accommodating individual members—provided additional assets for southerners whenever they were in tension with their northern fellow partisans.

So a continuing and statistically solid Democratic majority for the nation as a whole meant reliable Democratic presidencies, though not so reliable that the Republican threat did not seem prospectively real, year after year. And the same national party balance provided continuing Democratic majorities in Congress, though these were hardly reliable for policy-making, in that they depended on holding the bulk of

Figure 2.2. Factional Composition of the Two Parties in Congress: The Late New Deal Era

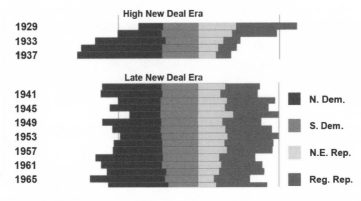

A. The House

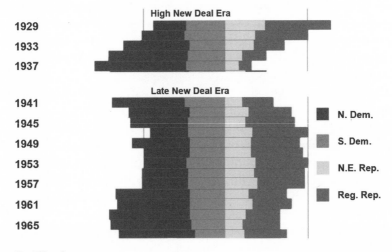

B. The Senate

Southern Democrats within the party fold or picking off dissident Republicans if that did not work, in an institution where there were normally more Republicans than Northern Democrats.

How polarized was this modulated but apparently stable party system? When the question becomes the level of *ideological polarization* within this new party balance, the answer is nearly opposite to that for the High New Deal Era. During the High New Deal, a dominant Democratic Party had been effectively unipolar, with Northern Democrats holding the presidency and dominating Congress as well. Despite that, a striking institutional conflict between presidency and Court had characterized—and polarized—the political system as a whole. In the Late New Deal Era, a remarkably few years later, a party system still featuring a substantial Democratic edge had become (and would remain) impressively depolarized—in effect, multipolar—with the Supreme Court just one more contributor to a much more complicated partisan situation.

Inside this new but lasting partisan context, a stable but multifactional array—four major factions, plus occasional subclusters specific to particular issues—would by itself have ensured a considerably less polarized process of policy-making than the unipolar world that had characterized the preceding era. Or at least, majority-building had to be more complex when more than the unity of one partisan faction was at stake. Yet this multifactional array was now additionally augmented by whole new theaters for substantive conflict, in foreign affairs and civil rights rather than just economic welfare. And when four major factions did not line up in the same ideological order across what were now three major sources of policy struggle, partisan depolarization proved to be ubiquitous, inescapable, and diagnostic.

In truth, one could have recognized all four key factions in the preceding High New Deal Era. For some purposes, analysts at the time talked explicitly about the difference between Northern and Southern Democrats on one side of the partisan aisle, or between Old Guard (principally Northeastern) and Progressive (principally Midwestern/ Western) Republicans on the other. Yet the sheer fact that putting three of the four factions together still did not equal the fourth, the Northern Democrats, made such an exercise frequently irrelevant to policy-making. And this would have been true even if a healthy leaven of the Progressive Republicans had not agreed with substantial parts of the New Deal, which in fact they did.

Yet in the Late New Deal Era, when a solid but declining Democratic edge within the overall party balance featured disproportionate losses by Northern Democrats, the same multifactional alignment acquired very different implications. Most fundamentally, coalition-building around new policy initiatives instantly became more complex, requiring cross-factional agreements in order to produce public policy. Beyond that, a four-faction alignment where no faction was inconsequential meant that any single faction that insisted too completely on its own policy preferences—a risk presumably greatest for the previously dominant faction, the Northern Democrats—was likely to build the coalition *against* itself in the process of doing so.

To see the full range of consequences over time from this continuing four-faction array, it is necessary to jump ahead of the story, momentarily but in two key regards. In one, it is necessary to review the geographic distinctions associated with these factions. In the other, it is necessary to preview the expanded substantive domains for policy conflict that would characterize the new era. Only then is it possible to see how differing geographic factions were aligned differently by each of the newly consequential policy domains. This would yield a policy-making process that featured constant coalition-building and continuing policy adjustment, a process summarized ultimately through the notion of "incrementalism," the process centrally characterizing the Late New Deal Era.

In that light, the evolving majority party could be seen to possess two grand, obvious, and continuing pieces.[4] Its largest continuing faction, and indeed its national core, remained the Northern Democrats. They were already showing an internal fault line between old-fashioned patronage-based organizations and the growing reform clubs that relied instead on issues and ideology, but this split would not become consequential until the successor period.[5] In the meantime, their opposite numbers inside the party were the Southern Democrats, headquartered in the states of the Old Confederacy. They benefited from the security inherent in one-party domination of their region; they were stressed by the New Deal liberalism that could not possibly appeal to everyone inside a one-party region.[6]

That was a geographic division inside the national Democratic Party that would have been recognized for a very long time, in fact well before the coming of the New Deal. Its counterpart within the evolving, newly minority, Republican Party likewise remained geographically stable, while otherwise changing rapidly in a very different way.[7] Before the New Deal, this had largely been a divide between Progressive Republicans and an Old Guard. Afterward, it was much more a divide between those state and local Republican parties that were attempting to reach some accommodation with the New Deal versus those that continued to cast themselves in active opposition to it.

Remarkably, these two wings of the national Republican Party maintained their previous geographic headquarters but swapped their ideological preferences, thanks largely to the way that economic welfare had come to define liberalism and conservatism for an increasing share of Americans.[8] In the predecessor world of the High New Deal, the Old Guard, the most rock-ribbed opponents of the New Deal, had largely been found in the Northeast. By contrast, Progressive Republicans, sharing preferences like the antimonopoly sentiments of the New Dealers plus a unifying support for aid to farmers, had largely been found in the Midwest and West. Yet the New Deal had achieved its greatest fresh attraction in urban areas, most commonly located in the Northeast, while adding nearly nothing to the Democratic base on the farms and in the small towns of the Midwest and the West.[9]

Accordingly, in the new world of the Late New Deal, those who sought an accommodation with New Deal programs became headquartered in the Northeast, while the proponents of what they regarded as traditional Republican values—best viewed now as the Regular Republicans—came to be found more often in the Midwest and West. The Northeastern region did not yet lack for established Republican politicians, but these individuals faced an apparent and increasing need to make their peace with the New Deal. In this, they still reflexively presented themselves as trying to impose some fiscal sanity on the new Democratic program. Yet they knew that their constituents were attracted to many elements within this program, so that appearing to go back to the policies associated with the world before the Great Depression was not an attractive option.

The relevance of these partisan factions—all four of them—had been submerged during the High New Deal Era by the force of economic crisis, by the scale of the resulting partisan shift, and by the implicit dominance of one faction within that shift, namely, the Northern Democrats. During the Late New Deal Era, all four regional factions resurfaced explicitly and unavoidably, becoming in effect the building blocks through which public policies in an expanding array of policy realms could be proposed, constructed, amended, or derailed. An entirely different interfactional dynamic surfaced simultaneously with them.

Table 2.1A begins this particular analysis in the House of Representatives, focusing on the two Congresses in which the Republicans actually did secure a majority of the full body, contrasted with the election before and after each. These constitute the largest shifts in aggregate partisan balance during the entire Late New Deal, though they are also the only Republican majorities during the period. Both the size of these

Table 2.1. Partisan Dynamics in the Late New Deal Era, the House

A. Democratic and Republican Parties

	Democratic Seats	Republican Seats	Other Seats
1944	244	189	2
1946	188	246	1
1948	263	171	1
1950	235	199	1
1952	213	221	1
1954	232	203	0

B. Democratic and Republican Factions

	Northern Democrats	Southern Democrats	Regular Republicans	Northeastern Republicans	All Others
1944	140	104	72	72	2
1946	85	103	96	96	1
1948	160	103	135	64	1
1950	135	103	126	73	1
1952	114	99	142	79	1
1954	133	99	132	71	0

shifts and their rapid dissolution stand out in this form of presentation. Yet the crucial operative points are actually contained in table 2.1B, which breaks this initial picture into four main factions rather than just two major parties.

The larger point that jumps out of this rearrangement concerns the internal structure of the Democratic Party. To wit: when Democrats lost seats overall, these losses were entirely within the Northern Democratic faction. Whether the party won or lost nationwide, the Southern Democrats were essentially static. A less dramatic point illustrated by the same table is that the factional structure of the Republican Party was different in kind from its Democratic counterpart. When Northern Democrats shed seats, the gains—transferred automatically into Republican hands—were proportionate as between Regular and Northeastern Republicans. The Regulars were reliably more numerous from start to finish, but the balance between them and the Northeastern Republicans changed very little during these years. In that sense, the Republican Party in the House was not at all a mirror image of the Democrats.

Table 2.2 tells the same story about the Senate, just less schematically—in a more modulated way, probably because only one-third of the

Table 2.2. Partisan Dynamics in the Late New Deal Era, the Senate

A. Democratic and Republican Parties

	Democratic Seats	Republican Seats	Other Seats
1944	57	38	1
1946	45	51	0
1948	54	42	0
1950	49	47	0
1952	47	48	1
1954	48	47	1

B. Democratic and Republican Factions

	Northern Democrats	Southern Democrats	Regular Republicans	Northeastern Republicans	All Others
1944	35	22	27	11	1
1946	23	22	35	16	0
1948	32	22	28	14	0
1950	27	22	32	15	0
1952	25	22	31	17	1
1954	26	22	30	17	1

Senate is elected in any given year, while even that third is not a random sample of the full body. In any case, aggregate volatility in the Senate was slightly less than aggregate volatility in the House (table 2.2A). Percentage swings both for and against the minority Republicans were thus more restrained. Nevertheless, what can be said about the internal structure of the parties, their factional dynamics, was the same for both bodies.

Accordingly, in good years and in bad, the Southern Democrats possessed the same number of senators (table 2.2B). Gains and losses for the Democratic Party were accrued entirely in the North. Across the aisle, lingering damage from the Great Depression and the New Deal was still evident among Northeastern Republicans in 1944. But after the 1946 pickup, both Northeastern and Regular Republicans in the Senate, like their counterparts in the House, shared triumphs and reverses in a roughly proportionate fashion.

Two implications of this resurgence of internal party factions became extremely important in describing the structure of *substantive conflict* that resulted. First, even in the major and continuing realm of economic welfare, partisan depolarization became the obvious and dominant theme after the disappearance of Northern Democratic hegemony. The Southern Democrats in particular could often award ultimate legislative power to either side. Yet second, two newly consequential realms, first foreign affairs and then civil rights, did not even align the four main factions in the same manner as they did with economic welfare. Accordingly, partisan depolarization did not just extend to new policy areas. It also differed among them, making the interaction of three distinctively organized policy domains even more inherently complex—and presumably even more malleable.[10]

The main focus for policy conflict within this revised mix of party balance and ideological polarization remained economic welfare, the substantive heart of the New Deal.[11] Operational concerns were to include questions about the proper scope of key New Deal initiatives, as with Social Security. They were to include questions about further areas that were arguable extensions, as with health care. They were to include cognate issues of the day, as with housing and rent controls. They were to include public expenditures for education, from the building of public schools at one end of the educational continuum to the implementation of the GI Bill at the other. And on the reverse side of the expenditure coin, they were always to include taxation, both its appropriate level and its proper degree of progressivity.

The factional dynamic surrounding these concerns was in turn very straightforward. Northern Democrats tended to be reliably liberal—supportive—on issues of economic welfare. Regular Republicans tended to be reliably conservative—unenthusiastic—about welfare initiatives. In such an environment, legislative fortunes tended to turn on the other two main factions, the Southern Democrats and the Northeastern Republicans. Holding a greater share of the Southern Democrats in line with their Northern colleagues, or compensating with an expanded share of Northeastern Republicans when that proved impossible, produced a liberal legislative coalition on economic welfare. Losing a greater share of the Southern Democrats, especially while failing to obtain an expanded share of Northeastern Republicans, produced a conservative legislative coalition instead.

Indeed, the possibility of generating this conservative coalition was widely understood in its time to be the central strategic concern of welfare politics.[12] Within this politics, the principal faction in play between the two national parties remained the Southern Democrats. As a dominant one-party region, the South inevitably contained the full ideological spectrum within its Democratic Party. From one side, Southern Democratic members of Congress were pressed leftward by a low standard of living in their general public. From the other side, an established Southern Democracy augmented the influence of an older pre–New Deal elite that continued on, courtesy of the lack of regularized internal competition.

The secondary faction in play was, then, those Northeastern Republicans, who had survived the Democratic surge of the Great Depression and were now seeking an uneasy peace with the New Deal. Failing to impose fiscal responsibility on the liberal welfare coalition put them at risk within their own party. Failing to support popular welfare initiatives put them at risk from the wider electorate. There were always fewer of them than there were of the Southern Democrats, in both houses of Congress. Yet they remained of a sufficient size that when the Southern Democrats split, as they easily could on welfare matters, the nature of the simultaneous division among these Northeastern Republicans could prove crucial to the overall result.

The New Deal programs at the heart of this array at the point when the High New Deal gave way to the Late New Deal were, however, to be joined in a remarkably short time by an insistent focus on foreign affairs. A response to World War II as an external phenomenon from 1939 onward, and then to active American participation after 1941, began this secondary substantive focus on a massive scale. Yet it was to be the extended Cold War after World War II had ended that would keep foreign affairs near the center of American domestic politics for the entire Late New Deal Era. At bottom, this involved nothing less than a new American role in constructing a standing military at home but especially in building the international institutions of the war against international Communism.[13]

A newly organized Department of Defense and a truly new North Atlantic Treaty Organization (NATO) were only leading examples among many. Yet there were to be major, associated, "hot" wars in Korea and Vietnam, while numerous other geographic theaters would draw American foreign policy into some relationship to the Cold War. Moreover, there would be major impacts on domestic society from concerns for national security, most often symbolized in what became known as the "Red Scare" but hardly limited to it. And there would be further international organizations, as with the United Nations or the World Bank, which, while focused well beyond the Cold War, would feature deep

American involvement—and intermittently turn up in domestic politics, too.

A sitting Democratic administration had to take the lead in managing the World War II effort, and a sitting Democratic administration then had to take the lead in constructing the international institutions of the Cold War.[14] In that limited but very practical sense, welfare liberalism blended seamlessly with international democratization. As a result, the particular historical situation served as an explanation for why postwar liberalism as an ideology blended support for the welfare state at home with support for resistance to totalitarianism abroad and, by extension, why postwar conservatism emphasized resistance to the welfare state and continuing caution with regard to international conflicts.

Yet the factional alignments characterizing foreign affairs were never to be drawn into parallel with those characterizing economic welfare during the long Late New Deal. To begin with, neither party was neatly consensual on foreign affairs. Moreover and more to the practical point, the factional structure surrounding foreign affairs, and thus the political dynamic that resulted from confronting these issues through those factions, was sufficiently different from the factional dynamic characterizing welfare politics as to augment partisan *de*polarization. With foreign affairs, the Southern Democrats were the most reliably internationalist—they were the left in this alignment—as they had been for a long time.[15] The bulk of Northern Democrats could be relied on to join them, though they possessed a vocal minority that was never enthusiastic about pursuing a contest with international Communism.

The great resistance to pursuit of the Cold War—the right on the same alignment—resided inside the Republican Party, among those elements that continued to prefer an isolationist approach to international affairs.[16] The surviving (and now recovering) body of Republicans from outside the Northeast anchored this position. Northeastern Republicans then provided an internationalist exception that was crucial to the creation of Cold War institutions. Moreover, in perhaps the greatest policy triumph of his presidency, Dwight Eisenhower went on to move the Republican Party as a whole away from isolationism and toward the evolving Cold War consensus. Though if that party was no longer devoted to a defense build-down, it remained more cautious about using American forces in international conflicts.

In any case, by the time the National Election Study could tap mass preferences for public policy, it was clear that the public gave the Republicans credit for being better able to handle foreign affairs generally, just as it continued to give the Democrats credit for being better able to handle domestic welfare.[17] On his way into office, Dwight Eisenhower, the lone Republican president of the Late New Deal Era, was to bene- fit critically from this generalized perception, as focused concretely in 1952 by the ongoing hot war in Korea. Yet while foreign affairs did join economic welfare as the main secondary realm of public policy (and substantive conflict) for the rest of the Late New Deal Era, surveys con- firmed that foreign affairs remained secondary to economic welfare as an organizing principle for partisan politics in the public mind.

The major further complication to this policy picture then in- volved civil rights, consciously and conspicuously avoided by Franklin Roosevelt during the High New Deal but claiming national attention more and more insistently as the Late New Deal matured. The issue was hardly absent in the previous period, breaking through in 1937, for ex- ample, while Roosevelt was attempting to secure his court-packing plan and executive reorganization. Antilynching legislation, inching its way through Congress, finally arrived on the floor of the House in that year and passed by 282–108 before stalling in the Senate. Roosevelt, while privately committed to the evenhanded implementation of New Deal programs, was even more committed to holding the Democratic Party behind his economic welfare agenda and so had nothing public to say about the antilynching bill.[18]

In the postwar world, however, this policy straddle became harder and harder to execute.[19] In fact, there were three distinguishable routes to increased prominence for civil rights as a matter of substantive con- flict. First, liberal Democrats began to press the issue within national party councils. Thus the first postwar Democratic convention, the Dem- ocratic National Convention of 1948, featured a successful insurgent effort to adopt a strong civil rights plank, leading to a Southern walk- out and the subsequent "Dixiecrat" campaign for president. Second, civil rights groups and their allies consistently pursued the issue in the courts. There, the possibility of suppressing the issue really ended with the *Brown v. Board of Education* decision of 1954, overturning the *Plessy v. Ferguson* decision of 1896 whose "separate but equal" formulation had been the critical defense for those wanting to sustain racial seg- regation. And third, last but not least, civil rights protests, dating in a major way to at least the Montgomery bus boycott of 1955, became only more insistent as time passed, raising the stakes for policy conflict over civil rights in a fashion that, from the late 1950s onward, would not go away.

In a sense, Congress first entered the fray in the postwar period by *refusing* to advance the proposed Fair Employment Practices Commission introduced repeatedly by President Harry Truman. Congress reentered the fray in the opposite direction with the Civil Rights Act of 1957, the first such legislation since Reconstruction and, more pointedly, since President Woodrow Wilson had introduced the practices of southern racial segregation to the federal government. The Civil Rights Act of 1964 and then the Voting Rights Act of 1965 ultimately addressed these matters much more forcefully than the largely anodyne act of 1957, enunciating the full-blown principles of antidiscrimination, while the Open Housing Act of 1968 was probably the most consequential subsequent effort to take those principles into critical substantive realms.

Yet whether or not the issue was embodied in current legislation at any given point during the Late New Deal Era, it was always there in the background, instantiated by its own continuing factional structure—a structure once again different from the counterpart structures on both economic welfare and foreign affairs, thereby contributing additionally and powerfully to the depolarized character of the Late New Deal. In this factional structure, the Democratic Party in Congress was split roughly down the middle. Yet with civil rights as opposed to economic welfare, where the party was also split, Northern Democrats anchored the liberal end of the ideological continuum while Southern Democrats anchored the conservative end.

Inevitably, such a split left the Republicans as effective arbiters of the details of civil rights legislation. On the one hand, the Republican Party had a long and hallowed tradition of support. Emancipation and Reconstruction had, after all, been Republican initiatives. On the other hand, the party was increasingly losing the black Americans who were the obvious beneficiaries of civil rights legislation, while it had many nonblack legislators who were responsive to general arguments about limiting the powers of central government. Accordingly, both Republican factions contributed the ideological center for civil rights politicking, and both were in play with any specific piece of legislation. Northeastern Republicans were more reliably sympathetic but simultaneously less numerous. Regular Republicans were less automatic in their support but more likely to be decisive if they broke clearly to one side or the other.

That factional alignment also made it difficult for the general public to judge the position of the national parties on civil rights. With economic welfare, Democrats were liberal, Republicans were conservative, and public concern favored the Democrats during the entire Late New Deal Era. With foreign affairs, Democrats were internationalist and Republicans at least more cautious, while public concern favored the Republicans during all but the dissident contest of 1964. Yet partisan perceptions of civil rights were vacillating and ambiguous well into the 1960s.[20] Even when the parties began to have a reliable partisan drift, Democrats liberal and Republicans conservative, it is worth remembering that had the Republican Party in Congress not *remained* more liberal than the Democratic Party in the domain of civil rights, there would have been neither a Civil Rights Act nor a Voting Rights Act to characterize the period.

The fight for civil rights was also the policy theater where the Supreme Court played its greatest role in the Late New Deal Era. The Court was already chipping away at the old racial order during the late years of the Roosevelt presidency, in decisions like *Smith v. Allwright* in 1944.[21] That ruling banned the white (segregated) primary, on grounds that it could not meet even the old standard of "separate but equal" imposed by *Plessy v. Ferguson*.[22] Yet the bombshell decisions were actually to be two bites of *Brown v. Board of Education* in 1954 and 1955,[23] the first striking down *Plessy* and the second specifying the proper course of relief from its former strictures.

That decision was pivotal on its own terms, moving doctrinally from a world of separate but equal to a world of equality before the law in every regard.[24] The substantive content of civil rights conflict was thereby changed qualitatively. But the decision was additionally pivotal by confirming the death of the old policy conflict between the Supreme Court and the elective institutions of national government along with the birth, at least in hindsight, of a potential new conflict between the same institutions. In the old world, this conflict had been about the ability of the government to regulate economic life. The resolution of that conflict had settled the nature of the policy-making process for the High New Deal. In the new world, this conflict would instead be about the ability of the government to regulate social life, through a focus on civil rights and civil liberties.

Brown and its successors were thus to be consequential not just on their face but also as a giant opening wedge in an even larger cluster of issues that would largely come into its own by way of the Supreme Court during the successor Era of Divided Government. In their initial appearance, these were embodied most centrally in key civil rights decisions, by way of *Brown* and its progeny. In the subsequent era, they would go on to encompass a much broader array of what would come to be recognized as "cultural" issues, including major decisions on criminal justice, school prayer, and abortion policy. Though while these latter would intermittently annoy both presidents and congressional majorities, sometimes in a major way, they would never again constitute one side of the ideological polarization characterizing a period, as their economic welfare predecessors had in the High New Deal Era.

Where the Late New Deal Era did, however, resemble the High New Deal in matters involving the Supreme Court was in the irrelevance of explicitly partisan attachments to the policy contributions produced by that Court. In the High New Deal Era, neither the partisan attachments of the presidents appointing Supreme Court justices nor the partisan attachments of those justices themselves had had much to do with the great and diagnostic split between presidency and Court. Appointees of both Democratic and Republican presidents had been on both sides of that great conflict, as were self-identified Democrats and self-identified Republicans among the justices themselves.

Precisely the same could be said of partisan attachments during the Late New Deal Era. All the justices on the Supreme Court by the time Dwight Eisenhower became president had been appointed by Democrats, so the partisanship of past presidents provided no clue about future divisions on the Court.[25] Yet Eisenhower, moderate Republican president, was to appoint the key figures on what became the Warren Court—that is, the key figures in building a liberal activist majority—including William J. Brennan Jr., widely regarded as the intellectual architect of the doctrinal transformation underwritten by the Warren Court and, of course, Chief Justice Earl Warren himself.

In formally partisan terms, Warren had been the Republican governor of California and then the running mate of Republican presidential candidate Thomas E. Dewey in 1948. In turn, the all-Democratic Court that he inherited was split between conservative defenders of precedent, led by Justices Felix Frankfurter and Robert H. Jackson, and liberal supporters of interpretation, led by Justices Hugo Black and William O. Douglas. Warren and Brennan became simultaneously the opening Republican appointees *and* the men who would lead the Court away from Frankfurter and Jackson and toward Black and Douglas (though Brennan was actually a committed Democrat). Alonzo Hamby summed up the lack of explicitly partisan cues in all of this by noting, "Strangely, Warren's leadership of the most radical Supreme Court in American history was the most enduring legacy of Eisenhower moderation."[26]

In any case, the resulting summary portrait of enduring party factions, evolving factional ideologies, and grand policy realms to which these ideologies were applied can go a long way toward explaining the ideological depolarization characteristic of the period, while suggesting the contours of the policy-making process that followed more or less inevitably from them. Such a portrait must be slightly stylized, since specific pieces of prospective legislation could affect individual states or districts in idiosyncratic ways, drawing their elected representatives away from normal factional preferences, while the interaction of two different policy domains within one piece of prospective legislation—foreign policy implications of domestic welfare legislation, for example, or civil rights implications of foreign policy legislation—could cause factions to split in less stereotypical fashion.

That said, there was at bottom a stereotypical array of party factions and factional ideologies specialized to policy realms, an array that imparted a clear if implicit structure to the politics of the period:

- With *economic welfare*, Northern Democrats were the left, the pro-welfare side; Regular Republicans were the right, the laissez-faire side; and Southern Democrats and Northeastern Republicans were the factions in play, the crucial pivots.
- On *foreign affairs*, Southern Democrats were the left, the internationalist wing; Regular Republicans were the right, the isolationist wing; and Northern Democrats and Northeastern Republicans were the crucial pivots, the factions in play.
- And on *civil rights*, Northern Democrats were the left, the interventionists; Southern Democrats were the right, asserting state autonomy; and both the Regular and the Northeastern Republicans were in play, joint pivots this time.

The best way to see this overall structure of party balance, ideological polarization, and substantive conflict at work is to select a few diagnostic legislative acts from the three main substantive areas across the Late New Deal Era and observe their fortunes through the lens of the policy-making process that characterized and distinguished the era. No one of these bills is definitively representative of an entire policy domain or a full political era. Yet most major legislative products make the ongoing linkage of key analytic elements in their politics look surprisingly straightforward: among factional alignments, substantive preferences, and the policy-making process itself. Results across the entire era do vary according to the specifics of the legislation at issue, the balance of parties and factions at that point in time, and the surrounding mix of other policy conflicts. Yet ongoing factional arrays and their differences across policy realms still shine through.

To help them do so, it is useful to have some external standard to separate major from minor legislative products of the period. One well-known set of external judgments, created for other purposes but extremely useful for ours as well, is found in David R. Mayhew's book *Divided We Govern*; his is the policy roster used here.[27] To achieve it, Mayhew applied two different "filters," one surveying written judgments of the time about the consequences of laws passed in every session of every Congress from 1945 onward, the other asking modern analysts for judgments about which of these laws proved additionally consequential with the benefit of hindsight.[28] Sometimes, especially in the realm of foreign policy where the transitions into World War II and then the Cold War are central to the Late New Deal Era, it is necessary to reach back before 1945 and the Mayhew list, but this is easily done.

Economic welfare had been more or less the sole—monolithic—policy focus of the High New Deal Era, and it continued as the policy spine for what came to be recognized as the New Deal party system. Programmatic specifics would inevitably change with the policy in question, but the primary thrust of this substantive realm remained as it had been during the High New Deal, just extended, retrenched, adjusted, or redirected. What was different was the factional balance around this thrust. The predominance of Northern Democrats was a thing of the past—revealed now to have been a short-run interlude. Earlier party factions resurfaced, but rebalanced and in some cases with changing policy preferences attached. Thereafter, the factional alignments characterizing the legislative politics of economic welfare would look impressively stable for the entire Late New Deal Era.

Thus the Congress that assembled for an era-opening session in 1939, the first in which the Northern Democratic dominance of the High New Deal was gone, proved sharply different in policy terms.[29]

Gone was any prospect for another round of comprehensive initiatives in the economic welfare domain. In its place were the beginnings of a counterattack on the New Deal project, though it would really be the one-two punch of the 1938 and 1942 midterms that confirmed the arrival of a new world of policy conflict in the domain of economic welfare. By 1943, this welfare "correction" was being implicitly but additionally reinforced by the growing consequence of foreign affairs as a policy focus for national government:

- Casualties included the Works Projects Administration, the Civilian Conservation Corps, and the National Youth Administration, all products of the second major tranche of New Deal programs in 1935 and all concentrated on provision of direct relief. The Farm Security Administration and the Rural Electrification Administration, also under attack, survived but as defunded shells of their former selves.
- On the other hand, the main social insurance and regulatory elements of the New Deal not only survived but endured no serious counterattack. Social Security, farm price supports, child labor laws, the minimum wage, plus banking and securities regulation became recognized as the "untouchable pillars of the new social and economic order that Roosevelt had wrought out of the Depression crisis."[30]

The Federal Housing Act of 1949 was then a good introduction to the contours of postwar conflict over welfare policy, being especially good at suggesting the complexity of the links among party factions, substantive preferences, and policy conflict. A severe housing shortage accompanied the demobilization of millions of servicemen at the end of World War II. Rent and price controls had been the first available response of the Truman administration in the aftermath of V-J Day. When that was followed by the partisan upset of the 1946 midterm elections, a new Republican majority had other priorities: the Taft-Hartley labor law was their most lasting contribution to the domain of social welfare.[31] So the first real push for major housing legislation had to await the Truman reelection of 1948 and resumption of Democratic control of Congress.

In that environment, the Federal Housing Act of 1949 became the first comprehensive effort to create a framework for housing policy in the postwar United States, including not just public housing but urban

redevelopment more generally.[32] Creating that framework required decisions about four main elements: the locus of planning, the degree
of public provision, the nature of targeted recipients, and associated
arrangements for funding. The bill that the White House introduced
was in effect what Northern Democrats preferred in each of these areas:
federally driven, publicly provided, reaching into the middle class, and
funded through long-term borrowing.

Yet each of the other major party factions had distinct preferences
on these central aspects of housing policy. Southern Democrats wanted
policy to be locally driven; had no problem with public provision of
such housing; preferred limiting it to low-income constituents; and
were unenthusiastic about borrowing for the long term. Northeastern
Republicans agreed with Northern Democrats on national planning;
disagreed strongly on public provision, preferring market-based incentives; liked extension to middle-income residents; and favored pay-as-
you-go funding. Regular Republicans, finally, preferred local planning;
were strongly opposed to direct public provision; saw such provision as
best limited to the truly disadvantaged; and preferred that it be as close
to self-financing as possible.

The result of that matrix of party factions and substantive preferences would drive compromises within the original plan, leading some
critics to complain that the result was an early triumph of the conservative coalition, isolating the Northern Democrats, though the fact that
the resulting policy was comprehensive and lasting could as easily be
grounds for noting what a major initiative it was. Either way, the Federal
Housing Act of 1949 was an excellent introduction to welfare politics
during the Late New Deal Era:

- Overall, the bill pitted the two parties against each other in the
  House, passing by a total vote of 232–191, with Democrats voting
  196–55 but Republicans voting 34–136. That was a classic split on
  welfare policy, the underlying spine of the New Deal party system.
- Still, the ultimate package could not have passed without Republican support. Or, said the other way around, Democratic desertions
  were sufficient to scuttle the plan as written, absent compensating
  Republican defections.
- This only emphasizes the further importance of factional divisions:
  Northern Democrats 147–6, Southern Democrats 49–49, Northeastern Republicans 19–46, and Regular Republicans 15–90.

- The Senate then proved anticlimactic, with all factions in positive territory for a total of 57–13.

A dozen years later, the Area Redevelopment Act of 1961, intended as a keystone achievement of the Kennedy administration in economic welfare, was still strikingly similar in partisan divisions and factional underpinnings, despite a very different substantive focus. From the mid-1950s onward, the national Democratic Party had begun to emphasize welfare programs targeted at geographic regions that were being left behind in the postwar boom. The idea now was, rather than a national attack on a specific problem, a regional attack on comprehensive problems. Appalachia served as a poster child for the alleged need, though from the other side, the strategy left itself open to the contention that it was merely an update on the old "pork-barrel" approach to policy-making.[33]

Either way, internal divisions for the area redevelopment vote were about as close to those of the housing vote a dozen years earlier as such tallies are likely to get, despite a radically different surface focus. Much had changed contextually. Postwar demobilization was a distant memory; the Eisenhower administration had dominated the years since. Yet the House vote was 231–200 as opposed to the earlier 232–191. The two parties were 200–59 versus 196–55 among Democrats and 31–141 versus 34–136 among Republicans. And the factions were Northern Democrats 158–4 versus 147–6, Southern Democrats 42–55 versus 49–49, Northeastern Republicans 22–38 versus 19–46, and Regular Republicans 9–103 versus 15–90. The Senate was again easier, with a grand total of 63–27.

Factional divisions were thus impressively stable across the Truman, Eisenhower, and Kennedy years. What this should not be taken to imply was that the partisan balance around them was therefore irrelevant to the resulting outputs. A useful example arrived only four years later with the Elementary and Secondary Education Act of 1965. This was landmark legislation, bringing the federal government into educational policy at the state and local level in a fashion never before experienced.[34] Seen one way, then, even landmark *change* confirmed the continuity of interactions among party balance, ideological polarization, substantive conflict, and their associated policy-making process that distinguished the Late New Deal Era.

Yet the shifting partisan balance that arrived with the Johnson landslide in 1964 was simultaneously critical to the ability of the federal government to enter a policy realm previously reserved to the states. Once again, the House was the key theater for conflict. This time, there was some factional movement: Southern Democrats had become progressively less enthusiastic as legislation moved from housing to area redevelopment to education, while Northeastern Republicans had become correspondingly more enthusiastic. But the main fresh point was the *forty* additional Northern Democrats available in 1965 but unavailable in 1949 or even 1961, a scant four years earlier. Hence for these Northern Democrats: 147–6 in 1949, 158–4 in 1961, but 199–4 in 1965. By extension, among all Democrats: 196–55 in 1949, 200–59 in 1961, but 232–57 in 1965.[35]

That was an evolutionary snapshot of the interaction among factional structure, substantive preference, and policy-making process during the Late New Deal Era for the domain embodying the original New Deal focus, namely, economic welfare. Yet the domain that would both distinguish this era from the High New Deal and continue as a major substantive focus thereafter was foreign affairs. Foreign affairs would be similar to economic welfare in that factional alignments were established early and remained remarkably stable. Yet foreign affairs would be sharply different in the ideological positions attached to the four major factions, and thus to the policy-making dynamic that followed from those positions. As a result, this latter difference would be additionally crucial to the ideological depolarization characterizing the entire era.

That difference was not slow in arriving. The election of 1938 effectively ended the High New Deal. The German invasion of Poland in 1939 effectively began the Second World War. Yet what it did in American domestic politics was to thrust foreign affairs to the attention of national policy-makers, beginning with a pointed struggle over amendment of the neutrality legislation governing foreign policy at the time.[36] Thereafter, foreign affairs would sometimes dominate economic welfare and sometimes be subordinate to it, but it would never again be absent from the national policy agenda in all the years of the Late New Deal.

The long surge of isolationist ideology within American society in the aftermath of World War I meant that the United States was still governed in 1939 by neutrality laws requiring an arms embargo on all belligerents upon the outbreak of war. Constrained by isolationist preferences in public opinion but believing that world war would inevitably involve the United States, while being specifically supportive of England

and France in their response to the German invasion of Poland, Franklin Roosevelt set out to repeal the arms embargo through a cash-and-carry policy. The United States would help to shape the course of the war by selling military matériel to chosen nations, as long as they paid for this matériel up front and removed it in their own vessels.

In the struggle for passage, public opinion appeared to flow, ebb, and flow again, being initially sympathetic to the victims of aggression, showing a resurgent desire to remain detached, then drifting back as disastrous international events continued to unfold. The president was nevertheless at his weakest with Congress in the aftermath of the 1938 election, having failed at court packing, failed at executive reorganization, and failed in his attempt to purge the most conservative Southern Democrats. Two critical if ironic events thus became crucial to the effort to secure bipartisan support for repeal: an early endorsement by Senator Robert A. Taft (R-OH), a recognized leader of the Regular Republicans, along with the unflinching support of the Southern Democrats, despite major policy differences in other realms.

In the end, in October 1939, the result was decisive but still diagnostic of the factional alignment associated with it. Repeal was first addressed in the Senate, claiming its usual priority in foreign affairs. The results there were 63 yes and only 30 no, led by Southern Democrats at 19–2, followed by Northern Democrats at 35–10, splitting Northeastern Republicans at 4–4, and opposed by Regular Republicans at 4–11, plus four minor-party senators at 1–3. The House Rules Committee cooperated by sharply limiting debate on this Senate result, and when the House rejected an amendment endorsing continuation of the embargo, the battle was over. That key tally was 181 yes and 243 no, with an internal division of 4–93 among Southern Democrats, 32–127 among Northern Democrats, 56–15 among Northeastern Republicans, and 87–6 among Regular Republicans, with a 2–2 split among the others.

In both bodies, then, the Southern Democrats led the internationalist bloc, despite that all-too-recent effort by the president to purge key players among them. Their 19–2 edge in the Senate was impressive; their 4–93 edge in the House contributed the entire margin of victory. Moreover, the same story would be repeated in the crucial opening conflict of the Cold War, perhaps the single greatest turning point in all of American foreign policy. This arrived over the proposal of aid to Greece and Turkey in what became recognized as the Truman Doctrine, promising that the United States would come to the aid of free nations facing Communist insurrection, ideally through economic stabilization but with the buttressing of military force when necessary.[37]

By the time of this debate in 1947, President Truman needed his Southern Democratic internationalists more than ever, having lost control of Congress in the 1946 midterm elections, which meant especially a decrease of Northern Democrats and an increase of Regular Republicans. On the other hand, the drift of postwar events continued to run in a supportive direction, such that the eventual vote was not close. The Senate tally—the Senate again going first—was 67 yes and 23 no, with Southern Democrats 17–4, Northern Democrats 15–3, Northeastern Republicans 12–4, and even Regular Republicans 23–12. The House tally, while likewise not close at 295–115, did spread the factions more characteristically: Southern Democrats 94–2; Northern Democrats and Northeastern Republicans in the middle at 70–11 and 64–24, respectively; Regular Republicans in opposition, still showing an isolationist majority at 66–77; and others at 1–1.

The Mayhew roster features many additional bills collectively creating the institutional framework for the long-running Cold War. These included the Marshall Plan (European Recovery Act) of 1948; the creation of NATO in 1949; the Mutual Defense Assistance Act of that same year; Point Four Foreign Aid in 1950, bringing the developing nations into the Cold War framework; and the Mutual Security Act of 1951. Their votes did shuffle the major factions in modest fashion, sometimes featuring a bit less support from Southern Democrats and a bit more from Northeastern Republicans, though the continuing resistance of the Regular Republicans was a constant. A different way to summarize this entire development was provided by Richard E. Neustadt, the great postwar student of the American presidency. His purpose was to defend the Truman administration; ours is more to note the huge policy-making consequences of this second major substantive domain of the Late New Deal Era:

> On no previous occasion has American foreign policy required—much less received—comparable congressional participation for such a span of time. Rarely before, save at the outset of our greatest wars, had the Congress broken so much new and unfamiliar ground. Rarely, if ever, has momentum been so long sustained . . .
>
> This raises a crucial point: the internationalist coalition which supported Truman's foreign policy existed, cheek by jowl, with a "conservative" coali-

tion which opposed administration policies at home. What's more, the two most vital elements in the conservative alignment were also participants in the internationalist bloc . . . the Vandenberg Midwest Republicans and the Russell Southern Democrats.[38]

Yet it was the third major substantive area for policy conflict in the Late New Deal Era, civil rights, that was largely idiosyncratic to the period and thus truly distinguished its policy focus. Like foreign affairs, civil rights was an additionally major domain for policy conflict in the aftermath of the High New Deal. Like both foreign affairs and economic welfare, civil rights had a factional alignment all its own, contributing additionally to the ideological depolarization of the era. Both economic welfare and foreign affairs would generate more legislation than civil rights during the Late New Deal. On the other hand, if there was a domain that generated the most singular and lasting policy contributions of the period, it was surely this one. Two comprehensive bills, the Civil Rights Act of 1957 and the Civil Rights Act of 1964, so very different in their ultimate impact, are in that sense all the better for highlighting yet another continuing mix of factional structure, substantive preference, and policy-making process.

Those seeking action on civil rights ordinarily began by trying to extract as strong a bill as possible from the House Judiciary Committee, under Northern Democratic leadership from Emanuel Celler (D-NY), just as they tried to avoid for as long as possible the Senate Judiciary Committee, under Southern Democratic leadership from James Eastland (D-MS).[39] The fate of such bills was then determined by negotiations with the two great Republican factions. Northeastern Republicans often came from states or districts with substantial minority populations, where traditional Republican support for civil rights might generate concrete rewards at the polls. Regular Republicans more often came from states or districts without substantial minority populations, where traditional Republican support for civil rights brought the risk of unforeseen consequences for nonminority voters.

The coming of the 1956 election caused national Republican strategists to sense potential gains among black voters, partly in response to the president's mobilization of the National Guard in Little Rock, Arkansas, in the aftermath of *Brown v. Board*, partly in response to the dramatic role of Democratic senators and representatives in the local resistance to that decision. Responding to these incentives became the responsibility of Attorney General Herbert Brownell, who brought forward the classic four-part civil rights initiative: creation of a new regulatory body, the Civil Rights Commission; expansion of voting rights to include primary and special elections; authorization for the attorney general to seek injunctive relief where voting rights were not being observed; and extension of injunctive power to include deprivations of civil rights more generally.

A bill to that effect actually passed the House, but only in the week it adjourned and thus never moved on to the Senate. The same bill passed the House again at the beginning of the 1957 session. Yet from that point onward, both the substance of the bill and the coalition around it began to unravel.[40] For the Southern Democrats, Richard Russell (D-GA) argued that what was being treated as a "voting rights bill" was actually a subterfuge, with a focus far beyond voting and with prosecutorial powers greater than previously authorized in any realm. For the Northeastern Republicans, Jacob Javits (R-NY) argued that Russell was correct, and that this was a good thing. The combination—apparent agreement between the extremes that the proposed act was far more sweeping than publicly acknowledged—caused Regular Republican support to hemorrhage.

A coalition of Northern Democrats and Northeastern Republicans subsequently agreed to strike both the prosecutorial powers of the attorney general and the ability to exercise them beyond voting. What remained was sufficiently anodyne as not to generate a coordinated Senate filibuster, though Strom Thurmond (D-SC), the presidential candidate of the Dixiecrat splinter in 1948, did produce a record-breaking, twenty-four-hour, one-man effort. Thereafter, the bill passed the Senate 72–18, though the factional breakout highlighted residual Democratic tensions: Regular Republicans 27–0, Northeastern Republicans 16–0, Northern Democrats 24–1, and Southern Democrats 5–17. Returned to the House, the bill passed with equal ease, 294–131, with similar factional results: Northern Democrats 122–11; Northeastern Republicans 70–3; Regular Republicans 102–19; Southern Democrats 0–98.

Seen one way, the result was the first civil rights bill since 1875, giving it nominally historic status in any list of postwar legislative accomplishments. Seen the other way, the absence of a reach beyond voting rights, but especially the limitation of legal relief to civil suits, meant that the law was quickly dismissed as toothless even by its supporters. Seven years later, a largely similar bill, containing the same four generic elements as the original Brownell proposal, (1) followed a roughly similar institutional trajectory, (2) produced a similar ultimate vote in Congress, yet (3) generated another landmark civil rights bill with serious policy teeth this time. Factional alignments were similar at the start. Factional votes were similar at the end. But ultimate substance was radically different, shaped by differing compromises along the way and driven by a different external context.[41]

Once again, the bill began in the House rather than the Senate. Once again, a comprehensive bill contained all the major parts: a permanent Civil Rights Commission to supervise extension of the franchise; expansion of voting rights to apply to all elections; authority for the government (both the Civil Rights Commission *and* the attorney general) to bring prosecutions; extension of this prosecutorial authority into civil rights generally, beyond the ballot box. But at this point Attorney General Robert Kennedy intervened to prevent the bill from being another empty rallying call and began cutting deals with the crucial factions.

Kennedy agreed with committee Republicans to strip out provisions affecting racial balance in the North. He agreed to narrow the focus of employment discrimination. He agreed that voting provisions would apply to federal elections only. That brought the bill out of the full Judiciary Committee. President John Kennedy was assassinated shortly thereafter; a new president, Lyndon Johnson, committed himself publicly to the bill; and Howard Smith, chairman of the House Rules Committee, found himself boxed into reporting it.[42] The bill then passed easily to the Senate, 292–132, with Northeastern Republicans 55–2, Northern Democrats 146–10, Regular Republicans 84–33, and Southern Democrats 7–87. The 1957 act had passed the House on an almost identical vote, 294–131. Yet the 1964 version going forward to the Senate was much stiffer on substantive grounds.

The Senate Democratic leadership then put this bill directly onto the calendar rather than sending it to the Judiciary Committee and managed to sustain its decision. Critical negotiations took place this time between President Johnson and Everett Dirksen (R-IL), Senate minority leader. Dirksen managed to remove the investigative authority of the new Equal Employment Opportunity Commission (EEOC) from those states that already possessed a Fair Employment Practices Commission (FEPC), thereby further limiting the impact of the bill to the South, where FEPCs were nonexistent. He succeeded in moving prosecutorial powers away from this reformed EEOC and sending them to the Justice Department, fully experienced in these matters but with a smaller staff and broader responsibilities elsewhere. And he further narrowed the employment focus away from family-owned businesses: "Mrs. Murphy's boardinghouse" was the recurrent metaphor.

Those compromises left Southern Democrats profoundly isolated, and while they did mount a comprehensive filibuster, they no longer had the votes to sustain it. Cloture was voted in June 1964 by 71–29: Northeastern Republicans 16–0, Northern Democrats 43–3, Regular Republicans 9–6, and Southern Democrats 1–20. The bill itself passed the Senate two days later on a vote of 73–27.[43] The overall tally thus resembled the vote in 1957, and the aspects of the bill that had had to be adjusted to reach these votes were pretty much identical. Yet the resulting product was fundamentally different. Much of this difference was the result of specific negotiations *within* a constant factional alignment, though an important further element was the increase in the raw number of Northern Democrats as between the two civil rights acts: 24–1 on final passage in 1957, but 45–1 in 1964.

The last big bill of the civil rights period was the Open Housing Act of 1968, taking rights legislation farther into the realm of substantive policy than either the 1957 Civil Rights Act or the 1964 Civil Rights Act.[44] By 1968, support for civil rights in the general public was actually in retreat, courtesy of widespread racial rioting, while the supportive cross-party coalition of Northern Democrats and Northeastern Republicans would be additionally stressed by open housing rules, with their obvious application to the North. An open housing bill from the White House had thus languished in 1967, and the biggest rights bill for 1968 was slated to be a minor one, protecting civil rights workers in the South. That bill passed the House easily. The Senate Judiciary Committee reported it without incident. And Mike Mansfield (D-MT), Senate majority leader, put it on the floor calendar.

But at that point, Walter Mondale (D-MN) appended the entire 1967 housing act onto this minor proposal, as senators (but not representatives) were entitled to do. His move made a Southern Democratic filibuster inevitable, and Sam Ervin (D-NC) organized the comprehensive response. Yet an opening test vote on cloture was surprisingly close, a result that returned Everett Dirksen to the center of negotiations. Dirksen's members were high on the list of those whose enthusiasm for civil rights was being cooled by the riotous degradation of the movement.

Yet Dirksen had also acquired a new cadre of Senate Republicans courtesy of the midterm elections of 1966, one that contained a number of senators with actively liberal credentials on civil rights.

Dirksen thus returned to the role that he had played with the Civil Rights Act of 1964, reinforced by better numbers. He succeeded in reducing the coverage of open housing rules modestly, and he removed owner-occupied dwellings that rented out three or fewer units. With those amendments, he endorsed the bill. A vote followed on March 4, and while Republicans generally could no longer be as confident as they had once been that such a bill would not fall disruptively on their home districts, cloture did squeak through, 65–32: Northern Democrats 39–3, Northeastern Republicans 9–12, Regular Republicans 15–11, and Southern Democrats 2–17. Passage occurred a week later, 71–20, when Dirksen brought almost his entire cohort with him: Northern Democrats 40–0, Northeastern Republicans 9–1, Regular Republicans 20–2, and Southern Democrats 2–17.

The bill then returned to the House, which had considered only the original draft involving the protection of civil rights workers. By this time, the two main contenders for a Republican presidential nomination, Richard Nixon and Nelson Rockefeller, had both endorsed the Senate bill. Shortly thereafter, Martin Luther King Jr. was assassinated in Memphis, and Gerald Ford, the new minority leader in the House, agreed to put the Senate version directly to a vote. That tally was 251–173, with supportive majorities in both parties. Factional divisions remained familiar, though Regular Republicans were decreasingly reassured about the risk of unintended local effects: Northern Democrats 140–19, Northeastern Republicans 38–7, Regular Republicans 62–77, Southern Democrats 11–70.

Those were some diagnostic policy outcomes from a four-faction alignment across three policy domains, where the factions lined up in a different ideological order in each major domain. Yet they do not exhaust the patterned complexity of this policy-making environment without some further attention to the fact that successful efforts at coalition-building within any one domain always required at least implicit disruption of the coalitional patterns characteristic of the others. Moreover, all the main players knew this. That is, they knew that they had to engage in coalition-building for their current policy focus with one eye on what these maneuvers would do to coalitional prospects in two other major domains.

On occasion, this could alter the dominant coalitions in each substantive realm—economic welfare, foreign affairs, and civil rights—though such alterations, like nearly everything else in the Late New Deal Era, were themselves patterned. To wit: there were two different but recurrent ways in which dominant patterns of factional support and substantive compromise could be disrupted and rearranged. The first surfaced with major legislation that was superficially consensual but had the alignments typical of one of the big-three policy areas hidden just below the surface. The second appeared with major legislation that belonged to one of the major substantive areas on its face, but where policy became entangled with another major domain for one or more factions.

Perhaps the best example of the first type of cross-domain politics, where one of the major domains is sitting right below an apparently consensual surface, was presented by the Federal Highway Act of 1956, keystone legislation for creation of the interstate highway system in the United States.[45] On its face, this was major legislation that, while it had huge programmatic implications, was universally acceptable, both across the political parties and among their factions. Completion of that system would have policy ramifications across substantive areas and down through time. It would cement into place the American preference for the automobile rather than mass transit. It would facilitate the growth of some industries while presenting major challenges for others. And it would shape the geographic pattern of subsequent economic development.

Still, with all those economic and social ramifications in so many places for such a very long time, the activating legislation appeared to be desired by almost everyone. Or at least, the legislation producing these effects was to secure a final vote of 388–19 in the House and 89–1 in the Senate. Nevertheless, below the surface, in a phenomenon that could be found in other apparently consensual realms, there were key disputes that had to be resolved on the way to this overwhelming support, disputes embodying one of the three great policy domains of the era, to be resolved either by a compromise satisfactory to the disputants or one that was so clearly the winning position that major players had to accept it or forfeit all potential rewards.

For the Federal Highway Act of 1956, there were actually two such disputes. The first involved funding for the new interstate highway system. When Dwight Eisenhower introduced his preferred bill in 1955, he called for creation of a national highway authority that would issue bonds, build roads, and use proceeds to pay off the loan. Apart from a few Northeastern Republicans, no one was attracted by his funding solution, and the bill languished. Eisenhower brought it back in 1956 after deleting his autonomous operating body and attempting a balanced funding plan that gave something to all sides. Discussion then shifted to disbursement of the cornucopia of jobs, contracts, and favors that would inevitably follow from the new law, a topic perennially of interest to representatives, senators, and their home districts.

Yet beyond the immediate questions of who would get to do the necessary construction and who would get credit for assigning the contracts—matters easily resolved by conventional logrolling—there lurked one of the major economic welfare concerns of the post–New Deal world, namely, what would be the prevailing *labor rules* governing this work. Revised legislation came forward with the provision that prevailing wage rules in the country as a whole would apply, the Northern Democratic preference. This was amended to substitute prevailing wage rates in the state where the construction would occur, the Regular Republican preference. But a stable resolution was not secured until the two sides in effect split the difference, leaving it to the secretary of labor to assign appropriate rates after considering a variety of locally relevant factors.

The key vote came in the Senate. Only when this passed did the bill become an "inevitability." This crucial tally saw the factions aligned not by highway mileage but from most to least tolerance of organized labor: Northern Democrats 24–1, Northeastern Republicans 9–6, Regular Republicans 6–19, and Southern Democrats 3–11. By a vote of 42–37, then, the question of labor relations was resolved—or, really, fudged and put off—so that the bill could move on to an 89–1 victory among the same senators. In hindsight, had three Northeastern Republicans moved, taking their 9–6 faction in the other direction, or had those three Southern Democratic "yes" votes gone "no," an apparently overwhelming consensus would at a minimum have been stalled.

The other way in which familiar patterns could reappear in initially unfamiliar fashion during the Late New Deal Era involved major legislation that belonged on its face to one of the three great substantive realms of the period—economic welfare, foreign affairs, or civil rights— but had implications that mobilized another of these realms for one of the big-four party factions, thereby generating a hybrid of substantive conflicts and factional coalitions. Despite the added complexity, this effect was usually recognizable from the character of the two substantive realms that were being conjoined—and tangled. Perhaps the best example was the long struggle, also during the Eisenhower years, over what became known as the Bricker Amendment to the US Constitution.[46]

John Bricker was a senator from Ohio, a Regular Republican, and an isolationist. He became the point man for those who feared that the Cold War was magnifying the power of the president not just through treaties but also by way of executive agreements, while at the same time expanding the policy-making clout of the federal bureaucracy and effectively short-circuiting Congress. His proposed amendment required that all executive agreements and even all agreed treaties remain inoperative until Congress passed implementing legislation. At its high point, the proposal had the endorsement of more than sixty senators, enough to send a constitutional amendment forward to the states.

Judged by the surface content of the proposal, this should have produced an alignment similar to the ones repealing neutrality provisions at the beginning of World War II or enunciating the Truman Doctrine at the opening of the Cold War. Yet in the mid-1950s, the Bricker Amendment became caught up in legislative maneuvering over civil rights because Southern Democrats feared that increasingly insistent resolutions from the United Nations about racial segregation might be smuggled into public policy in the United States by way of executive agreements. Only such an understanding—the Bricker Amendment as foreign affairs for three major factions but as civil rights for the fourth—could explain the otherwise curious ultimate tally.

Overall, the resolution narrowly failed to achieve the necessary two-thirds majority, 60–31, and thus failed to advance to the House.[47] Yet inside that aggregate vote, the factions fell out as Regular Republicans 29–0, Southern Democrats 19–3, Northeastern Republicans 5–12, and Northern Democrats 7–16. Three factions were thus largely on form with their usual behavior in foreign affairs, namely, Regular Republicans, Northeastern Republicans, and Northern Democrats, with a bit of extra support for the White House from Northeastern Republicans, who viewed Dwight Eisenhower as one of their own. But the remaining faction, the Southern Democrats, was wildly out of line with its usual internationalism, instead doing what it always did on *civil rights*.

That tour of major legislation during the Late New Deal Era speaks to the ideological depolarization that characterized the period. Four partisan factions had to be treated strategically and distinctly whenever prospective legislation was at stake. The same tour speaks to the further complexity introduced by having three main policy domains. Each was shaped by the calculations of the four main partisan factions, but each aligned these four factions in different ways. And just to add to this de-polarized complexity: while strategic calculations in one policy domain not did not carry over to the others, they did often come with strategic implications for policy-making in these other domains. Accordingly, strategic implications for policy-making in the two other substantive do-mains had to be considered, constantly and simultaneously, when pur-suing legislation in the policy realm most directly in question.

In the end, then, the tour also suggests the perpetual—and inter-locked—negotiations and renegotiations that were diagnostic of policy-making in their era. It was a gradual but growing recognition by pro-fessional students of American politics of these patterned calculations that would lead on to a summary concept, "incrementalism," widely recognized though not always saluted, that distinguished this era from all three of the other periods of modern politics since 1932. Which is to say: as scholars worked on major aspects of politics during the Late New Deal Era, they came more and more to converge on a picture of its policy-making process. So a different way to see the resulting system of policy-making in action is to revisit three classic scholarly works from the period, each intended to explain how some major aspect of Ameri-can politics did indeed function. With hindsight, however, it is clear that what each accomplished was to explain major aspects of politics as these worked in the policy-making system *peculiar to the Late New Deal.*

Fortunately, all three of these works took major steps toward synthe-sizing this politics at a level well above individual bills. In one, David Truman in *The Congressional Party* used the enduring factional structure of the period as a means of analyzing the overall lawmaking process.[48] In a second, Richard Fenno in *The Power of the Purse* pasted all of that into the institutional mechanics of appropriations politics.[49] And in a third, Aaron Wildavsky in *The Politics of the Budgetary Process* examined the recurring dynamic by which factions and institutions produced the single document that underwrites policy-making most generally, the federal budget, while giving this process the summary label that has in fact become diagnostic of its time, namely, incrementalism.[50]

The factional situation impelling the policy-making process that distinguished the Late New Deal Era was already becoming evident to serious scholars when Truman published his landmark look at party factions and legislative lawmaking, *The Congressional Party*. Focusing on the first and second sessions of the Eighty-First Congress, from 1949 to 1952, Truman worked from agreement scores between each legislator and every other, while categorizing legislative actions as featuring either high or low cohesion for each of the political parties as a whole. He then applied internal cluster analysis to those cohesion categories, in search not just of the critical party factions but of how these interacted with various leadership and institutional structures.[51]

Already by those early dates, Congress was tussling with housing, labor relations, education, health insurance, Social Security, rent control, and the minimum wage, just within the overarching domain of economic welfare. Yet in the two sessions of this Eighty-First Congress, it also found itself contending over national security, the creation of NATO, treatment of displaced persons, internal security, foreign economic aid, and mutual defense assistance in the policy domain of foreign affairs. And all the while, these Congresses could no longer escape from continuing disputes in the realm of civil rights, including struggles over abolition of the poll tax and creation of the Fair Employment Protection Commission plus the 21-Day Rule in the House (a discharge arrangement) and Rule XXII in the Senate (the cloture rule), procedural arrangements relevant to all major policy realms but where civil rights tended to crystallize the debate.

Truman began with the Senate, on grounds that its factional alignments were more direct, that is, less additionally shaped by the more restrictive rules and procedures that were necessary to allow the House to do its business. What he found essentially confirmed—ratified—the general but often more impressionistic observations of other political scientists and political historians about the simple but far-reaching distinction between Northern and Southern Democrats, the lesser but still clear-cut distinction between Regular and Northeastern Republicans, and the way that the alignment of these divisions differed across major issue areas. For the Democratic story:

> The Southern bloc, consistently the smaller of the two major groupings, was a dissenting agreement of a particular sort. It did not as a unit offer continuous, unremitting opposition to the remainder of the party. Rather, the composition of the bloc showed a good deal of variation from issue to issue. . . . In the first session, six of the seven of its agreements were the

prevailing side in the Senate, while only half were on the side of the party majority. This excess of agreements on the prevailing side is an indication of successful coalition voting in association with one or more Republican factions and in opposition to a majority of Democrats.[52]

The Republican story followed:

> Given the substance of the crucial divisions among the Republicans, one would expect to find rather marked differences among the various blocs with respect to their identification with the party majority and with respect to the frequency with which they appeared on the prevailing side in the Senate. This is indeed the case. In both sessions Bloc I [Northeastern Republicans] clearly was the spearhead element within the Republicans who joined forces with the majority wing of the Democrats, frequently at the expense of deserting the bulk of their own colleagues.[53]

When he moved on to the House, Truman found some modest further structure to the Democratic Party, especially when agricultural issues cut across its bedrock factionalism in anomalous ways. Superficially, his cluster analysis made House Republicans look additionally complex, with seven internal factions. Yet a look backward through the lens of the Late New Deal, searching particularly for its Northeastern versus Regular division, makes it easy to recognize his first three House clusters as the Northeastern Republicans and his last four as their Regular Republican counterparts.

Truman would take this factional lens onward, to speculate about some additional roles for majority and minority status within the partisan cohorts, especially as these roles visited particular responsibilities for managing the larger body upon one (usually the Democratic) or the other (very occasionally the Republican) party. He would pay special attention to the placement of floor leaders within their parties, reliably located inside the dominant faction but leaning slightly away from that faction in the direction of its main alternative. And he would contrast the regularized behavior of these party leaders with the largely autonomous—and wildly heterogeneous—behavior of the formal heads of congressional committees, who provided an alternative leadership structure, narrower in every case and idiosyncratic in many.

That was a complex picture of party factions and legislative struggles. Yet scholars of the time implicitly took this analysis to an even higher level of abstraction, asking whether it was possible to characterize the overall policy-making process that resulted when three major domains for policy conflict were addressed by four major partisan factions in the extended period gathered here as the Late New Deal Era. Because this process is so central to our analysis, it seems important to revisit the comprehensive portrait that emerged. On the one hand, its authors could not know that they were describing a process with temporal limits, and they certainly could not know when those limits would be reached. On the other hand, they addressed this process with a richness that can never be recaptured after the fact.

The great comprehensive analysis of the appropriations politics underpinning this comprehensive policy-making process was Fenno, *The Power of the Purse*. With evidence drawn from an extensive reading of the public documents, supplemented crucially by personal interviews with major actors, Fenno focused on the budgetary requests (and their fortunes) of thirty-six executive agencies drawn from seven cabinet departments for the eighteen-year period from 1947 to 1965. By happy accident, this captured the larger half of the entire Late New Deal Era: "The power of the purse is the historic bulwark of legislative activity. The exercise of that power constitutes the core legislative process— underpinning all other legislative decisions and regulating the balance of influence between the legislative and executive branches of government."[54]

What emerged was a richly textured picture of the world of all the main players: (1) major institutions from the separation of powers, including the White House, bureaucratic agencies, and of course Congress; (2) the main operative parts of both the House and the Senate, in their subcommittees, their full committees, the floor, and the conference; as well as (3) key further distinctions within these operative elements, on the part of formal leaders and their rank and file. This proved to be a world where all these players were more or less reliably integrated, in the sense that they shared mutual expectations and recognized the regularized patterns of behavior that these interlocking expectations generated.

The result was that these regularized patterns of behavior—not personalities, not even the occasionally dramatic conflicts of politics—actually determined outcomes and distributed benefits. The policy-making process was almost mechanistic in many regards. Aspiring participants served an apprenticeship in order to claim their place in this process. Apprentices adapted to the shared goals of protecting the congressional power of the purse, guarding the federal treasury, reducing budget requests, but also serving constituency interests. And a socialization process with real sanctions needed only barely implicit norms, widely acknowledged, to keep the members focused on these goals and to coordinate the financial machinery of government.

There were, in the nature of appropriations politics, modestly disappointed players everywhere. Yet the system was remarkably stable and impressively predictable. Indeed, it was so strongly integrated, with the critical center of this integration inside the House Appropriations Committee, that major dissents were infrequent, while frequent dissenters were irrelevant. In the Late New Deal Era, this appropriations politics—and by extension much other legislative activity—was about mastering the machinery of policy-making and maximizing available policy increments when they occurred: "Furthermore, in an overall sense, the Committee meets both expectations [of responding to external demands but preventing unnecessary expenditure of funds] by avoiding drastic action of any kind in any direction. Its decisions are mostly marginal or incremental—whether measured by the relation of budget estimates to appropriations or by the relation of appropriations to last year's appropriations—and they tend to sustain existing relationships."[55]

Fenno notes in passing that a fully integrated but constantly self-adjusting process like appropriations was inevitably incremental. That notion had been the analytical centerpiece for a nearly simultaneous study of the entire budgeting process: from the individual bureaus, to their departments, to the Bureau of the Budget, past the president, into the House, and onward to the Senate, until it was ultimately converted into operative behavior in the bureaus once again. This was Aaron Wildavsky in *The Politics of the Budgetary Process*, whose central analytic notion of "incrementalism" can stand as a kind of grand summary term for the larger policy-making process that was at the center of analysis here.

Wildavsky began with the budgetary hearings for twenty-five agencies across the period from 1946 to 1960, again the temporal core of the Late New Deal Era, though the author would have had no way of knowing this retrospective fact. His initial reading was supplemented with 160 interviews with major participants in the budgetary process: agency heads, budget officers, Budget Bureau staff, appropriations committee staff, and members of Congress. Like Fenno, Wildavsky was struck by the near-mechanical character of what he observed:

The burden of calculation is enormously reduced for three primary reasons: first, only the small number of alternatives politically feasible at any one time are considered; second, these policies in a democracy typically differ only in small increments from previous policies on which there is a store of relevant information; and, third, each participant may ordinarily assume that he need consider only his preferences and those of his powerful opponents. . . . Since only a relatively few interest groups contend on any given issue and no single item is considered in conjunction with all others (because budgets are made in bits and pieces), a huge and confusing array of interests is not activated all at once.[56]

Wildavsky would go on to take the incremental logic of the budgetary process as he found it and attempt first to formalize it,[57] then to integrate even the larger increments within this process into this formalized picture, such that its outliers became merely the "expected" outer limits of an integrated and stable politics.[58] More than Fenno, however, Wildavsky was willing to go on and analogize the budgetary process that he discovered to the larger processes of policy-making in the United States of the time, within which budgeting was still only one, albeit crucial, arena. For both, it was the shifting political coalitions at their core that simultaneously distinguished individual policy domains and constrained the possible outcomes within them:

In the American context, a typical result is that bargaining takes place among many dispersed centers of influence and that favors are swapped as in the case of log-rolling public-works appropriations. Since there is no one group of men who can necessarily impose their preferences upon others within the American political system, special coalitions are formed to support or oppose specific policies. Support is sought in this system of fragmented power at numerous centers of influence—Congressional committees, the Congressional leadership, the President, the Budget Bureau, interdepartmental committees, departments, bureaus, private groups, and so on.[59]

It is this larger process of policy-making that was gathered and summarized for the Late New Deal Era through the notion of incrementalism, a grand summary term that would work much less well in the Era of Divided Government to follow, and one that would largely have collapsed by the successor Era of Partisan Volatility. Yet an even larger implication lurked in the background, though barely, of this diagnostic process of policy-making, an implication following more or less ineluctably from the incrementalism summarizing that process. To wit: this was very much a centripetal, not a centrifugal, process, drawing both political parties toward the ideological center.

That particular result was explicit and straightforward—hence easiest to see—inside Congress. It was obvious for economic welfare, where the disposition of the centrist factions, Southern Democrats and/or Northeastern Republicans, was widely understood to be decisive. Northern Democrats and Regular Republicans might anchor the ideological extremes, but Southern Democrats and Northeastern Republicans determined the outcome. This meant that expansion of some very popular welfare initiatives from the High New Deal was easy, as with Social Security, receiving major coverage expansions plus benefit increases in 1950 and 1954, along with further benefit boosts in 1958, 1961, and 1967. But it meant that the contraction of unpopular initiatives from the preceding period was easy as well, as with the facilitative regulation of organized labor, constrained by the Taft-Hartley Act of 1949 and the Landrum-Griffin Act of 1959.

The same formal logic governed the other two great policy domains of the era, foreign affairs and civil rights: one faction anchoring the left and one anchoring the right, with two up for grabs in the middle. It was just that the centrist factions were different there: Northern Democrats and Northeastern Republicans on foreign affairs, Northeastern Republicans and Regular Republicans on civil rights. Moreover, this centripetal dynamic within Congress was further reinforced by the fact that the critical membership of these centrist factions itself varied from domain to domain: Southern Democrats on economic welfare, Northern Democrats on foreign affairs, Regular Republicans on civil rights. Only the Northeastern Republicans were actually in this centrist bloc all the time.

Moreover, the same logic governed presidential politics during the Late New Deal Era, though it was less often noted because the locus of its operation and the measure of its impact had to be different with the presidency than with Congress. As a single institution without multiple members, any centripetal dynamic had to appear in the *electoral* politics of presidential selection if it was to characterize the presidency. And in all but one contest of the Late New Deal Era, it did. In all of those contests, the Republican Party, being on the wrong side of a national party imbalance, had to find a presidential candidate who could hold Northeastern Republicans in their voting coalition and pick off a substantial minority of Northern Democrats. Else there would be no Republican president.

The Southern Democrats, with a blanketing one-party system in their geographic region, could harvest their congressmen and senators more or less automatically, while allowing these elected officials to decide *subsequently* whether they would remain in coalition with Northern Democratic counterparts or defect to the Republicans on an issue-by-issue basis. And with the presidential vote, until the coming of the successor Era of Divided Government, the Southern Democratic edge was so overwhelming in its region that only a Republican candidate who was sweeping everything else—and certainly not one who was focused on holding Northeastern Republicans and peeling away Northern Democrats—could crack this Southern edge in a major way.

So the presidential pivot was always in the territory of the Northeastern Republicans. From one side, the party failed only once to understand this electoral logic and respond accordingly. Which is to say: every Republican nominee from 1948 through 1960 represented this pivot, denominated in its time as the "eastern establishment." Wendell Willkie in 1940, Thomas Dewey in 1944, Dewey again in 1948, Dwight Eisenhower in 1952, Eisenhower again in 1956, and Richard Nixon in 1960—eastern establishment by courtesy of being a New York lawyer but also by virtue of his programmatic attachments—all catered to this strategic imperative. Only two of the six (the two Eisenhower contests) were ultimately successful, but that disappointing result was largely an inescapable reflection of the overall nationwide disadvantage in party balance. The strategic imperative was itself invariant.

From the other side, the power of this strategic logic was to be powerfully confirmed in the one breach, the one contest where it was violated. In this, Barry Goldwater led his party to its most crushing defeat in any of these elections, while providing a crucial contribution to the realization of Lyndon Johnson's Great Society, probably the one thing that Goldwater and his supporters least wanted to do. Yet as large as the associated electoral debacle was, it looked remarkably like the major partisan disruptions from the early years of the Late New Deal (see figure 2.1). Then, one-term bounces in favor of the Republicans had quickly restabilized around the Democratic edge. Twenty years later, a one-term bounce in favor of the Democrats just as quickly restabilized around the status quo ante (table 2.3).

Table 2.3. Partisan Perturbations in the Late New Deal Era

A. The House

	Democratic Seats	Republican Seats	Other Seats
1962	259	176	0
1964	295	140	0
1966	247	187	0

B. The Senate

	Democratic Seats	Republican Seats	Other Seats
1962	66	34	0
1964	68	32	0
1966	64	36	0

Year in and year out, then, the Late New Deal Era was reliably characterized by centripetal political forces and regularized but incremental policy-making. Nothing in the shift from 1962 to 1964 and then back again in 1966 suggested that what looked like a familiar pattern of loss and recovery was instead the prelude to a fundamentally unfamiliar world. With hindsight, of course, we know that it was. Party balance, ideological polarization, and substantive conflict would all be different in a successor era, and so would the policy-making process that these different political inputs produced.

3 | The Rise of Participatory Politics

The Political Structure of an Era of Divided Government, 1969–1992

Party balance: *a narrowing imbalance of partisan attachments that become more ambiguous in their impact;* **ideological polarization:** *the growing polarization of party activists, resisted by elected officials;* **substantive conflict:** *economic welfare joined by cultural values as dual, dominant, and crosscutting issue concerns;* **policymaking process:** *cross-partisan and cross-institutional negotiations to reassemble these otherwise fragmenting pressures.*

No one at the time could have known that the Late New Deal Era had come to an end with the presidential election of 1968.[1] The Democrats once again controlled the House, as they had for all but four years since 1930. The Republicans did pick up the presidency, but only over a Democratic Party suffering internal disarray on a cosmic scale within a faltering economy in the midst of an unpopular war. Top it all off with widespread racial rioting, extensive war protest, plus surging public anxieties about crime, and commentators at the time could be excused for seeing the collective outcome of 1968 not as the harbinger of some new and stable patterning to American politics but rather as an amazing combination of anomalous, idiosyncratic, transitory, and in most ways disastrous events.

In hindsight, however, it is easy to see—it is hard to avoid seeing—the same election as the first in a sequence of contests that was to be distinctive in all of American history.[2] Its hallmark would be "divided government," split partisan control of the elective institutions of American national government, but with further and stable specifics inside it. To wit: this was to be an era of Republican presidencies stapled onto Democratic Congresses. Indeed, again in hindsight, the only real anomaly in this extended period was not the election of Republican Richard Nixon in 1968 but the election of Democrat Jimmy Carter in 1976, bringing with him a single term of unified partisan control. Otherwise, the era was to be characterized by lockstep repetition of one specific version of split control, in which Republican presidents faced Democratic Congresses.

The unexpected and unconventional nature of this partisan balance made it additionally difficult to notice the peculiar nature of the ideological polarization that accompanied it. From one side, party activists, led by the Democrats but followed closely by the Republicans, were moving rapidly away from the ideological center. A fundamental change in the nature of American political parties, coupled with a major shift in the substantive conflicts at the heart of American politics, were impelling this activist polarization. Yet from the other side, public officeholders responded as much or more to a voting public that was changing only gradually and that often manifested a different mix of substantive conflicts than the one favored by partisan activists. In the face of divided government and despite widespread unease among political commentators about this division, it was these elected officials who managed to construct a policy-making process featuring cross-partisan and cross-institutional negotiations. Working *across* split partisan control, this process managed not just to distinguish its era but to make the era an apparently productive one in policy terms.

In the beginning, however, even scholarly analysts, with their professional caution and their systematic methods, might have been excused for failing to recognize the new period as it arrived,[3] since each of the available indicators of *party balance* told a different story—and all of them were wrong. Mass partisan self-identification, as measured by social surveys, told a tale of stability and continuity within a modest Democratic decline. Congressional elections, likewise stable, showed an arguable if modest improvement over the established Democratic edge. And presidential elections, last but certainly not least, suggested nothing less than the arrival of a new and reliable Republican majority.

Survey evidence of party identification, the modern gold standard for party balance, did attest to two clear changes. In the first, it was now possible, courtesy of the National Election Studies, to know that the Era of Divided Government offered a modestly reduced Democratic edge when compared with the Late New Deal Era. During the Late New Deal, an absolute majority of all Americans had defined themselves as Democrats (figure 3.1A). During the Era of Divided Government, a majority

Figure 3.1. Party Identification in the Nation as a Whole:
An Era of Divided Government

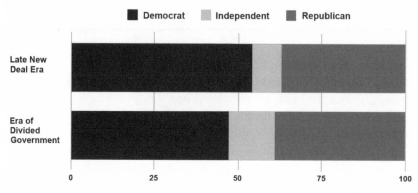

A. The Three-Point Scale

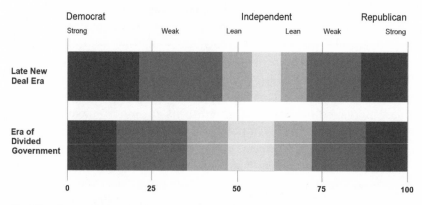

B. The Seven-Point Scale

of all *identifiers* remained Democratic, but they no longer constituted a majority of all Americans. That was clearly a shift in party balance nationwide, though its scale and potential impact should not be overdone. For in the face of this modest Democratic decline, the Republicans managed to gain nothing at all. So if existing Democratic identifiers voted Democratic, as they conventionally did, then Republicans could still forge a national majority only by ensuring that Republican identifiers likewise voted Republican *and* that effectively all independents did the same. That remained a substantial and demanding requirement.

In the second clear change of party balance between electoral eras, the share of both Democratic and Republican identifiers who styled themselves as independent partisans—partisan "leaners" in the vernacular, refusing initially to claim a party identification but then confessing to a preference for one party or the other—had increased as well (figure 3.1B). This too might have qualified as a first contribution to split partisan results, if analysts had begun with the theory that divided government had arrived to stay rather than that it was just an idiosyncratic product of the dramatic politics of 1968. Yet in very short order, and well before professional analysts began to tackle the implications of lasting divided government, analysts who specialized in partisan attachments had moved to dismiss this entire possibility.

Instead, students of party identification came to believe that the burgeoning independent leaners who did arguably characterize the new era, those self-proclaimed Independent Democrats and Independent Republicans, represented a nominal but not a practical change. In this view and despite their personal claims, they were little more than closet partisans.[4] Their collective propensity to assert independence had obviously increased. That was not in dispute. But their voting behavior did not otherwise change. Newly self-designated Independent Democrats voted as Democratic as their non-Independent brethren, and newly self-designated Independent Republicans did the same. If the attractiveness of the label had obviously changed, then, the behavior associated with choosing that label had apparently not. So a very modest decline in Democratic identifications, still larger than Republican identifications and still an effective majority, remained the proper verdict on party balance.

By contrast, the longest-running, most concrete, and least disputable indicator of party balance, the partisan outcome of congressional elections, told a different story (figure 3.2). The problem was that in this story, depending on where one looked, Democratic prospects might actually have improved. In the Late New Deal Era, Republicans had seized control of the House of Representatives only twice out of fifteen efforts, in 1946 and 1952. That was hardly a happy performance. Yet in the Era of Divided Government, they never succeeded at all (figure 3.2A). In fact, the stretch between 1952 and 1994, the bracketing elections for a Republican majority in the House and a period subsuming the entire Era of Divided Government, was quite literally the longest such stretch in American history.[5]

By that measure, Republican prospects within a continuing Democratic hegemony, rather than improving, had marginally decayed. As

Figure 3.2. Factional Composition of the Two Parties in Congress: An Era of Divided Government

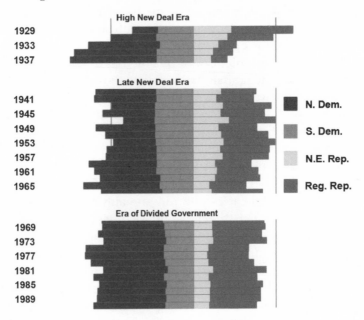

A. The House

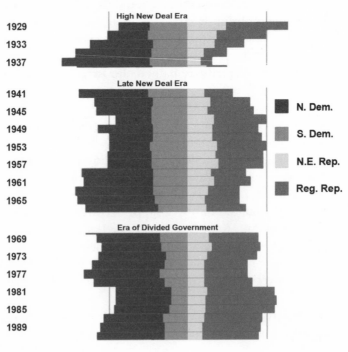

B. The Senate

it turned out, the Senate leaned the other way, being slightly kinder to the minority party, thereby reversing this emphasis (figure 3.2B). Two Republican majorities for the Late New Deal Era became three majorities in the Era of Divided Government when the Republican Senate class of 1980 managed to remain in the majority for their entire (six-year) term. Accordingly, Congress as a whole told a story that was either slightly tougher or slightly kinder to the minority party than was aggregate party identification, depending on which house was used as a partisan measure. Though just to complete the analytic confusion, *presidential* elections told a very clear partisan story—no shifts at the margin here—and that story was profoundly different from either congressional counterpart.

To begin at the end: the imposition of this evidently new presidential story is, after all, why the period became an extended era of *divided* government. By the least charitable count, Republicans were to secure the presidency in five of the six presidential elections during the Era of Divided Government, a better statistical performance than the Democrats had managed during the Late New Deal Era, when they had secured five out of seven. Yet many and perhaps most analysts, even at the time, felt that this understated Republican presidential success, since the one-term Carter presidency was often characterized as fundamentally a product of the Watergate crisis and its presidential resignation. By this final (presidential) measure, then, the country had moved from regular Democratic dominance to unfailing Republican hegemony.[6]

So what *can* explain a string of Republican presidencies to go with an unbroken chain of Democratic Congresses, and thus differentiate the Era of Divided Government from the Late New Deal Era? Party identification could never be made to carry this load, since party identification as a concept can never explain why self-conscious Democrats choose Republican presidents and/or why self-conscious Republicans choose Democratic Congresses. Election outcomes are not similarly constrained. They can produce exactly this combination, being the outputs of, not the inputs to, electoral politics. Yet in practice, election outcomes in this case tell two different—and polar opposite—stories. That is, after all, the essential precondition for an extended era of split partisan control.

In our terms, then: What was it that translated a fresh interaction among party balance, ideological polarization, and substantive conflict into a stable but not eternal sequence of electoral outcomes, different from those of the Late New Deal Era and characterized by its own continuing but distinctive partisan mix? Two obvious, alternative, proximate places to search for an answer appear immediately, given the analysis to this point. One is ideological polarization; the other is substantive conflict. Either something was different about the *political parties* during the new period, something capable of encouraging and sustaining a new and divided pattern of partisan outcomes. Or something was different about the *policy issues* characterizing the period, such that their substantive interaction was capable of generating and sustaining the new and divided partisan pattern. Or, of course, both—which proved to be the correct answer.

Perhaps the best way to start unpacking an answer is to begin with a major element structuring politics in the preceding era, the one that blended ideological polarization and substantive conflict most diagnostically. In this, the behavior of regional factions within the two national parties had been crucial to explaining the nature of political combat during the Late New Deal Era—crucial, that is, both to the depolarized character of that era and to the fact that the major issues that dominated the era were not aligned in parallel ways by these key regional factions. Regional factions would hardly evaporate in the successor era, and they could still occasionally color its policy outcomes in decisive ways. In their place as the dominant operative influence, however, was a changing structure to both political parties nationwide, a change that would be crucial to explaining the split partisan control distinguishing the Era of Divided Government as well as the way the diagnostic substantive conflicts associated with the new era played into its structure.

Yet this time, the critical distinction within what was a changed party structure would not feature horizontal stratification by political geography, that is, region versus region. Instead, this critical distinction would feature vertical stratification by operating level, elite versus mass, that is, partisan activists versus party rank and files. A kind of *split-level polarization* would thus be key to the new period, though its ability to generate and sustain divided partisan control of the elective institutions of American national government was also to depend on the two-dimensional nature of the policy conflict that arrived in tandem with it.

There had been major operational differences between the two parties during the Late New Deal Era, and it was in part the attenuation of these differences that helped to underpin an Era of Divided Government. In that previous era, the Democratic Party nationwide had remained much more of an old-fashioned political organization, despite the coming of a new policy program with revised ideological alignments. This older Democratic Party had still been characterized by a hierarchy of party offices whose incumbents expected to rise up through the party structure and be rewarded (by politics) for their labors along the way. While the party had been riven by a great regional divide, North versus South, each region had featured its version of this common operating structure, in the form of what were known as urban machines in the North and courthouse rings in the South.[7]

By contrast, the machine-based part of the Republican Party—the city of Philadelphia, for example, had long been home to a famous Republican organization—had been staggered by the Great Depression and fatally undermined by the New Deal.[8] From one side, a depression arriving under national party auspices had seriously discredited this Republican machinery. From the other side, a huge new increment of divisible rewards, courtesy of the New Deal, had reinvigorated Democratic organizations, though this would prove to be a kind of "Indian summer" for party machinery.[9] As a result, the Republican Party as a collectivity moved much earlier than its Democratic counterpart to become a recognizably modern political organization. In this, the party was increasingly constituted from a network of issue activists, whose rewards were basically ideological rather than financial or even programmatic. It was just that during the Late New Deal Era, as we have seen, party officialdom retained sufficient authority within its increasingly skeletal structure to allow an office-based Republican hierarchy to continue seeking ways to overcome, though never to displace, the Democratic majority. In that sense, this had been an Indian summer for Republican Party organizations as well.

What happened in the Era of Divided Government, then, was that the Democratic Party too was increasingly captured by this alternative—participatory—model of party structure, while the formal hierarchy in both parties increasingly lost control over the nomination of party candidates and the substance of party programs. Some such development had been long anticipated by students of American political parties. Scholarly theorists had predicted it as an ostensible concomitant of modernity: a more middle-class society, more highly educated and increasingly located in suburbia, was going to demand a different kind of politics. Practical reformers had actively aspired to just such an outcome: it was often the intended *point* of institutional reform.[10]

Nevertheless, the coming of a new practical structure to internal party politics was a major event in its own right—as well as a major surprise—when it actually arrived in the 1970s. More to the point here, this major internal change went on to become a key element in the creation and sustenance of an Era of Divided Government. Yet it did not accomplish this alone. It was simultaneously facilitated, then buttressed, by a new substantive matrix for policy conflict, now juxtaposing economic welfare, that is, economic and welfare issues, with *cultural values*, in the form of social and behavioral concerns. And just to knit this new world together, these newly ascendant cultural issues generated major new interest groups whose active participants were to generate the issue activists who benefited from (and hence drove) the evolving intermediary structure of politics

What resulted, most diagnostically, was a divergence within both parties between newly influential issue activists and a general public that changed much more slowly, when it changed at all. This divergence was to give the Era of Divided Government not only its theretofore peculiar pattern of split electoral outcomes but also the policy-making process that was to characterize—and sustain—the new era. Unchanging rank-and-file partisans, rapidly changing party activists, and public office-holders facing the need to mediate between the two were to provide a new dynamic to underpin a new era.

Once again, there was a literature of its time that, in attempting to capture the structure of contemporary politics, simultaneously captured the story of a new political era in rich and textured fashion. Yet unlike the counterpart situation in the Late New Deal, where leading authors aspired to elicit the lasting essence of American politics, those attempting to unpack the structure of politics during the Era of Divided Government were spurred by a sense that this politics was profoundly in flux. Accordingly, they thought of themselves variously as:

- Setting out an abstract framework for understanding party structure, and thus the theoretical basis for interpreting a shift from parties as official hierarchies to parties as activist networks. James Q. Wilson, *Political Organizations*, was the cornerstone here.[11]
- Examining the operational dynamics by which this abstract framework became a concrete road map to the Era of Divided Government, by way of a major change in party structure. Alan Ware, *The Breakdown of Democratic Party Organization*, played this role crucially.[12]

- Or surveying the distribution of the different types of party structure in the nation as a whole at the point when this great transition
was occurring, thus capturing an old world in comprehensive detail while it was in fact saying good-bye. David R. Mayhew, *Placing
Parties in American Politics,* added this final piece.[13]

In the abstract—in what we might call classical political science—
intermediary organizations transmit preferences from society to government. That is, they transmit substantive preferences from the general
public, at the social base for politics, into governmental institutions, the
bodies that actually make public policy. In doing so, however, these organized intermediaries partially transform those grassroots preferences,
sometimes modestly, sometimes more so. Either way, the crucial organization in this transmission is expected to be the political party, where
efforts to think about the structure of American parties often begin with
the work of James Q. Wilson.

Most fully realized in *Political Organizations,* the argument was pre-
figured by an earlier article from Wilson and Peter B. Clark on incentive systems and their organizational impacts.[14] In this earlier framework, Clark and Wilson argued that the crucial maintenance activity
of any organization was to distribute incentives; that all incentives had
consequences for behavior; and that changing incentives would thus
change organizational and not just individual behavior. They went on
to classify incentives into three general categories: material, the most
tangible and fungible; solidary, the most social and associational; and
purposive, the most substantive and ends-related. These general types
of incentives then fueled three archetypal forms of organization, which
converted their diagnostic incentives into different patterns of recruitment, different operating priorities, and different contributions to policy outputs.

Wilson was to take this theory onward and apply it in book form to
the range of organizations regularly involved in American politics. Not
all such organizations *existed for* politics, of course. Yet political parties
did, so that his crucial elaboration was chapter 6 of *Political Organizations,*
applying the theory explicitly to American party organizations. "The political party, at least in the United States, is a conspicuous exception
to the general tendency for society to become increasingly organized,
rationalized, and bureaucratized."[15] With that opening observation,
Wilson tied his three types of incentives to the three types of partisan

organizations available in the American context, "The Machine," "The Purposive Party," and "Solidary Parties."[16]

By the time he applied his theoretical argument to concrete contexts, Wilson believed that the balance of party types in the United States was clearly shifting from the first category to the second, from material incentives and machine organization to purposive incentives and the participatory party. Barely implicit in his analysis was a further assumption, that the third category, solidary organizations with their focus on promoting sociability, was a residual. These organizations could ultimately be made to work inside (and thus to be subsumed by) whichever of the other great categories of party organization proved ultimately dominant:

> In this country, parties seek resources—offices and influence—that are chiefly available locally rather than nationally. As a result, parties have been highly decentralized. Furthermore, the value of some of the resources available to parties has been declining relative to the value of equivalent resources available through extra-party channels. Patronage jobs and material favors are increasingly less attractive when compared with nonpolitical opportunities for employment and business, at least for the rank and file. Social solidarity is an incentive available from a host of nonparty clubs and voluntary associations, and often more cheaply; that is, in nonpolitical clubs, the member is asked to do less in return for the opportunity for camaraderie. And the value of solidarity is often debased in a political organization because it must strive to be inclusive.[17]

Not long after the publication of *Political Organizations*, Alan Ware began a book-length attempt to unpack the operational specifics of this transition, away from material incentives and their traditional machinery among formal officeholders and toward purposive incentives and their social networks among issue activists. To that end, Ware focused on three very different locales with three very different Democratic parties that were nevertheless caught up in the same overarching development: New York City, once the stereotypical home of the party machine; the Denver metropolis, a voluntaristic culture that had nevertheless managed to generate a Democratic Party capable of contributing to multiple, partially coordinated campaigns; and the East Bay in the San Francisco Bay Area, stereotypically hostile to machine politics but generating a network of reform clubs that performed many of the functions of old-fashioned organizations.

Each of Ware's three locales began at a different point. Each evolved in distinctive ways. Yet all experienced, and thus embodied concretely and dynamically, the variety of changes that Wilson had perceived in his theoretical framework. Initially, however, careful and rich consideration of three archetypically diverse Democratic parties convinced Ware—as they would convince Mayhew in his national survey—that the demise of material incentives and machine-type structures had been overstated during what is here called the Late New Deal Era: "The main thrust of our argument differs from a popular contemporary view. For we claim that in the 1940s and 1950s, the parties were not becoming so weak that complete collapse in the 1960s was inevitable. Far from being in continual decline since the height of the New Deal, in some respects the parties actually had a brief revival about the middle of the century."[18]

As a result, it was to be the late 1960s and 1970s (and hence the Era of Divided Government) that threw up a set of further challenges to these continuing structures, challenges that would ultimately—yet with surprising rapidity when they finally arrived—bring about the demise of old structural arrangements. Moreover, regardless of their idiosyncratic starting points and regardless of the particular mix of stressors that fell upon these differing incarnations of old-fashioned party structure, the result was generalized, sweeping, and qualitatively different: "There can be little doubt that what happened to the Democratic Parties in America between the early 1960s and the late 1970s was truly extraordinary. Within a few years, most of them were transformed."[19]

Ware began *The Breakdown* with an explicit lament about the absence of the kind of comparative measures—a record of careers in party rather than public office, an inventory of the resources available to official parties—that would have been ideal for a systematic study of this national transition. In *Placing Parties in American Politics*, David Mayhew, working on the same problem at roughly the same time, began by acknowledging the same basic problem but chose the opposite strategy for research. Mayhew noted that students of political parties were often more interested in what happens between them, which is to say, in party competition, rather than by what happens inside them, that is, by party structure. In taking the opposite tack, he asked, "What if the more fundamental policy-related distinction in the American party sphere of the last century or so has indeed had to do with structure rather than competition?"[20]

In pursuit of that possibility, Mayhew turned to defining his central focus as clearly as possible and then to applying any and all available historical or journalistic reports—a data set that was encyclopedic but also impressionistic and nothing like a random sample—to party politics in the fifty states. For Mayhew, the central phenomenon was what he called "traditional party organizations," his "TPOs":

> Finally, the special term *traditional party organization* is needed since no other has quite the right meaning. . . . Its acronym TPO will be used interchangeably in the following chapters to refer to any organization at the level of county, city, city ward, township, or other local jurisdiction about which all five of the following statements can be made:
>
> 1) It has substantial autonomy.
> 2) It lasts a long time.
> 3) Its internal structure has an important element of hierarchy.
> 4) It regularly tries to bring about the nomination of candidates for a wide range of public offices.
> 5) It relies substantially on "material" incentives, and not much on "purposive" incentives, in engaging people to do organization work or to supply organization support.[21]

In his search for the distribution and evolution of these TPOs, Mayhew came to much the same conclusion as Ware: previous reports of the death of "the organization" had been much overstated. Ware referred to the period immediately after the Second World War—the Late New Deal Era but not the Era of Divided Government—as the Indian summer of organized political parties. Mayhew extended the point: "It is not even decisively clear that local organizations counted for less in, say, the late 1940s than in 1900."[22]

What could be much clearer with the thinner but wider research net that Mayhew was able to cast over American political parties was that the clustering of surviving TPOs was uneven, with a strong geographic pattern. His "Regular Organization States" and "States with Persistent Factionalism" were found largely in the Northeast, the Ohio River Valley, the Mississippi River Valley, and not much elsewhere. Figure 3.3A recasts his crucial summary map to set out the situation circa 1950. Figure 3.3B is Mayhew's own adjustment of that map to suggest the proportionate size of states that still did (and did not) possess traditional party organizations at the time of their imminent demise, making it

Figure 3.3. The Organizational Character of State Democratic Parties at the Inception of the Era of Divided Government

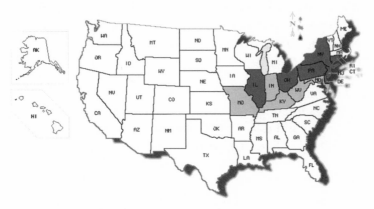

A. Traditional Party Organizations by State

Dark gray = Regular Organization States; Light gray = States with Persistent Factionalism

B. Traditional Party Organizations by Population

States weighted by population with TPO score indicated. Population based on 1970 census figures; TPO scores range from light (1) to dark (5).

additionally clear that TPOs remained a substantial force in American party politics in the immediate postwar years.[23]

Like Ware, however, Mayhew concluded that the era of these TPOs really did come to an end as the 1960s gave way to the 1970s. For an analysis built around party balance, ideological polarization, and substantive conflict, this has two immediate implications. In the first, the two periods associated most closely with the New Deal as a policy influence, namely, the High and the Late New Deal Eras, are connected by the survival of substantial and serious TPOs. Different forms of ideological polarization and different substantive foci do go on to distinguish one era from the other, making them operate very differently in their policy-making. But it is not state and local party structure that distinguishes these eras.

On the other hand, the break between the Late New Deal Era and the Era of Divided Government does fit neatly with the break between the long-running survival and then the serious diminution of the TPOs. By itself, this structural break did not demand the associated break in the pattern of election outcomes. Yet the relationship between the two must be pursued.[24] Indeed, Mayhew himself pursued the first of these implications, the link between TPOs and the substantive agenda of the New Deal. He began with an opening irony, that Franklin Roosevelt actually came out of the Progressive wing of the Democratic Party, whose seminal thinkers were critics and opponents of New York politics as practiced by its TPOs.

Once in office, however, a different bargain between the nominal Progressive and the organization men, his old adversaries, was not hard to strike. The president was looking for reliable links to the voting public and reliable support within Congress. Organization Democrats were quick to see that the New Deal could be the source of fresh, concrete, divisible benefits. A marriage of convenience that would sustain both the New Deal and the TPOs during its first generation was quickly arranged:

> Whatever they amounted to at the local level, it became evident that traditional party organizations could agreeably supply strength to, as well as draw benefits from, politicians who built and tended coalitions at the national level. This contributed a key combinatorial element to the Democratic Party's formula for presidential leadership from the mid-1930s through the late 1960s. . . .
>
> But reaching the Presidency was one thing, using and keeping it another. After he took office, Roosevelt came to a quick understanding with the lo-

cal Democratic organizations on the terms of support downward in federal money and jobs in exchange for loyalty upward in elections, national conventions, and Congress. This easy and basic accommodation was evidently [to be] honored and valued by Democratic Presidents for three decades.[25]

Ongoing social change might have been sufficient by itself to undermine this refreshed link between an older form of partisan intermediation and policy substance. Or at least, volunteer activist branches continued to proliferate within both parties, while the governmental bureaucracy that blossomed with the New Deal and then World War II came to dominate not just programmatic implementation but actual policy planning.[26] Traditional party organizations were hobbled by both in an ongoing fashion. Yet the termination of those refreshed links was hugely facilitated by self-conscious, participatory, structural reforms, aimed essentially at maximizing the power of issue activists. Which is to say: political change was more than just evolutionary and informal. Rather, devotees of the new style of party politics attempted to create formal institutions that would allow issue activists to penetrate the official party and guarantee ideological payoffs from this penetration.[27]

Best known among the resulting structural reforms was the root and branch reworking of the process of presidential selection, with its burgeoning presidential primaries coupled with newly participatory caucuses in states where the primary did not prevail.[28] When the Democratic National Convention of 1968 exploded at the end of its presidential nominating contest, only a minority of Democratic delegates had come from states where the general public had direct access to selection politics, just as only a minority of these Democratic delegates had come from states where the identity of presidential candidates was linked automatically and transparently to their selection (table 3.1A).[29]

Among primary states, more delegates were still selected under their own names (delegate primaries) than under the names of their chosen candidate (candidate primaries). Among caucus states, more delegates were still selected at gatherings of party officeholders (traditional caucuses) than at gatherings of rank-and-file identifiers (participatory caucuses). And those relationships had remained roughly stable through the entire Late New Deal.[30] As if to emphasize the situation symbolically—and thus the lingering power of the formal party structure—13 percent of the total was still chosen by sitting central committees of state Democratic parties, without the need for so much as a gathering

Table 3.1. The Spread of Participatory Politics: A Changing Institutional Matrix for Delegate Selection (%)

A. The Democrats

Year	Committee Selections	Traditional Caucuses	Delegate Primaries	Participatory Caucuses	Candidate Primaries
2008	0	0	0	17	83
—	—	—	—	—	—
—	—	—	—	—	—
1976	0	0	9	24	66
1972	2	2	14	36	46
—	—	—	—	—	—
1968	13	24	19	21	23
—	—	—	—	—	—
1952	8	27	26	19	19
—	—	—	—	—	—
—	—	—	—	—	—
1936	8	31	31	15	14

B. The Republicans

Year	Committee Selections	Traditional Caucuses	Delegate Primaries	Participatory Caucuses	Candidate Primaries
2008	0	0	0	16	84
—	—	—	—	—	—
—	—	—	—	—	—
1976	1	4	11	24	60
1972	3	16	20	24	37
—	—	—	—	—	—
1968	5	24	23	28	20
—	—	—	—	—	—
1952	4	26	25	25	19
—	—	—	—	—	—
—	—	—	—	—	—
1936	4	31	32	20	14

of other party officeholders, much less the participation of the general public.

Only four years later, none of that remained true. By 1972, a solid majority of delegates to the Democratic National Convention was selected in presidential primaries, while an even more crushing majority was selected through arrangements that explicitly linked delegate selection to candidate support. Among primary states, candidate primaries dominated delegate primaries. Among caucus states, participatory caucuses dominated traditional caucuses. And the archetypically old-school committee selections were on life support, at 2 percent of the total. Four years after that, the transformation of this institutional matrix was essentially complete. Two-thirds of all Democratic delegates were selected through candidate primaries—the only serious holdout among primary states being Roosevelt's old bête noire and coalition partner, the Democratic Party of New York—while literally all remaining caucus delegates were chosen through participatory caucuses. And old-school committee selections were extinct.

The more dramatic public conflicts over state-level pieces of this institutional shift were fought out within state Democratic parties, yet the result quickly came to characterize Republican counterparts as well (table 3.1B). Partly, this was because the minority party had actually been forced to move toward the modern archetype earlier than its majority counterpart, courtesy of the collapse of the old Republican machines. Partly, parallel change resulted because the social changes and ideological currents moving the Democrats—rising levels of education, an increasing tendency to assert independence, the touted virtues of "unbossed" participation—inevitably fell upon both parties. Finally, when state Democratic parties resisted reform but lost the battle, the winners often preferred to drag their Republican counterparts along, whereas when state Democratic parties implemented the proposed reforms easily, they tended to go on and impose them on state Republicans too.

Yet participatory ideology and associated institutional preferences, while most easily gathered and exemplified through reform of the process of delegate selection, were hardly limited to political parties and presidential nominations. Rather, the same intellectual currents and the same procedural preferences reached comprehensively across American politics. Thus they reached into Congress in a clearly parallel fashion, just as they reached into much of the federal bureaucracy. Both institutional theaters were characterized previously by the power of an internal hierarchy of formal officeholders and their management of the relevant procedural rules. Both were to be addressed—assaulted, really—by structural reforms embodying the participatory ideology associated with an Era of Divided Government.

For Congress, this meant, first and foremost, an assault on the role and power of committee chairs. The essence of congressional politics had long been committee politics. The High New Deal Era had appeared to undermine this generalization, courtesy of its presidential dominance. Yet the Late New Deal restored committee dominance, re-creating multiple decentralized satrapies, whose leaders were the product of long internal service. So it fell to the Era of Divided Government to bring a conscious and concentrated assault on these individuals, from both directions. From below, there was an extensive new "subcommittee bill of rights," intended to democratize the power of committee chairs by empowering subcommittees, dispersing committee staff to them, and making chairs of the full committee procedurally accountable to the collective body. From above, there was a double-barreled effort to make committee chairs more responsive to party leadership in the chamber as a whole, while making party leaders themselves more accountable to the collective body.[31]

The Senate, beginning as a much less rule-bound institution, saw less of this reform thrust than the House, though both bodies had their version of overall participatory currents. The Democratic Party, being in control of both bodies, was again the primary theater for this reform politics. Yet there was always a Republican counterpart that, while reflecting some inherent differences between the parties, still embodied the same reform thrust. In any case, a detailed account of this reform politics within Congress could easily be constructed from the same general elements that told this story with regard to presidential selection: new issues in general, especially cultural issues; new personnel, who responded to these new issues as well as to the simple passage of time; the Vietnam War (and its resistance) in particular; cognate social movements, especially the environmental and women's movements; plus the lingering politics of civil rights and emerging problems of fiscal policy-making.

The story could be rolled on and on. Even the federal bureaucracy, that stereotypical embodiment of a rule-bound formal hierarchy, was not immune to participatory reform currents. There was a panoply of open-government reforms: sunshine laws to guarantee public access to bureaucratic decision making; freedom-of-information laws to ensure that a public with access could see both what was happening and what had happened; stringent procedural requirements to avoid informal collusion by insiders along the way; even the creation of proxy advocates—varieties of ombudsmen—to speak for those who might not be able to speak for themselves within a newly participatory process.[32] Moreover, all of these reform streams, from participatory parties to participatory legislatures to participatory bureaucracies, were not merely national-level (federal) developments. They had widespread echoes in state governments as well.

Yet political parties remained at the heart of these developments, both procedurally and ideologically, and the result would be parties—two of them—that were increasingly best viewed as social networks of issue activists, rather than as formal hierarchies of long-serving office-holders. That result, the centrality of issue activists, more or less automatically amplified the importance of whatever proved to be the dominant *substantive content* of the main policy conflicts of the time. The particular conflicts of the 1968 campaign were inevitably the opening route into this dominant content. But in the longer run, these conflicts would come to be characterized—gathered and subsumed—by two great, underlying and generic, policy dimensions.

One of these was economic welfare, continuing in roughly the form that it had manifested since the High New Deal. In other words, despite the scope of overall substantive change, one great pillar of policy conflict did not change much at all. A powerful focus on the cluster of policy issues that can be gathered under the rubric of economic welfare continued into the Era of Divided Government, as it had continued into the Late New Deal Era and as it would continue into the Era of Partisan Volatility. What made the central substantive conflicts of this new era different, then, was the fact that welfare issues were joined by, and now in tension with, a second powerful cluster of policy concerns, one that did not align rank-and-file voters in the same way.

The election of 1968 had featured pointed and specific incarnations of the new and growing substantive divisions from this essentially cultural realm, not just via the Vietnam War but also by way of racial rioting, student protests, a galloping concern with public order, and even the apparent arrival of a self-conscious "counterculture." Yet beyond the antiwar movement and behind all those election-specific incarnations, gathering them all into one hugely divisive cluster, was a much more general divide over proper *behavioral norms* for American society.[33] On one side were traditional values and their concern for maintenance of the family, the neighborhood, the community, and the nation. On the other side were progressive values and their concern for individual choice and self-realization in those same realms.

The larger result for the realm of substantive conflict was that continuing battles over economic management and social welfare were to be joined by a second cluster of conflicts over cultural values and social life, that is, over the appropriate distribution of behavioral norms in American society. Ultimately, public preferences in what were now two grand policy domains were to make the new era strategically complicated in a fashion that underpinned divided government, not so much because there were two fundamental policy domains rather than one— there had, after all, been three in the Late New Deal Era—but rather because public preferences in these two domains were *socially crosscutting*.[34] Though as we are about to see, what made them socially crosscutting was largely the changing structure of the political parties.

In any case, the critical harbinger of new policy splits among cultural concerns (and of their socially crosscutting character) arrived first in the realm of national security. Dissent on the Vietnam War among party activists had already begun to pull the Democratic Party out of the Cold War consensus during the Johnson administration, the last presidency of the previous electoral period. During the High New Deal and well into the Late New Deal, it had been Republicans who disproportionately resisted international involvements and Democrats who were more prepared to assume them, though as the Cold War escalated and the Late New Deal aged, both parties solidified behind the effort to contain international Communism.

Yet what had been a rough cross-party agreement during the Late New Deal Era was on its way to becoming a clear partisan divide during the Era of Divided Government, but the other way around this time, pitting isolationist Democrats against internationalist Republicans. Or at least, that was what happened in the burgeoning, participatory, activist strata of both parties. Among their rank and files, it would take much longer for this alignment to be recapitulated. Accordingly, an initial elite-mass difference—active partisans versus *their own* rank and files—came to characterize conflicts over foreign affairs in the Era of Divided Government, while proving to be only one instance of the burgeoning elite-mass differences so central to the structure of politics during the new era.

Part and parcel of this change in party alignment on foreign affairs was a key associated social movement, a widespread antiwar movement calling for an end to the major Cold War engagement of its time, the Vietnam War.[35] This movement would find its partisan expression principally within the Democratic Party and its operational home among Democratic activists. Ware emphasizes the way in which the antiwar movement levied a major policy strain on the decaying world of Mayhew's TPOs, in effect providing a flash point for long-term forces that were finally eroding the latter for good. In Wilson's terms, this was profoundly a purposive and not a materialistic movement. By extension, it mobilized individuals who were socially unlike those most attached to the existing TPOs.[36]

The antiwar movement, while it would lose its specific focus with the end of the Vietnam War, remains a helpful introduction to the generic interaction among (1) new substantive conflicts, (2) changing party structures, and (3) emergent interest groups, the groups that in effect carried those substantive conflicts into partisan politics. In this dynamic, through a kind of chicken-and-egg logic, new interest groups sprang up to generate the issue activists who would increasingly populate the political parties, while new issue activists moved to align party policies in a fashion different—to them, more ideologically coherent—than the one that had characterized the long Late New Deal. For the Democrats, these newly consequential organized interests would include not just peace groups but also environmentalists, feminists, and homosexuals. For the Republicans, they would include antiabortionists, gun owners, religious fundamentalists, and supporters of the traditional family. And on and on in both cases.

Among Democrats, the movements for a cleaner environment and for women's rights proved to share many characteristics with the antiwar movement, characteristics that all three shared with the civil rights movement that had preceded them.[37] Thus all arose on issues that had historically been focused more on the Republican Party nationwide. All mobilized political activists who had largely been outside both major parties in the period before their mobilization. All were attracted to the participatory ideology of the 1960s and 1970s. And all found a more comfortable home within a changing (and reformed) Democratic Party.

Among Republicans, much of the new universe of interest groups resulted instead from reactions to the opening (or reopening) of previously settled cultural issues. For these, the impetus to group formation often lay with the Supreme Court rather than with a social movement, at least in the first instance, until Evangelical Protestants became fully mobilized (back) into politics.[38] In truth, many of these issues had been given their initial impetus by the *Warren* Court, so that many were in fact initiated—announced—in the waning days of the Late New Deal Era. Yet it was in the Era of Divided Government that public reaction to these issues would be registered, and this registration would become a further, major, substantive and structural buttress to the new era.

The cultural issues that were forced into national politics by the Supreme Court arrived in intermittent and interspersed fashion during the 1960s and 1970s. Earliest in line were major new conflicts over the role of religion in public life. In *Engel v. Vitale* in 1962, the Court confronted the issue of readings from the Bible in public schools and concluded that such readings did indeed violate the establishment clause of the First Amendment, forbidding public sponsorship of religious practices. It restated its view a year later, more forcefully, in *Abington School District v. Schempp* and *Murray v. Curlett*. In their aftermath, the Gallup Poll showed more than three-quarters of all Americans in favor of a constitutional amendment to reverse those decisions.[39]

Next came major new conflicts over criminal justice. The critical run-up to these was *Gideon v. Wainwright*, where the Court read the due process clause of the Fourteenth Amendment into state politics, potentially affecting state and local police procedures nationwide. Yet this was followed much more crucially by *Miranda v. Arizona*, directly specifying what this application of the due process clause implied in operational terms. In an era of sharply rising crime rates, this particular minoritarian cultural initiative became what the *Oxford Companion to the Supreme Court of the United States* would call "the most famous, and bitterly contested, confession case in the nation's history."[40]

After that came a set of cases returning to the desegregation decisions of the Late New Deal Era. This time, the concern was with implementation of *Brown v. Board of Education II*. In 1968, in *Green v. County School Board of New Kent County*, the Court averred that "freedom of choice" plans could not in principle produce desegregation. Yet when the Court moved on to *Swann v. Charlotte-Mecklenburg Board of Education* in 1971, potentially requiring cross-busing of children to achieve school integration, it managed to nationalize the whole issue, bringing justiciable concerns about de facto segregation into the North and not just the South.[41]

Finally, the Court took perhaps its longest leap into concerns for individual rights and liberties when it moved into the territory of abortion policy. A predecessor decision for the Era of Divided Government had been *Griswold v. Connecticut* in 1965, where the Supreme Court found that a Connecticut statute barring the distribution of medical advice on contraception was unconstitutional, violating an implied right to privacy in the US Constitution. Far more of a practical policy change—and a symbolic fire bell in the night—was *Roe v. Wade* in 1973, where the Court found that both the traditional and the modern forms of laws restricting abortion were unconstitutional, again based on an abstract right to privacy but effectively creating a concrete entitlement to abortion on demand.[42]

Seen one way, all of these decisions—on school prayer, criminal justice, racial busing, and abortion policy—were classic embodiments of the great substantive shift that had occurred earlier within the Court. The High New Deal had seen the end of the long period, dating from the conclusion of the Civil War, when the Court was principally focused on economic rights and liberties. The Late New Deal opened what has become an equally long successor period focused instead on personal rights and liberties. Racial discrimination and its remedies did inaugurate that era. Yet the multiple further initiatives from the Warren Court, the ones that were to help roil politics in the Era of Divided Government, were classic incarnations of the cultural issues that would jointly (with economic welfare) come to characterize politics in this new era.

In narrow partisan terms, these decisions on rights and liberties continued the pattern by which both the partisanship of the presidents who appointed federal judges and the partisanship of the justices themselves were largely unrelated to their preferred outcomes. Yet the Court nevertheless managed to contribute powerfully to the ideological polarization of the period. In the High New Deal Era, this had meant that the Supreme Court had literally created one end of the dominant policy continuum. For the Era of Divided Government, it meant instead that the Court reinforced one of two dominant and polarizing conflicts, by fueling the cluster of newly invigorated cultural issues that were so central to an evolving political structure while simultaneously indulging its (increasing) penchant for siding with minorities rather than majorities in the policy substance of its decisions.

Perhaps inevitably, again in hindsight, what resulted from all of that—social change, participatory ideology, institutional reform, and

Supreme Court decisions—was a diagnostic elite-mass split inside the political parties. Partisan activists, those who did the actual work of restructured parties, moved away from the ideological center of American society, even on the old and continuing concerns of economic welfare. Yet simultaneously, they brought with them the new set of largely cultural issues that had drawn them into American politics in the first place. And while they worked at integrating these into both party programs, they moved away from the ideological center on these new concerns as well. Their putative rank and files, however, the party identifiers who came out to vote but were not otherwise active in party affairs, moved much more slowly. They had long constituted the ideological center, and they still did. They had long since acquired a set of policy attachments that they associated with their partisan identifications, and if these were subject to amendment in the long run, they were not likely to change much in the short.[43]

Movement away from the ideological center on the part of party activists was easiest to see by focusing on what is in some sense their peak embodiment in American politics, as delegates to the national party conventions. The ideological attachments of these delegates are always colored by the fortunes of the specific candidates to whom they hitch their wagons. Yet those candidates also always need to find a way to attract the party activists of their time in order to construct nominating campaigns, and offending the ideological prejudices of the latter— more developed, more explicit, and more extreme than those of the rank and file—is not an obvious strategy for doing so. Fortunately, we possess collective portraits of these delegates for many of the presidential nominating contests of the postwar years. Fortunately as well, these collective portraits tell a story powerfully consistent with the evolution of the parties and their internal processes (table 3.2).

The oldest world of presidential nominating politics available through these data, from 1956 in the Late New Deal Era, shows only the slightest difference in liberalism or conservatism between Democratic and Republican rank and files, along with a body of Democratic activists who were modestly left of their identifiers and a body of Republican activists who were sharply off to the right of theirs.[44] Perhaps these latter were still tapping the ideological world of the pre–New Deal period. Perhaps they were just the logical product of a heavy Democratic majority in the aftermath of the New Deal, where only activists with deep ideological commitments would have bothered to mount constantly los-

Table 3.2. Polarization of the Activists: Ideological Representation at National Party Conventions

	Republican Delegates	Republican Identifiers	All Voters	Democratic Identifiers	Democratic Delegates
2008	+62	+48	0	–20	–50
2004	+48	+39	0	–29	–52
—	—	—	—	—	—
1980	+49	+15	0	–11	–54
1976	+49	+14	0	–8	–42
1972	+24	+12	0	–9	–55
—	—	—	—	—	—
1956	+45	+6	0	–6	–9

ing efforts for the Republicans. Without the ability to ask retrospective questions, we cannot really know.

What we can know is that the McGovern campaign of 1972, a Democratic counterpart to the disastrous Goldwater campaign of 1964 among Republicans, initially reversed this picture. Rank-and-file Democrats and Republicans were still only modestly left and right of the national average, with Republican activists additionally off to the right of their rank and file but Democratic activists now sharply off to the left of theirs. For our purposes, however, the point is that after 1972 this alignment did not settle back into the old pattern. Instead, a fresh alignment appeared, featuring greater but more symmetric polarization by both active parties. This became in effect the generic picture of activist politics for an Era of Divided Government. The new pattern is readily visible in the first two nominating contests to follow. Activists in both parties had indeed polarized sharply—Republicans now sharply off to the right, Democrats now sharply off to the left—*while their respective rank and files had hardly moved at all.*

Moreover, this picture cannot plausibly be attributed to the ideologies of the candidates around whom these delegates rallied. The Republicans in 1976 nominated an obviously centrist Republican in Gerald Ford. The Republicans in 1980 nominated a clearly conservative Republican in Ronald Reagan. Yet the delegates favoring the two men lived in ideological territory that was effectively identical. The Democrats in 1972 had fronted their most liberal candidate of the postwar period in George McGovern. The Democrats of 1976 nominated their most moderate candidate of the postwar period in Jimmy Carter. Yet the

Figure 3.4. Crosscutting Economic and Cultural Preferences:
Democrats and Republicans in an Era of Divided Government

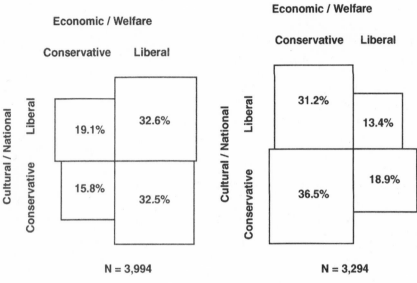

A. The Democrats   B. The Republicans

delegates favoring these two men likewise lived in similar ideological
territory, becoming effectively identical by 1980.

Table 3.2 confirms a second major aspect of the newly institutionalized alignment by demonstrating that the relevant rank and files remained impressively unmoved by the evolution of their party activists.
Between 1956 (deep in the Late New Deal) and 1976 (well into the Era
of Divided Government), party activists had indeed moved far apart. Yet
their rank and files showed only the tiniest echo of this activist effect. In
fact, the resulting ideological disjunction was so great by 1976 that the
two partisan rank and files were closer to each other than either rank
and file was to its own active party! Split-level polarization had become
an institutionalized fact of active political life.

That is a powerful disjunction on its own terms, between active partisans and their putative rank and files. On the other hand, it is still based
on aggregate self-designations of "liberal" and "conservative." Which is to
say, what table 3.2 cannot do is to separate the influence on these resis-
tant rank and files of the economic welfare issues that were so central to
the Late New Deal Era *as opposed to* the cultural value issues that were be-

coming so central to the issue-driven activists of a new, participatory party system. It is, however, relatively easy to capture and set out these relationships too. To that end, figure 3.4 presents the situation in 1984, where a particularly large and careful in-person survey, funded by the Times Mirror Company and executed by the Gallup Organization, allowed a fuller examination of the relationship both between and within the overarching liberal versus conservative designation for the general public.[45]

In this picture and as expected, Democratic identifiers were predominantly liberal on economic welfare, as opinion surveys had long suggested that they would be, dividing 65/35 liberal-over-conservative in figure 3.4A. As expected, Republican identifiers were predominantly conservative on those same issues, the ones that had dominated partisan attachments through the High New Deal Era and the Late New Deal Era, dividing 68/32 conservative-over-liberal in figure 3.4B. Yet Republican identifiers were only slightly conservative on cultural values—pretty much 55/45 conservative-over-liberal—while Democratic identifiers were just a whisper more liberal: 52/48 in the other direction, liberal-over-conservative. Two conclusions emerge:

- Apparently, an election revolving around economic welfare could still, fifty years after the coming of the New Deal, align the mass base of the political parties in the fashion that Harry Truman himself would have recognized from early in the Late New Deal Era.
- Yet simultaneously, an election revolving instead around cultural values could split the mass bases of both parties more or less down the middle. Indeed, given that figure 3.4 includes activists and not just their rank and files, an election that emphasized cultural issues surely did align *more than half* of the Democratic Party with its Republican opposition.

To say the same thing more pungently: the new world of ideological polarization and substantive conflict pitted Democratic activists *against* a large body of Democratic identifiers, Republican activists *against* a large body of Republican counterparts. Perhaps it should not have been surprising that the rank and file of the two parties did not immediately and naturally populate new social movements, so that they did not move readily and easily into the new policy alignments associated with them. In any case, it was this type of division, not just Republican versus Democrat, not just economic welfare versus cultural values, but now activist *versus* rank and file, that would lead more or less ineluctably to split partisan control of American national government.

Said the other way around, the newly augmented cultural conflicts, whether traditional or progressive in their roots, were distinguished not just by policy substance but also by the fact that they fit remarkably badly with the partisan coalitions built on social class that had characterized both New Deal eras. To begin at the end, then, the critical polarization characterizing politics during the Era of Divided Government was not ideological in the simple and direct sense, as when a Democratic Party with a new view of the role of government had faced a Supreme Court championing an old view during the High New Deal. On the other hand, this critical division was certainly not depolarized, as it had been when four major party factions combined and recombined across additionally varying policy domains in the Late New Deal.

Rather, there was now an elite-mass polarization within both parties, in which party activists became aligned in one fashion while their rank and file remained aligned in another. As a result, there was not just heightened *interparty* conflict between increasingly polarized liberals and increasingly polarized conservatives among those who did the actual work of the political parties. Now, there was an additional *intraparty* conflict, an elite-mass conflict as well, between party activists and their own putative rank and file:

- Democratic activists were consistently liberal. They remained liberal on economic welfare—that did not change—and they added a strident liberalism on cultural values.
- Yet Democratic mass identifiers retained a huge body of supporters who remained liberal on economic welfare but had never been liberal on cultural values.
- Republican activists were consistently conservative. They remained conservative on economic welfare, while they added a stiff conservatism on cultural values.
- Yet Republican mass identifiers retained a huge body of supporters who were conservative on economic welfare but had never been conservative on cultural values.[46]

So there were crosscutting majorities on economic versus cultural issues at the social base for American politics. Seen from below, from the grass roots, these majorities were crosscutting largely because the intermediary organizations of this politics, its political parties and associated interest groups, put policy programs together in fashions very different from the preferences of large segments of the general public. Seen from above, by party strategists, these majorities were crosscutting because dominant public preferences on the two great underlying policy domains of the era could not be captured simultaneously and successfully by the possible programs of either party.

Seen either way—though again, not forever—there appeared to be continuing majorities during the Era of Divided Government in favor of the liberal (and hence Democratic) position on the main economic and welfare programs introduced by the New Deal. If a Democratic presidential nominee lurched off to the left of these, as George McGovern did in 1972, the Democrats could still lose control of the policy domain. Yet Republicans were otherwise judged less positively in this domain on a regular basis, so that if the Republican nominee moved additionally off to the right, as Barry Goldwater did in 1964, the result could be catastrophic.

On the other hand, there appeared to be continuing and simultaneous majorities in favor of the conservative (and hence Republican) position on the main cultural issues of the new period. In the beginning, while large swaths of the public were unhappy with the (non-)progress of the Vietnam War, they could not easily connect this unhappiness to available partisan choices. A real difference on the war was clearly embodied in the independent candidacy of George Wallace, governor of Alabama—he promised to win that war—but the public otherwise had great difficulty recognizing (and being sure of) the differences between Democrat Hubert Humphrey and Republican Richard Nixon.[47]

Yet beyond the war, the main issues of the day even in 1968—racial rioting, student protest, street crime—showed reliable public majorities for the conservative position.[48] Going forward, these majorities would prove to be connected to cultural preferences more generally, with their focus on behavioral norms for American society. Those concerns would last into the successor period, the Era of Partisan Volatility, when they would come to encompass new issues on which electoral majorities were not reliably conservative or Republican. Yet in the Era of Divided Government, such issues—including those being pumped into politics by the Supreme Court, as with school prayer or abortion provision— appeared to be pretty much a one-way play, like economic welfare but in the opposite partisan direction.

As a result, crosscutting majorities on the two major substantive domains for politicking during the Era of Divided Government were a straightforward product of the split-level relationship between ideological polarization and substantive conflict characterizing the period—elites versus masses, active partisans versus the rank and files. Yet the structure of American government facilitated a simple solution for policy-making in the face of this apparent strategic conundrum, namely, colonize one branch of elective national government with one majority and one branch with the other. Abstractly, that might seem a formula for instability on the grand scale, with rolling and tumbling party control of each of the three elective institutions of American national politics in quick succession. Concretely, however, the same structure that facilitated an initial solution by way of divided government went on to impart a remarkable stability to this resolution. This further outcome seemed anomalous in its time; it seems obvious looking backward.

For in fact, all that such a setup required for a stable pattern of split partisan outcomes to emerge over an extended period was for one set of issues to be attached principally to voting for the presidency, the other set to be attached principally to voting for Congress. When the new era first arrived, few analysts would have known how to specify those attachments. In short order—with the gift of hindsight—everyone did. Economic and welfare matters stayed rooted in Congress. Tending to such matters on a districted basis was, after all, what members of Congress and senators historically did. Foreign policy and cultural values, by contrast, found their way to the presidency. This was partly because these were more "holistic" concerns, less easily subdivided by districts. It was partly because presidential aspirants shifted their policy focus more regularly than congressional candidates, being more responsive to emergent issues. And it was partly because newly consequential issue activists had more immediate and concentrated access to the politics of presidential selection than to the many-headed (and incumbency-constrained) selection of congressional candidates.

Accordingly, divided government—split partisan control of the elective institutions of American national government—became not just a logical and lasting electoral outcome. It also became the continuing world that would have to generate a new policy-making process, one characteristic of an Era of Divided Government, if policy were to be made at all. Moreover, because the Republicans nearly always controlled the presidency while Democrats nearly always controlled Congress, it was possible to specify further requirements for policy-making to occur on a regular basis. To wit: the new era appeared to require both *cross-partisan* and *cross-institutional* negotiations. If these were regularized, a fresh but ongoing process of policy-making should emerge. If they were not, the policy process would presumably be characterized by a descent into extended gridlock.

Initially, as pundits and analysts began to recognize what is here being dubbed an *Era* of Divided Government—as they came to see that split partisan control might not readily go away—some offered just such a dire hypothesis about the new policy-making environment. To wit: that recurrent partisan outcomes characteristic of the period had ushered in a new world where partisan officeholders could not agree and policy would not be made. That was the nightmare scenario, reached by a serious subset of commentators through simple extrapolation from the structure of a previous world. During what we have dubbed the Late New Deal Era, multiple party factions, multiple issue domains, and a lack of alignment between the two had meant that policy-making majorities could often be built (though of course also derailed) across the parties. Simplify the issue structure, downgrade the importance of factions, polarize the active parties, but divide partisan control within the matrix of governmental institutions, and you might bring a screeching halt to that previous policy-making resolution.

In remarkably short order, it would become clear that most such analyses were unduly alarmist. The requirements for policy-making under the new conditions characterizing the Era of Divided Government would indeed be satisfied. Gridlock would thus be avoided. In this period as in any period, there were still critics who argued that more problems could have been addressed and more policy could have been produced had politics been structured differently, that is, had split partisan control not been the central feature of an extended era.[49] Yet the era was to produce a steady stream of new public policies, distinguished additionally by the number of major pieces of legislation that passed by overwhelming congressional votes, sometimes nearly unanimously, other times at least featuring majorities of both parties.

These latter votes, so diagnostic of their period, did not imply that the major players—a Republican president, Democratic congressional leaders, and the Republican congressional minority—focused only on areas that began with an easy consensus. Nor did these votes imply that those players secured the legislation that each would have preferred in the absence of the others. There was to be sharp negotiating all along the way, and there could be sharp voting divisions in the run-up to ultimate legislation. In fact, losing the White House and facing up to stable divided government encouraged a Democratic Congress to arm itself additionally, for example, with its own sources of fiscal analysis in the form of the Congressional Budget Office, the better to *resist* a Republican president.[50]

Yet an overwhelming and thus bipartisan vote for final passage remained noteworthy by comparison to the Late New Deal Era, not to mention the Era of Partisan Volatility to follow. Perhaps surprisingly, the Nixon administration, viewed by many analysts as inherently conflictual and potentially incendiary, with a president dedicated to creating a new Republican majority,[51] featured this surface bipartisanship more or less from day one. Thus the first five legislative acts with a recorded vote on Mayhew's list of consequential laws were the following:

Coal mine safety: 334–12 in the House and 73–0 in the Senate
Social Security increase: 399–0 in the House, bundled into tax
 reform in the Senate
Draft lottery system: 383–12 in the House and a voice vote in the
 Senate
Comprehensive tax reform: 391–2 in the House and 71–6 in the
 Senate
National Environmental Policy Act (NEPA): 372–15 in the House
 and a voice vote in the Senate

While it is easy to imagine members of Congress falling in line behind a big increase in Social Security payments, it is harder to imagine them doing the same with reinstitution of the draft, or with the most comprehensive rewrite of the existing tax schedule since its inception, or with NEPA, with its reorganization of governmental institutions and its environmental impact statements. These latter were all high-impact laws with great inherent potential for political controversy. Yet they understate the situation even then. For of the thirty-four bills with a recorded vote on the Mayhew list during the entire first term of the Nixon presidency, only one featured a majority of Democrats against a majority of Republicans.[52]

For theoretical supporters of bipartisanship, there was a nasty irony in the fact that the one-term Carter administration—the lone instance of unified partisan control during the Era of Divided Government—

would feature more of those classic partisan divisions, one party versus the other. Yet the larger irony, and the one diagnostic of the Era of Divided Government, is easily seen in the landmark deregulation bills that would distinguish the policy-making of the Carter presidency, in the same way that landmark environmental legislation would distinguish the Nixon administration:

Airline deregulation: 363–8 in the House and 83–9 in the Senate
Banking deregulation: 380–13 in the House and 76–9 in the
    Senate
Trucking deregulation: 367–13 in the House and 70–20 in the
    Senate
Staggers Rail Act: 337–20 in the House and 91–4 in the Senate

Moreover, the same could be said of the major environmental initiatives that continued to appear during the Carter administration:

Surface Mining Control Act of 1977: 325–68 in the House and
    25–8 in the Senate
Clean Water Act of 1977: 346–2 in the House and 96–0 in the
    Senate
Clean Air Act Amendments of 1977: 326–49 in the House and
    73–7 in the Senate
Toxic Wastes Superfund of 1980: 274–94 in the House and a voice
    vote in the Senate

How did this work? How *could* the institutionalization of split partisan control feature so much major and ongoing legislative productivity, and how could so much of this be apparently consensual or at least ultimately bipartisan? The overall pattern did appear productive. In a comparison of policy outcomes designed for other purposes, Mayhew himself was implicitly kind to these years, emphasizing their productivity.[53] By the time the Era of Divided Government had morphed into the Era of Partisan Polarization, other scholars would have had the chance to quarrel with the Mayhew framework, asking about legislation that did not pass or about what might have passed under unified control. Yet few were to deny that there were major realms—environmental policy and fiscal policy would head most lists—where the Era of Divided Government was highly consequential, which only makes the Mayhew list of further policies that were enacted outside these areas during this period look all the more imposing.

In short, the requisite negotiations, both cross-partisan and cross-institutional, did ensue. Moreover, in hindsight, it was the very nature of the institutional division distinguishing the period—Republicans almost always in control of the presidency, Democrats almost always in control of Congress—that came more or less automatically to the rescue. This too was not obvious prospectively. But once the political structure of the era and the consequential character of its policy outcomes are acknowledged, it becomes possible to work backward and ask: Why *did* cross-partisan and cross-institutional negotiations rather than simple gridlock characterize the policy-making process of the Era of Divided Government?

A large part of an answer was to lie in another ironic fact: that this particular and recurrent institutional split implied that the two parties could not hope to be rescued electorally, at least in the short run. Split institutional control was effectively permanent for an extended period. By extension, the parties had little or no hope of ending divided government through simple obstinacy and obstruction. Presidents and congressional leaders, Democratic and Republican, remained fully capable of derailing legislation, or at least of stalling it for the two years necessary to bring about a new congressional election, perhaps even the four years necessary to bring a fresh presidential ballot. But the point is that neither outcome promised a reliable payoff. Republicans would probably again win the presidency; Democrats would probably again win Congress. Obstructionists could thus garner the blame for failure. What they could not do was to secure success.

Among major players as time passed, some acknowledged this fact openly. Others (both Republican and Democratic) preferred not to, spinning infinite adumbrations—aka infinite excuses—for why the diagnostic outcome of 1968 would be gone with the next election, and then the next, and then the next. Yet all labored within a recurrent structural context that they came to know intuitively through experience, one that formed the basic backdrop to a new process of policy-making. Within this, the one thing that appeared potentially able to generate public restiveness on a scale that might be sufficient to end split partisan control would have been a generalized public perception that one party or the other really was centrally responsible for the failure to act on consensually major national concerns.

So the crucial fact completing the story of policy-making in this era was that such concerns did indeed exist. Environmental policy concerns helped to kick off the era and lasted for a long time within it. Economic policy concerns, rooted in the dreaded stagflation, followed shortly and likewise endured for a long time.[54] Eventually, public worries about the governmental deficit itself, a noteworthy offshoot of policy responses to those economic concerns, acquired its own partially autonomous public compulsions. In any case, the point is that all three generated a major and continuing flow of legislation through a policy-making process that reflected the interactions of party balance, ideological polarization, and substantive conflict peculiar to the Era of Divided Government. A different process would surely have produced different specifics to the resulting legislation. *This* process generated legislative products that were substantial and ongoing in response to all three consensually major public concerns.

A quick tour of policy-making on the natural environment, the private economy, and then the governmental deficit is a good way to make the dynamics of this process concrete. In passing, this tour has the further virtue of unpacking a set of idiosyncratic puzzles about policy-making in its extended period. To wit: Why was the Republican administration of Richard Nixon arguably the great environmental lawmaker in all of American history?[55] Conversely, why was the Democratic administration of Jimmy Carter arguably the great deregulatory lawmaker?[56] And how could the administration of Ronald Reagan, self-consciously attempting to reverse the full drift of public policy since the New Deal, have generated so much legislation that fit comfortably within the policy-making contours of the Era of Divided Government, being ultimately bipartisan much of the time?

With the first of these concerns, the Era of Divided Government did become the great period of environmental legislation in all of American history. Dramatic instances of environmental degradation came together in public attention during this period: air too fouled for jogging, rivers that caught fire, depletion of plant or animal species, human medicines whose effects went awry, toxic wastes impinging on urban environments.[57] These were surely a crucial context for the policy-making that ensued. Yet the list of new environmental policies, in a world where policy-making was said to have become complicated, was impressive on its own terms and might always have been less (rather than just more) impressive if filtered through the policy-making process of a different era. In any case, the following acts meet the Mayhew test of significance:

National Environmental Policy Act of 1969
Clean Air Act of 1970
Water Quality Improvement Act of 1970
Pesticide Control Act of 1972
Water Pollution Control Act of 1972
National Forest Management Act of 1976
Resource Conservation and Recovery Act of 1976
Toxic Substances Control Act of 1976
Clean Water Act of 1977
Surface Mining Control and Reclamation Act of 1977
Alaska Lands Preservation Act of 1980
Nuclear Waste Repository Act of 1982
Major expansion of Superfund in 1986
Water Quality Act of 1987 (over a veto)
Clean Air Act of 1990

Two of the cornerstones of modern environmental policy in the United States arrived early in the Nixon administration, the National Environmental Policy Act of 1969 and the Clean Air Act of 1970. Both have always looked surprising in hindsight for the absence of serious conflict over groundbreaking substance, though the general lens of policy-making during the Era of Divided Government does make this appear less distinctive than a narrow retrospect focused on environmental policy alone might suggest. Seen through this general lens, both bills instead looked like much else in the legislation of their period, featuring cross-partisan and cross-institutional negotiations toward a lopsided ultimate outcome, though they stand out for having required so little partisan give-and-take even then.

The National Environmental Policy Act of 1969 assigned responsibility for the quality of the natural environment to the federal government; authorized a new institution, the Council on Environmental Quality, to pursue that responsibility; and created a major regulatory tool for its pursuit, via the environmental impact statements required of all new federal programs.[58] There was a catalytic event that contributed to policy-making in this general realm, in the Santa Barbara oil spill of early 1969, the largest such spill in American history to that date. Otherwise, the specifics of the ultimate bill were mainly the result of negotiations among major *institutions*—the presidency, the Senate, and the House—rather than among parties, factions, or even interests.[59]

The Santa Barbara spill encouraged Senator Henry Jackson (D-WA), chairman of the Senate Interior and Insular Affairs Committee, to reintroduce his bill establishing a national policy on environmental quality and setting up the Council on Environmental Quality in the Executive Office of the President. While he was holding hearings, however, Senator Edmund Muskie (D-ME), chairman of the Subcommittee on Air and Water Pollution of the Senate Public Works Committee, introduced a second Senate approach to the same general goals, through an amendment to the Omnibus Water Pollution Control Act. Jackson and Muskie turned to personal negotiations to resolve these differences.

While those proceeded, Congressman John Dingell (D-MI), chairman of the Subcommittee on Fisheries and Wildlife Conservation of the House Merchant Marine and Fisheries Committee, began work on his own bill, more modest in its aspirations in part because other House committee and subcommittee chairs were concerned with its impact on their jurisdictions and prerogatives. While all of that was going on, finally, the White House had to scramble to assert its own relevance. The original Jackson bill was introduced only three weeks after Richard Nixon was inaugurated. John Whitaker, secretary to the cabinet, summarized the atmosphere of the time in his account of environmental policy-making: "Yet there is still only one word, *hysteria,* to describe the Washington mood on the environmental issue in the Fall of 1969. The words *pollution* and *environment* were on every politician's lips. The press gave the issue extraordinary coverage. Congress responded by producing environment-related bills by the bushel, and the President was in danger of being left behind."[60]

Accordingly, President Nixon moved ahead and created the Council on Environmental Quality, so as to maximize presidential influence on the new body. The endgame to legislative politics then played out quickly. Senators Jackson and Muskie resolved their differences, especially on the action-forcing language that became the environmental impact statement. The full House did substitute the Dingell draft for this now-consensual Senate bill by a vote of 372–15. Yet this proved to be a very temporary detour. The Senate moved toward the House by confirming that its bill did not change the statutory responsibility of any established agency, but otherwise repassed its own bill by voice vote.

House and Senate versions went to conference, where even House conferees largely preferred the Senate bill. This was accepted on a voice vote by the Senate and then the House, going on to the president just before Christmas. Richard Nixon signed the bill on January 1, a day when he could hope that his signing ceremony would be (as it was) the major news event of the day.

Three things seemed noteworthy about this legislation in its aftermath. First was the absence of partisan, factional, or even interest-group contestation. Second, in some sense the obverse of the first, was the extent to which policy conflict was essentially among lawmaking institutions, partially for influence over the contents of legislation, partially just for claiming credit. Yet the third noteworthy fact about the bill was that its major operative substance, the automatic requirement for an environmental impact statement, appeared to be noncontroversial—to the point of being not worth a debate. This lack of conflict on the crucial operative provision probably reflected the fact that those signing onto the bill had only limited ability to foresee the edifice of institutions for environmental policy that would follow or, more particularly, how the reforms of the late 1960s in other realms—participatory access coupled with civil suits and judicial review—would convert environmental impact statements into major policy tools for environmental interest groups.[61]

In any case, an important element of that edifice arrived in the form of the Clean Air Act of 1970. Again, conflict over creating the act was largely structured by competition among presidency, Senate, and House. Again, competition between the parties was minimal. Where the two bills differed was that NEPA had failed even to draw much action from the organized interests on either side, while the main affected interests came to life in the case of the Clean Air Act. Yet the relevant economic interests, namely, manufacturing, electricity, and especially automobiles—about as "major" as organized interests come—were ultimately brushed aside in the rush to legislate, and to be seen to do so.[62]

There had been a series of modest prior clean-air acts, mandating study, then proposing standards, then introducing enforcement powers. But as the 1967 act came up for reauthorization in 1970, no state had comprehensive standards or implementation plans for any pollutant. In his State of the Union address in February, the president, out in front this time, called for reauthorization of the bill and followed with a special message to Congress calling for motor vehicle emission standards, improved testing, regulation of fuel composition, national standards for air quality, quality control regions, and national emission limits.

Chairman Harley Staggers (D-WV) of the Public Welfare and Health Subcommittee of the House Interstate and Foreign Commerce Committee moved expeditiously to hold hearings on the proposed bill, working from the White House draft but strengthening it in most areas, weakening only its provisions on auto emissions and fuel composition, where the auto and fuel industries were particularly active before his subcommittee. The full committee then converted these provisions into its own bill, which passed the House within a week, 374–1.

The Subcommittee on Air and Water Pollution of the Senate Public Works Committee, still under Chairman Edmund Muskie, ran longer in its deliberations, partly because the House bill stimulated aggressive testimony by the affected interests: the auto industry on the timing and severity of pollution targets, manufacturers on the absence of the technology necessary to achieve the bill's goals, and state governments on state autonomy in the face of national standards. Yet the subcommittee went on to propose a 90 percent reduction in auto pollution by 1975, to salute the priority of public health over technical feasibility, and to override state-level complaints. The full committee sent this bill to the full Senate, which substituted its bill for the House counterpart on a roll-call of 73–0.

Accordingly, the House and Senate bills again moved to conference. Eighty conference sessions, spread out over three months, ensued. Industry representatives continued to press both the White House and the House leaderships, yet the midterm elections played as much of a role in delaying a conference response. Ultimately, pollution requirements were slightly eased, while the calendar for appealing them was extended. Otherwise, it was largely the Senate bill—the toughest of three contenders—that went back to the two houses of Congress, both of which accepted the conference report on the same day in early December by voice votes. The president signed it on New Year's Eve, calling it a "cooperative effort" by both parties and the full government.[63]

Yet early on, while this flood of environmental actions was only cresting, a second major cluster of policy concerns began to impinge consistently on the public mind. These were most often gathered under the rubric of "stagflation." Inflation and unemployment were not supposed to rise together, while economic growth was supposed to cushion their mutual adjustment. Yet during the Era of Divided Government, the former appeared to be happening while the latter clearly was not. In response, a public accustomed to rising standards of living over the long run came to want the economy to be constantly "restarted." Presidents Nixon, Ford, Carter, Reagan, and Bush would all feel compelled to respond.[64]

The most symbolic affronts to these general public wishes were the oil embargo of 1973–1974 and the aftershock—another echoing energy crisis—of 1979. Yet those were just the most dramatic flash points for a continuing concern. Once again, a list of only those acts responding to this overall situation that meet the Mayhew test of significance is impressive:[65]

> Economic Stabilization Act of 1970
> Unemployment Compensation Expansion of 1970
> Emergency Employment Act of 1971
> Comprehensive Employment and Training Act of 1973
> Emergency Petroleum Allocation Act of 1973
> Congressional Budget and Impoundment Control Act of 1974
> Energy Policy and Conservation Act of 1975 (price controls)
> Tax Reduction Act of 1975
> Unemployment Compensation Overhaul of 1976
> Tax Cut of 1977
> Comprehensive Energy Package of 1978
> Tax Revision of 1978
> Chrysler Corporation Bailout of 1979

Yet the truly diagnostic embodiment of this public concern with stagflation—its signature legislative product—was to be a series of self-consciously deregulatory laws, intended to reduce the slowing effect on the national economy of governmental regulations while simultaneously improving service to consumers. The further aspect of this signature embodiment that attracted special attention from policy analysts was that it came in its most concentrated form not from Richard Nixon, Republican, but from Jimmy Carter, Democrat, that is, from a president of the party long recognized for pioneering governmental *regulation* of the private economy.

Two of the cornerstones of this deregulatory impulse were the Airline Deregulation Act of 1978 and the Trucking Deregulation Act of 1980. Like their environmental counterparts, both would generate only limited conflict between the political parties but serious efforts to shape their provisions by the president, the Senate, and the House. Like their environmental counterparts, both would reflect the overall policy-making process of the Era of Divided Government through near unanimity in ultimate support. Deregulatory initiatives would see more substantial pushback from the affected interests than their environmental counterparts. Yet they would also witness the defeat of the stereotypically dominant coalition of those interests.

The landscape of policy conflict over federal deregulation had begun to take shape during the Ford administration, pitting industries that were comfortable with their regulatory framework against consumer groups, while pitting geographic constituencies that felt underserved by the corporate response to existing regulations against areas which feared that greater competition might damage the companies that already served them. Such divisions jumbled the normal partisan alliances inside government. Thus, Gerald Ford, Republican president, could favor deregulation as a key device for tackling inflation but side with Edward Kennedy, Democratic senator from Massachusetts, who favored deregulation as a way to advantage the general public over the organized interests.[66]

The short Ford administration accomplished little directly in this realm, though the independent regulatory bodies, the Civil Aeronautics Board (CAB) for airlines and the Interstate Commerce Commission (ICC) for trucking, did begin some deregulatory initiatives of their own. With that as backdrop, the new Carter administration moved quickly to focus on airline deregulation, catering to a general public concern that airfares had become excessive while believing that previous congressional hearings might produce an early and easy victory for the new administration.[67] The Senate Commerce Committee did move quickly to take up the White House draft, though the House Public Works Committee did not, suggesting the scope of entrenched resistance: all six major carriers plus their major employee unions were lined up against deregulation.

In that environment, it took even the Senate Commerce Committee a full year to report a bill. When it finally did, however, the product was expansive, requiring the CAB to promote airline competition, speed its decisions, permit carriers to begin changing fares and routes without CAB approval, and ultimately phase itself out of existence. Small communities were brought into the proposal by subsidizing "essential" air services, though the industry and its unions continued to argue that the bill would produce only service cuts and job losses. Senator Kennedy strengthened this further on the Senate floor by instructing the CAB to presume approval of new transportation proposals unless *opponents* could prove that these were neither necessary nor convenient for the public, an amendment that passed with solid majorities of both parties. The Senate did add compensation for airline employees harmed by deregulation, but it also expanded the limits within which airlines could adjust fares without consulting the CAB, before passing the final version 83–9.

This apparent drift toward sweeping deregulation was, however, halted abruptly by the Aviation Subcommittee of the House Public Works Committee. Long a bastion of corporate and union support from the industry, the subcommittee produced a substitute bill eliminating most deregulatory provisions. On the other hand, its full committee, frustrated by subcommittee resistance, went on to report a *separate* companion bill with provisions more like those in the original Senate version. It was this strengthened bill that passed the House 363–8. House conferees then ceded further policy ground to Senate counterparts in conference, and the resulting product passed the Senate 82–4 and the House 356–6, despite a last-ditch effort by House opponents to insist on prior consideration of a bill on airline noise abatement.

The Trucking Deregulation Bill of 1980 would follow much the same overall course in the face of an additionally muscular industry-labor coalition, ultimately confirming the general drift toward deregulation in both parties and all institutions. Trucking was much more densely regulated than airlines: more firms, more categories of firms, and more detailed regulations, to the point where rules could be idiosyncratic nearly to the individual trucker. As an industry, trucking had first been addressed by the Motor Carrier Act of 1935, with regulations initially managed through the National Industrial Recovery Administration and transferred to the ICC when the Supreme Court struck down the NIRA. These regulations were sustained through the Late New Deal Era, after the Reed-Bulwinkle Act of 1948, passed over President Truman's veto, exempted trucking from antitrust laws.

During that long era, the industry boomed, propelled additionally by the success of the Federal Highway Act of 1956. By the Era of Divided Government, there were 17,000 regulated firms (though only one major union, the Teamsters, with 450,000 members), contributing three-quarters of the transport revenue in the entire national economy. The industry had also built strong relationships with Congress, to which it turned when the ICC began to implement deregulatory initiatives.[68] Industry leaders asked allies in Congress to assert their constitutional prerogative by reasserting regulatory control, and the Senate Commerce Committee duly asked the ICC to take no further action until what became the Trucking Deregulation Act of 1980 was completed.[69]

This potentially tougher landscape of affected interests caused President Carter and Senator Kennedy to hammer out a common bill for deregulating the industry, even as they were simultaneously running for the Democratic presidential nomination against each other. It was this bill that the Senate Commerce Committee addressed, and its draft, while weaker than the Carter-Kennedy proposal, gave considerably more to pro-competition forces than expected, though the end of antitrust immunity drew a fierce counterattack from the industry, beaten back by votes of only 8–9 and 7–9. This amended bill passed the full Senate by a vote of 70–20, albeit only after surviving a couple of further major attacks, in which a majority of Senate Republicans had to rescue the Carter-Kennedy draft from a narrower majority of Senate Democrats.

The Senate bill then went to the House Public Works and Transportation Committee and on to its Surface Transportation Subcommittee, widely thought to be the congressional body most responsive to the business-labor coalition. True to form, Chairman James J. Howard (D-NJ) refused even to open hearings on this Senate bill. Yet the fact of Senate passage did push Howard into private negotiations with President Carter and Senators Kennedy and Howard Cannon, and ultimately to compromises acceptable to them. Senate proposals on food haulage, industry entry, and antitrust immunity were moderated, but the draft House bill otherwise moved much closer to the Senate version. The House then passed its version 367–13; the Senate accepted that on a voice vote; and the president signed it on July 1, after a successful renomination campaign and in time to claim it as policy success for his administration.

The character of the attack on stagflation began to change with the coming of the Reagan presidency in 1980, as the federal budgetary deficit ballooned. In response, concerns about this growing federal deficit were increasingly mixed into more fundamental concerns about the private economy. Sometimes, policy remained a direct response to these presumed fundamentals. Other times, policy became a response to the belief that growing deficits might be contributing to stagflation on their own. Either way, the parade of policy responses continued:

Economic Recovery Tax Act (ERTA) of 1981
Omnibus Budget Reconciliation Act of 1981
Job Training Partnership Act of 1982
Tax Equity and Fiscal Responsibility Act (TEFRA) of 1982
Anti-recession Jobs Measure of 1983
Deficit Reduction Measure of 1984
Gramm-Rudman-Hollings Anti-deficit Act of 1985
Deficit Reduction Act of 1987
Deficit Reduction Package of 1990

In addressing stagflation, Jimmy Carter had featured deregulation as his great tool for (re)stimulating the economy. Ronald Reagan was to take a more fundamental and broad-based approach in his ERTA of 1981. Along the way, Carter had suffered a major expansion of the federal deficit during his presidency, due largely to those twin bugbears of stagflation, namely, rising inflation coupled with rising unemployment. Ronald Reagan (and then George H. W. Bush after him) would be called upon to address an additionally large deficit, first in the TEFRA of 1982, then in a succession of further legislation. ERTA and TEFRA are thus a good introduction to the shift in policy approaches for dealing with the running problem of deficit finance.

The new president was encouraged in offering the extensive tax cuts of ERTA not just by the historic Republican preference for tax cutting in the aftermath of the New Deal but by two newer trends driving in the same direction. The high road was a revisionist theory of the economics of taxation, a supply-side approach that argued prosperity without inflation was best attained through attending to supply rather than demand in the economy generally, via incentives to work, save, and invest. The low road was an enhanced economic populism favored by elements of the congressional party, arguing that tax reductions that went beyond stimulating business, that is, reductions in the general rate for the common man, should be an important part of the Republican policy arsenal. In effect, President Reagan put the two together in ERTA, proposing to cut individual income taxes by 10 percent in each of the next three years while proposing specific reforms for organized business.[70]

Early signs indicated that this proposal might not have sufficient support in the House, whose Ways and Means Committee had to begin the process, leading Ways and Means chairman Dan Rostenkowski (D-IL) to craft his own bill, cutting income taxes for a single year, targeting these cuts more toward the middle class, and adding alternative business proposals.[71] Yet two other events, one idiosyncratic and one strategic, were to influence the negotiating landscape. In the idiosyncratic event, the president was seriously wounded in an assassination attempt; courage mixed with humor in response caused his personal popularity to rise. In the strategic event, the White House largely succeeded in getting the budget resolution that it wanted from Congress, thereby framing tax cuts with the promise of spending reductions.

Worried by this budget resolution, Chairman Rostenkowski turned to discussions with Robert Dole (R-KS), chairman of the Senate Finance Committee and a traditional conservative known to be skeptical of supply-side arguments. Encouraged by the vote on budgetary reconciliation, however, the president retreated only to the 5/10/10 percent three-year cut being proposed by Barber Conable (R-NY), ranking minority member on House Ways and Means, and Kent Hance (D-TX), a central figure from the budget resolution fight. Subsequent politicking then focused on the "sweeteners" that could be added by each side, either to sustain or to undermine the coalition that had been victorious on the budget resolution. The Senate Finance Committee managed to hold its draft within range of the revised Reagan targets, but the full Senate could not be restrained, adding major amendments for a variety of interests large and small. In deference to House prerogatives on revenue measures, however, the Senate held off final passage of its bill.

The House Ways and Means Committee added a different mix of business benefits, actually outbid the Senate on others, but stuck with its original one-year cut. This version made it to the House floor, but no farther. On the floor, the other side substituted the Conable-Hance draft on a surprising 238–195 vote, drawing a substantial minority of Democrats across the line. That proved to be the decisive battle. The winning margin expanded sharply in the vote for final passage, 323–107, while on the same day, the Senate overwhelmingly endorsed its own amended proposal, 89–11. Both bills did have to go to conference, but their differences were small. On August 3, the House adopted the conference report by another large (and bipartisan) margin, 282–95, with

Republicans 169–1 and Democrats 113–94, while the Senate passed the same report by 67–8, Republicans 41–1 and Democrats 26–7.

ERTA thus became the largest tax cut in American history, though this result would otherwise come back to haunt all the major players when the combination of rate cuts and tax breaks reduced revenue both directly and indirectly, vastly expanding the federal deficit. Simultaneously, the economy fell into what would be a short but sharp recession, fueled in part by anti-inflationary contractions at the Federal Reserve Board. What followed was the first of many efforts to address public perceptions of the deficit itself as a cause of stagflation, an intermittent series that would not really expire until the mid-1990s, at a point when the Era of Divided Government had itself expired. It was the first initiative in this chain that produced the Tax Equity and Fiscal Responsibility Act of 1982.[72]

Prior experience with ERTA provided all the major players with a particular context for TEFRA. That experience left the House Democratic leadership in particular feeling badly burned, to such an extent that the Ways and Means Committee, normally jealous of its ability to go first on revenue matters, deliberately passed, in effect insisting that the Senate Finance Committee be responsible for a bill that had to be centered on tax increases. In part, such increases were the unavoidable response to public demands for action against a recession accompanied by burgeoning deficits. Yet in part, they were also an implicit bargain between the White House and the Federal Reserve: the president would reduce his tax cuts if the Fed would ease its monetary tightening.

In that light, the Senate Finance Committee generated a bill hewing closely to presidential wishes. This promised to raise approximately $98 billion in net revenues, mostly through increases in the income tax, while closing some loopholes, clamping down on tax evasion, and adding modest spending reductions to the mix. This bill passed the full Senate on a nearly pure party-line vote, 50–47, with Republicans 49–3 and Democrats 1–44. Yet the House leadership—recall that the Senate was now controlled by Republicans, but the House remained Democratic—was so allergic to any responsibility for tax increases or spending cuts that it proposed going directly to conference on the Senate bill, bypassing not just its own Ways and Means Committee but the House floor as well. The vote endorsing this strategic initiative was another party-line split at 208–197, with Democrats 197–22 and Republicans 32–147.

Conference negotiations expanded to include all the main players, including majority and minority leaders from the relevant Senate and House committees plus majority and minority leadership from the full bodies, though key aspects of these negotiations devolved directly to President Reagan and Thomas P. "Tip" O'Neill (D-MA), the Speaker of the House. Even with their intense engagement, a conference agreement took eight days before settling close to the bill approved by the full Senate. In this, the support of Speaker O'Neill remained critical as the bill squeaked through the House in a bipartisan fashion, 226–207, with Republicans 103–89 and Democrats 123–118.

This first incarnation of what would be an ongoing effort to deal with the federal deficit thus ultimately conformed to the general character of policy-making during the Era of Divided Government. The Senate, in Republican hands and with a president from its own party for the first time since 1952, did offer a more partisan final tally: 52–47, with Democrats 9–36 and Republicans 43–1. Yet note a different element of change from the Late New Deal Era, in that those nine Democratic votes for TEFRA, so crucial to its passage, were all from Northern Democrats. Southern Democrats voted 0–11 against. Beyond that, even in a realm that inherently engaged partisan preferences, the final vote on TEFRA in the House, the place where cross-partisan and cross-institutional negotiations had to be centrally registered, still pitted majorities of both parties against minorities of both for passage.

Environmental legislation had been largely a matter of attempting to gain credit for new initiatives in a widely supported policy area. Deregulatory legislation had been more a matter of generating policy responses to public unhappiness about a major ongoing problem. Budget balancing was unlike either of those in the sense that the two parties approached it with well-staked-out positions, so that party balance within institutions mattered more, as did the ideological distance between the parties. Yet each party still had to conduct budgetary negotiations within the policy-making content characteristic of the Era of Divided Government. Along the way, each thus kept one eye on prospects for escaping clear ownership of responsibility for the fiscal deficit, while at the end, majorities of both could still often be found on the same side of the ultimate solution.

That handful of concrete examples is one way to tell the story of policy-making in the Era of Divided Government, and thus to confirm that split partisan control could generate the recurrent pattern of cross-partisan and cross-institutional negotiations that characterized the policy-making process during this era. From one side, elected officeholders on Capitol Hill and in the White House clearly felt themselves under pressure to act—that is, to make policy. Beyond that, being impelled to act in the context of divided government, they apparently came to believe that the main way to avoid unified partisan control of national government in the hands of the *other* party was to avoid being seen as the ones who caused widely demanded policies not to be made. From the other side, and surely coloring their response, was the fact that these public officeholders were in large part, especially in Congress, established products of an older world, one in which they were sent to Washington for the precise purpose of handling problems and securing benefits.

The disappearance of major aspects of this older world affected Democratic and Republican congresspersons differently, yet it led both to the same ultimate destination. On their side of the partisan aisle, Democrats had thought of themselves as the engine of government for a very long time. Securing both district-level benefits and national-level policies was central to that vision. The quality of their policy-making experience declined with the arrival of reliably Republican presidents. Yet if they found the world after 1968 to be much less attractive, it was not one that suggested that a strategy of eschewing benefits for their districts and/or policies for the nation would somehow improve their prospects.

On the other side of the partisan aisle, Republicans found themselves dealt into policy-making in a fashion that had not characterized them for a very long time. They still could not control the main institutional levers in Congress, its committee chairs and floor leadership. But party leaders who had been resigned to seeking small adjustments to Democratic initiatives during the long Late New Deal now found themselves with expanded policy prospects, even if they were often personally frustrated by a process in which Republican presidents cut deals with Democratic congressional leaders rather than with them.

Moreover—and this too was crucial—elected officialdom was far less comprehensively penetrated by the ideological polarization that quickly came to characterize newly mobilized party activists in their newly participatory institutions, a polarization additionally reinforced by newly ascendant cultural issues. Many of these officials, instead, had been elected to public office in an earlier, depolarized era. Though lesser penetration also reflected (and was buttressed by) the fact that the constituencies for many of these officeholders did not reflect the newly ascendant issues, or actually reflected them in ways inconsistent with activist preferences—coupling liberal economics with conservative culture, or liberal culture with conservative economics.

So, in what many still regarded as an unappetizing context for policy-making, the main players reliably chose the course of cross-partisan and cross-institutional negotiations. In turn, it was this temporally extended policy-making process that helped to explain those great analytic conundrums of the period. How could Richard Nixon, from the party that was the natural home of private business, become the outstanding president of environmental intervention? How could Jimmy Carter, from the party that was the natural champion of the welfare state, become the outstanding president of *de*regulatory reform? And how could Ronald Reagan generate so much more consensus in legislative voting than either a chronicle of postwar politics or the rhetoric of all the main players in his time would suggest?

The answer in all three cases is that these presidents inherited a policy-making process that suggested trying to manage major demands for public policy rather than attempting to stonewall those demands and pay a public price. They did not have to love the result. They just had to deal themselves into the process and manage it. What was most impressive about this era in many ways, then, was the way in which split partisan control forced negotiations among institutions and between parties. The further result, still puzzling to analysts long after the fact, was that so many of the final legislative votes in Congress were so lopsided. Which is to say: cross-partisan and cross-institutional jousting on the way to framing a policy could nevertheless be concluded by an overwhelmingly cross-partisan and cross-institutional vote.

Again, the nature of an ongoing process of policy-making, diagnostic of the era, had to provide the answer. Or, to say the same thing backward: major bills on which both a Republican president and Democratic congressional leaders were not "bought in" were bills that never reached a final stage at all. Conversely, bills on which they became "bought in" were bills that featured critical choices earlier in the process. As a result, the number of major legislative successes that featured majorities of one party versus majorities of the other was notably smaller than in the preceding Late New Deal Era, and massively fewer than in the succeeding Era of Partisan Volatility.

The policies that emerged were surely not the ones that would have emerged had one party controlled all three elective institutions of national government. In particular, it is hard to overestimate how much the Republican ability to control the presidency shifted the specifics of these negotiations when compared with the Late New Deal Era, when Democrats could be expected to control just about everything. On the other hand, the force of new social movements in the cultural realm, plus new policy problems in the national economy, forced these Republican presidents (along with their Democratic Congresses) to enter into true negotiations, driving them to try to shape policy in realms where they might otherwise have preferred not to legislate at all. The Era of Divided Government was thus, professional Cassandras notwithstanding, an era in which new public policies did emerge, an era of policy productivity rather than policy gridlock. Moreover, in an obvious affront to abstract reasoning, regularized split partisan control was actually *the explanation.*

All that said, the policy-making dynamic at the heart of the Era of Divided Government remained centripetal, though for very different reasons and in a very different way from the Late New Deal Era. Then, centripetal tendencies in Congress had revolved around the need of Northern Democrats to hold their Southern Democratic brethren in line, while centripetal tendencies in the presidency stemmed from the need of Republican candidates to reach out to Northern Democratic voters. Now, the task of both parties was to negotiate successfully across institutions, in a world where neither could expect to be holding both Congress and the presidency at the same time. Negotiation was essential to any immediate policy gains in such a world, and most of the players understood that there was no point in waiting for the next election. Both parties and both institutions thus negotiated.

4 | A Political Structure for the Modern World

The Era of Partisan Volatility, 1993–2016

Party balance: an apparently stable balance, now coinciding with volatile electoral outcomes; **ideological polarization:** *previously damped by elected officialdom, now reaching into every corner of politics;* **substantive conflict:** *economic welfare, foreign affairs, civil rights, and cultural values simultaneously collapsing into a single dimension of issue alignment;* **policy-making process:** *long stretches of stasis punctuated by spikes of activity as the dynamic characterizing a modern world.*

Every bit as idiosyncratic as the presidential election of 1968, the one that kicked off the Era of Divided Government, was the presidential election of 1992, the one that kicked off its successor period—what has become the Era of Partisan Volatility in modern American politics.[1] In its time, the most idiosyncratic element of the 1992 contest was the presence of the biggest third-party vote, for independent candidate Ross Perot, since the Republicans split into two camps in 1912 and independent candidate (and former president) Teddy Roosevelt actually came in second. This raised the possibility—but only that—that a new and different *kind* of shift in party balance might be under way for the nation as a whole.

Yet the winning Democrat, William Jefferson "Bill" Clinton, insisted that he too was a new development, a "New Democrat" who would recast the meaning of Democratic partisanship, modernize his party, and thus activate a different vision of the new electoral era. Moreover, his plan effectively linked party balance and ideological polarization: by countervailing the activist polarization of the previous era, the Democrats would attract substantial new adherents within the general public and in effect restore the favorable Democratic (im)balance of the Late New Deal. There was even a Republican echo of Clinton's Democratic repositioning in the reelection campaign of President George H. W. Bush, hobbled by ideological division but still emphasizing leadership and experience rather than dogma and partisanship.

Neither of these intendedly major changes, a new kind of party balance fostered by growing partisan independence or revised partisan majorities built on moving against ideological polarization, ever came close to realization. Someone had to win, and Bill Clinton did. Yet none of these putative strategic theories were of any use in predicting the veritable kaleidoscope of electoral outcomes that would follow. Initially, Clinton managed to bring back unified partisan control of the institutions of American national government in Democratic hands. Two years later, however, he was a key influence in bringing back split control, albeit in a fashion opposite to the entire Era of Divided Government, with a Democratic presidency stapled onto a Republican Congress.

That was a rich and suggestive but hardly exhaustive introduction to the ensuing sequence of electoral outcomes. The next president, George W. Bush, brought back unified partisan control in Republican hands this time. Yet in his second term, he too contributed to resurrecting split control, though of the sort found in the predecessor era, coupling a Republican presidency with a Democratic Congress. This was in turn replaced by unified partisan control in the hands of Barack Obama and the Democrats in 2008, though that lasted only two years before being replaced by split control, once again in the new fashion, with a Democratic president and a Republican Congress.[2]

In one sense, there could be no unifying theme to such a kaleidoscopic succession of partisan outcomes. Neither the Late New Deal Era nor the Era of Divided Government had seen anything like it. Indeed, such a rapid succession of all four partisan possibilities had not been seen in American politics since the 1840s. Though in a different sense, the kaleidoscope itself—limitless electoral possibilities in very short order—was precisely the theme for a new Era of Partisan Volatility.[3] The Late New Deal Era had been characterized by Democratic dominance, broken by a few short Republican upticks. The Era of Divided Government had been characterized by Democratic control of Congress but Republican control of the presidency. The Era of Partisan Volatility would now be characterized by shifting mixes of absolutely everything.

So, the presence of all possible combinations of election outcomes and, even more strikingly, their rapid circulation and replacement, was what distinguished this period electorally from its predecessors. Yet the first of the main explanatory variables that had helped to frame the operation of those predecessors, namely, party balance, did not appear to be contributing much to this new world. Worse yet, the second of our key explanatory variables, ideological polarization, appeared to work opposite to the way it did in the Era of Divided Government. Then, it drove all the main players toward cross-party and cross-institutional negotiations. Now, it appeared to drive those same players away from such negotiations, to the point where principals who did undertake them stood in more or less explicit opposition to the strategic wishes of their fellow partisans.

Accordingly, the search for some new and patterned *interaction* among these elements, as joined by substantive conflict, must again be the central task in interpreting a new political era. The first such element, *party balance,* had featured a declining but still substantial Democratic edge during the Era of Divided Government when captured through the canonical measure of partisan self-identification. Although the big winner in a small shift had been not the Republicans but the self-proclaimed Independents, the so-called partisan leaners (figure 4.1A). For the Era of Partisan Volatility, this Democratic shrinkage was stanched. Instead, it was the share of independent identifiers that receded, and while it was the Republican Party that picked up the shrinkage this time, the result still left them well over on the wrong side of the national party balance.

A more complex measure of party identification, the seven-point rather than the three-point scale, adds only marginal elements to this story (figure 4.1B). In the Era of Divided Government, it had been not just the Pure Independents who had increased. The share of Independent Democrats and Independent Republicans had both been up as well, while the share of the more conventional partisans—Strong Democrats, Weak Democrats, Weak Republicans, and Strong Republicans—had all declined. For the Era of Partisan Volatility, the strong identifiers, both Democrats and Republicans, regained ground. Yet the independent identifiers held their own, so that it was the weak identifiers this time, again both Democratic and Republican, who continued to shed membership.

The analytic problem in all this, for the Era of Partisan Volatility as in the Era of Divided Government, was that these trends were more or

Figure 4.1. Party Identification in the Nation as a Whole: The Coming of an Era of Partisan Volatility

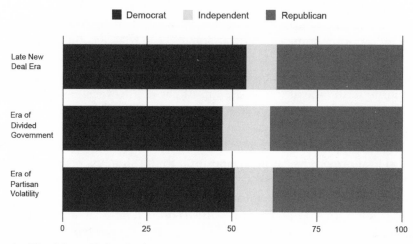

A. The Three-Point Scale

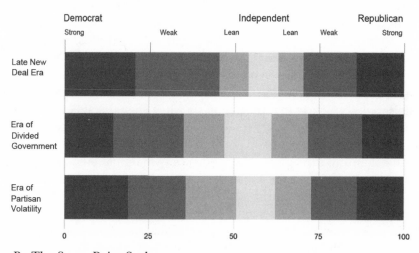

B. The Seven-Point Scale

less inconsistent with the mix of electoral outcomes that was to characterize the new era. If anything, modest Republican gains in the partisan balance nationwide would have been expected to solidify the previous Republican edge with the presidency, which they did not. Similarly, a stable Democratic edge would have been expected to sustain the previous Democratic margin in Congress, which it likewise—and much more strikingly—did not. An increase in the number of strong partisans while weak partisans continued to decline could fit with a world of sharply augmented ideological polarization, but it was not on a scale anywhere close to what would be needed to *generate* this new world.

The traditional (and main alternative) way to measure party balance is, as ever, by way of electoral outcomes. For Congress in the new era, the product of a focus on these outcomes was hugely consequential on its own terms, stunningly different from what party identification would have suggested, yet still more or less completely misleading. What jumped out from House outcomes in the Era of Partisan Volatility was the return to majority status of the Republican Party (figure 4.2A). The 1994 congressional election, viewed as an earthquake even in its time, produced the first Republican majority in the House since 1952. Literally no sitting Republican member had survived from those days. But in fact, Republicans were to go on and secure control of the House in eight of the ten elections to follow, a performance unequaled by them since before the High New Deal. The Senate would tell a slightly weaker version of the same story, with a Republican majority in seven of those ten elections (figure 4.2B).

Party identification notwithstanding, then, it was hard to argue that Republicans were condemned to the same sort of miserable minority status that they had suffered in both the Late New Deal Era and the Era of Divided Government. Indeed, it was hard to weep for a party that was so congressionally successful. On the other hand, it was hardly reasonable to declare the Republican Party the new and reliable majority in a period with the extreme variability in composite outcomes that was the distinguishing characteristic of the Era of Partisan Volatility, a period in which they were to shed their presidential dominance and secure unified partisan control of the elective institutions of American national government in only three of twelve elections to date.

Moreover, that was hardly the end of analytic confusion about party balance in the nation as a whole. For the kaleidoscopic character of the new period—its continuing variety of composite outcomes—could be made to tell yet a different story, one of true balance this time. In a provocative note on party voting, Frances Lee simply combined the vote by decade for Democratic versus Republican candidates for president, Senate, and House into one measure (figure 4.3).[4] Viewed this way, the Era of Partisan Volatility stood out dramatically as the most closely

Figure 4.2. Factional Composition of the Two Parties: The Coming of an Era of Partisan Volatility

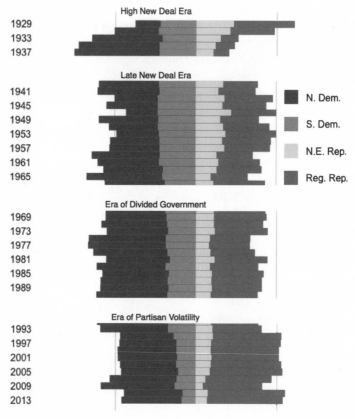

A. The House

balanced of any extended period since before the Civil War. There was an old world of Republican dominance from the 1860s through the 1920s. There was a successor period of Democratic dominance from the 1930s into the 1980s. And there was the Era of Partisan Volatility, 30 years that were by this measure unlike the previous 130.

In many ways, the Lee calculations are the most satisfying for our purposes—best, that is, at allowing party balance to underpin a new period characterized by volatile outcomes. Yet even these numbers fall a step short of capturing the full electoral patterning to modern politics, patterning that separated an Era of Divided Government from the

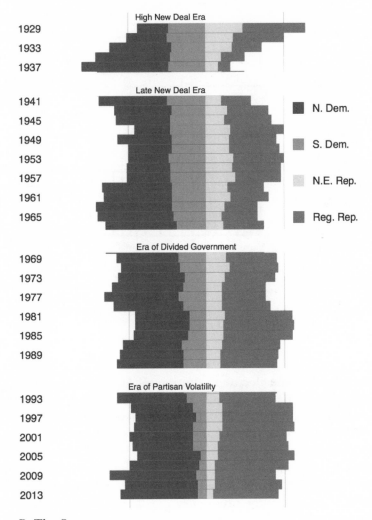

B. The Senate

Era of Partisan Volatility. Moreover, full explication of this patterning remains the prerequisite for describing a new policy-making process, one appropriate to (and distinguishing) the new era. In order to move from the interaction of three key elements to a composite process of policy-making, then, something additional is needed.

To that end, figure 4.4 reaches back before the High New Deal Era and then forward through 2015.[5] Solid bars reaching upward represent

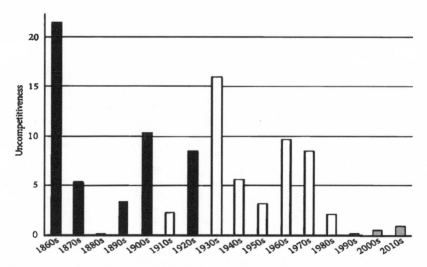

Figure 4.3. Party Balance as Reflected in Voting Behavior: The Presidency, the Senate, and the House Combined

Black bars reflect Republican edge; white bars show Democratic edge; gray bars show an edge of less than 1 percent either way.

unified control of the elective institutions of American national government in Democratic hands, while solid bars reaching downward represent unified control in Republican hands instead. Striped bars reaching upward represent split control of national government where the Democrats had majorities in both houses of Congress while Republicans controlled the presidency, while striped bars reaching downward represent split control with Republican majorities in both houses of Congress but Democratic control of the presidency. Finally, black bars represent control of the presidency plus one house of Congress in the hands of one party, with control of the other house in the hands of the other; these bars point up under a Democratic president, down under a Republican.

Yet even in the face of this complex portrait of collective outcomes, the story by political era is simple enough:

- The dominant result of both the High New Deal and the Late New Deal was solid bars reaching upward: unified partisan control of the institutions of American national government in Democratic hands.

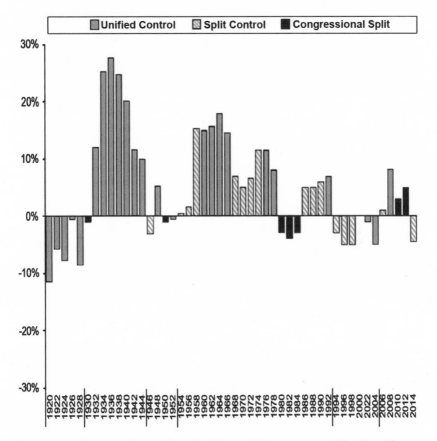

Figure 4.4. Partisan Control of the Elected Government: The Presidency, the Senate, and the House Distinguished

Bars are sized according to the percentage margin in the Senate of the time, calculated from the vote to organize the Senate at the opening of each session.

- The dominant result of the Era of Divided Government was instead striped bars reaching downward: split partisan control with Democrats sustaining their majorities in Congress but Republicans repeatedly picking up the presidency.
- From the perspective of the contemporary era, this shift from solid to striped bars testified, at a minimum, to the inability of American politics to sustain—and increasingly even to generate—unified partisan control after the New Deal Eras.

- The dominant result of the Era of Partisan Volatility, while graphically the most complex, is still easily summarized. Most striking to the eye is the addition of an ongoing *Republican* story in Congress, which had surfaced only once (in 1946) since the High New Deal.
- Yet what this contributes in summary terms is not the onward march of a newly majoritarian Republican Party, much less a countervailing recovery by a previously majoritarian Democratic counterpart. Instead, nearly every possible result is crammed into a political period characterized overall by rapid rotation and replacement.[6]

What this suggests most immediately is that the impact of any aggregate party balance remained crucially dependent on the nature of the *ideological polarization* with which it was associated. It is this linkage that becomes the inescapable next port of call in an effort to ask where the Era of Partisan Volatility came from, what sustained it, and what kind of policy-making process it acquired as a result.[7] Or at least, differing interactions between party balance and ideological polarization certainly distinguished the three preceding eras, one from the other and all from the Era of Partisan Volatility. In shorthand form, this interaction featured unipolarity in the High New Deal Era, multipolarity in the Late New Deal Era, and split-level polarity in the Era of Divided Government.

A different incarnation of the same interaction will prove essential to explaining the new era as well. This time, however, it is a stiff and all-encompassing *bipolarity* that demarcates the new era. This fresh bipolarity was to reach across and integrate diverse geographic areas, the ones whose regional divisions had characterized the Late New Deal Era so centrally. Bipolarity was likewise to reach across and integrate all levels of party structure, where an operational division between party activists and their officeholders had instead characterized the Era of Divided Government. And bipolarity was ultimately to reach across and integrate the varying substantive conflicts whose policy differences had characterized both the Late New Deal Era and the Era of Divided Government, albeit in different ways.

The great instantiation of ideological polarization among the elected officials of American national government—and it is the polarization of these officials that would cause the new era to operate in its distinctive way—is again most easily recognized in the US Congress, where both major parties are always present and where their representatives offer a trackable measure of polarization over an extended period, comfortably back to 1932 in this case and then up into the most recent legislative session. As measured by the degree of overlap between the two parties in Congress, polarization in the contemporary era surged to its highest level in all the years after 1932, not excluding even the High New Deal. As such, it would prove to be the dominant structural characteristic of the modern period. In the process, partisan overlap inside Congress would essentially disappear.

Numerous scholars were becoming curious about this polarization process by the early 1990s. What became the canonical index for tracking it derives from work by Richard Fleisher and Jon Bond, work that can be made to offer a simple graphic presentation of the situation in the Late New Deal Era, the Era of Divided Government, and the Era of Partisan Volatility.[8] To measure ideological polarization, Fleisher and Bond began with a simple left-right continuum based on congressional voting scores and went in search of their target population, the "partisan nonconformists."[9] That category combined two subpopulations: (1) "cross-pressured" members, who were actually closer to the ideological midpoint of the other party, and (2) "moderate" members, who, while less strikingly out of step, remained closer to the midpoint of Congress than to the midpoint of their fellow partisans.

For our purposes, the story that resulted was brutally straightforward (figure 4.5). Despite varying by party, by period, and by institution, and despite moving in fits and starts along the way, an ongoing process of ideological polarization ended up at one similar—stiff and encompassing—terminus:

- The political world of the Late New Deal brought a clear diminution of ideological diversity within both congressional Democratic parties, though Senate Democrats, having begun with a greater share of ideological nonconformists, also shed them more rapidly than their House counterparts. Across the partisan aisle, however, the Republican Party was effectively immune to this trend in the Senate, while actually gaining nonconformists in the House.
- House Republicans then surrendered all of this nonconformity during the Era of Divided Government, ultimately looking indistinguishable from House Democrats, who were essentially stable for the entire period. At the same time, both parties in the Senate

drifted modestly but continually toward conformity, though this meant that the Republicans continued to have a larger share of ideological nonconformists than the Democrats from beginning to end.

- Finally, the Era of Partisan Volatility was especially hard on ideological nonconformists in its early years, for both parties and within both chambers of Congress. Major shrinkage among these nonconformists was in fact what kicked the policy-making process diagnostic of a new era into gear, as we shall see. Nonconforming Democrats would rally a bit in the Senate, leaving the two parties roughly equivalent there, albeit at no more than a third of the level they had attained in the Late New Deal. Nonconforming Democrats enjoyed a mini-renaissance in the House at the elections of 2006 and 2008 before shedding—pretty much discarding—their nonconformists in 2010, while nonconforming House Republicans merely continued their downward trajectory, reaching essentially zero after 2000.

The break points in a parallel overall development did differ between the two parties, with Democrats beginning to polarize earlier but Republicans more than catching up in the long run. The same overall development differed between institutions as well, with the Senate featuring a more gradual evolution than the House, where Republicans became less ideologically conformist during the Late New Deal before plunging back toward conformity from the 1970s onward. Yet with these nuances noted, the comprehensive story remained one of increasing and ultimately blanketing ideological polarization among congresspersons in both parties and both institutions across political eras.[10] At the end of the day, then, it was this common evolution that was most striking about two formally autonomous parties in two formally autonomous institutions. Through the 1980s, it was still not unusual for each party to feature a third of its congressional delegation as ideologically dissident. Thereafter, the nonconforming bottom simply fell out.

Where had this augmented and striking ideological polarization—now including elected officials and not just party activists—come from? There are two main answers to this question, and they go a long way toward shaping the story of *substantive conflict* during the Era of Partisan Volatility. The first answer involves the penetration of one geographic region—the one-party South—by the national party system. Generically,

Figure 4.5. Partisan Polarization among Public Officials

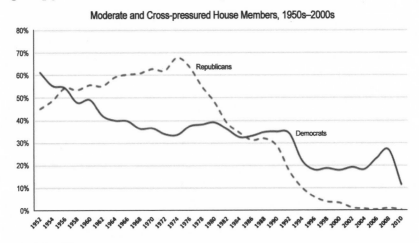

A. The House

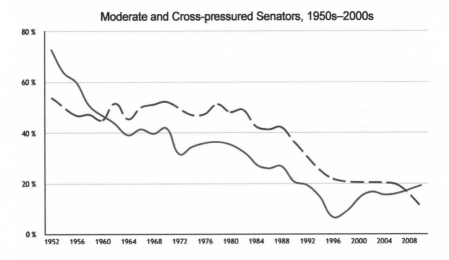

B. The Senate

when a substantial region is characterized by a single party, partisan divisions and their associated policy differences are perforce muted. All views are "represented"—that is, jumbled—within that one party. If external divisions then invade this region so as to integrate it with a national system, the region achieves implicit but inescapable polarization, at least on the substantive matters that differentiate national parties. In the process, composite national parties become additionally polarized as well.

That is an abstract way of describing the postwar evolution of the American South and its subsequent contribution to ideological polarization nationwide. A second answer to the question of the roots of a blanketing ideological polarization involves the penetration of one *level* of the party system—in this case, public officeholders from those parties—by another level of the system, here party activists. Generically, if officeholders are more polarized than activists when this occurs, then a national party system should actually depolarize. But if activists are more polarized than officeholders, as indeed they were in the American politics of the time, then a national party system should increasingly polarize instead. That is an abstract way of describing the growing ideological polarization of elected national officials during this period, including but certainly not limited to those in Congress.

The first answer, the demise of the one-party South, harks back to what was sometimes referred to (and usually derided) as the American three-party system—Northern Democrats, Southern Democrats, and National Republicans. Coming into existence in the 1870s, that system was still alive and well in the Late New Deal Era. It began to erode during the Era of Divided Government. And the eventual result, a two-party South in a nationalized party system, was realized in the early years of the Era of Partisan Volatility. The signature characteristic of this realization was the appearance of a serious Southern Republican Party. The Era of Divided Government had seen these Southern Republicans arrive. The Era of Partisan Volatility saw them rise all the way to majority status in their region, while going on to eclipse the old Northeastern Republicans as a regional bloc inside their national party.

Viewed through the lens of Southern Republican representatives and senators, the Late New Deal was still very much of a piece with the partisan structure of American politics that had arrived in the 1870s (figure 4.6). There was a tiny perturbation at the end of that period: a small diminution of Democratic dominance, the appearance of a handful of elected Republicans. Yet no one could have been sure in the context of the preceding hundred years that this was anything more than that, a perturbation. The Era of Divided Government began to suggest otherwise, though Southern Democratic contractions and Southern Republican expansions remained modest. Yet the era-opening election of

1992 and, in hindsight, the subsequent election of 1994 were to confirm a major change concentrated in the Era of Partisan Volatility, to the point where Southern Republican members of Congress almost immediately outnumbered Southern Democrats, a situation last seen 120 years earlier, in 1872.

At the same time, however, the surviving Southern Democrats were undergoing a transformation all their own. They too were in effect being 'nationalized,' meaning most pointedly that their nonconformist members (in the Fleisher and Bond vocabulary) were being eliminated. In the House, termination of these dissident members was dramatic (figure 4.7A). From the 1930s through the 1970s, and thus from the High New Deal into the Era of Divided Government, Southern Democratic members of the House had actually been majority-dissident, at roughly 60 percent. Late in the Divided Government Era, they had shed a third of these nonconformists. During the Era of Partisan Volatility, they effectively shed the rest. The Senate story is more mottled in its early years because Southern senators were actually becoming more nonconformist from the 1930s through the 1950s (figure 4.7B). After that, they were to mirror the House in featuring a clear decline of nonconformists. Southern Democratic senators did retain a larger percentage of ideological dissidents than their House counterparts during the Era of Partisan Volatility, though that percentage applied to a sharply dwindling aggregate population.

This development should simultaneously have annihilated one of the critical substantive divisions giving shape to American politics during the Late New Deal Era. This was the great factional division over civil rights, where Northern Democrats and Southern Democrats had once anchored the ideological extremes. That division was present for all to see in the battle over the Voting Rights Act of 1965, so that the evolution of the politics surrounding that act can serve as a kind of surrogate for the evolution of this substantive division more generally. The life-or-death moment for the Voting Rights Act, as with so many previous attempts to improve the lot of black Americans, had come in the Senate, where Southern Democrats waged a familiar but this time unsuccessful resistance (table 4.1A). Three of the major partisan factions were overwhelmingly supportive, the Southern Democrats were overwhelmingly opposed, but at the end of the day they were overwhelmed. And the same could be said, a bit less starkly, about the battle in the House (table 4.1B).

Figure 4.6. The "Missing Faction": The Rise of Southern Republicans

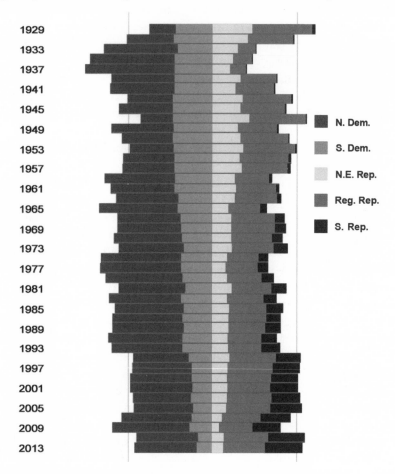

A. The House

One of the compromises associated with passage of the Voting Rights Act had been an agreement that it would require (and come up for) reauthorization five years later. When it duly did in 1970, factional alignments were remarkably unchanged. The Senate produced a nearly perfect copy of its geographic ballot from 1965. The House showed a bit less enthusiasm among Regular Republicans but was otherwise a carbon copy as well. Yet by the time reauthorization came up again in 1985, the factional world had been transformed. In the Senate, South-

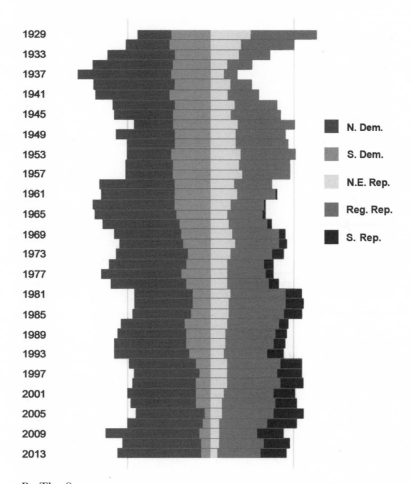

B. The Senate

ern Democrats were now indistinguishable from Northern Democrats or Northeastern Republicans. In the House, they had likewise been displaced by the Regular Republicans as the faction least enthusiastic, though the essential fact was really there were no serious factional divisions left.

The precise mix of influences that ultimately brought the old Southern world to an end remains contested among students of the phenomenon.[11] Yet the point here is different: effective extension of the national

Figure 4.7. The Nationalization of the South

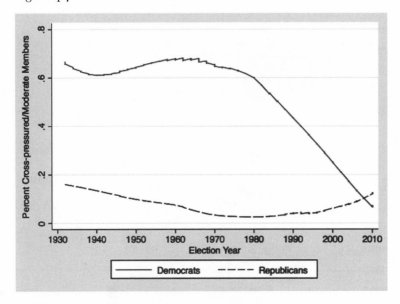

A. The House

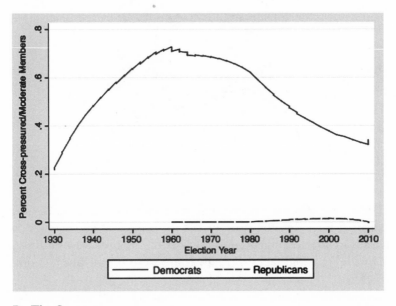

B. The Senate

Table 4.1. Evolution of the Factions: The Voting Rights Act of 1964

A. Senate Vote

	Northern Democrats	Northeastern Republicans	Regular Republicans	Southern Democrats
1965 original bill	44–0	10–0	20–2	3–17
1970 reauthorization	32–1	13–0	22–3	3–14
1985 reauthorization	31–0	11–1	32–6	11–1

B. House Vote

	Northern Democrats	Northeastern Republicans	Regular Republicans	Southern Democrats
1965 original bill	194–0	36–2	75–20	28–58
1970 reauthorization	147–7	33–14	69–64	27–51

party system into the South through creation of a serious Southern Republican Party automatically increased the degree of partisan polarization in both the region and the nation. Lesser one-party areas had come and gone naturally across the United States during the whole postwar period. Yet the South was different in kind, in the scope and depth of its one-party reach, but also in the ferocity of the formal rules used to help maintain this one-party character.[12] In any case, the general point remains that when a two-party system replaces such an arrangement, as long as these are the same two parties present in the rest of the country, two things must follow.

First, the region itself automatically becomes more polarized. Given the national party system at the point when the South began to join it, this meant liberals staying with the Democrats and conservatives moving to the Republicans. But second, the nation as a whole becomes more polarized as well, at least if the region driving this change is numerically large, as the South in fact was. It is surprisingly common to treat partisan change in the American South and partisan polarization nationwide as if they were separate topics. Yet when the one-party South finally collapsed, leaving a serious Southern Republican Party and a revised Democratic Party that was now largely integrated with its Northern counterpart, a huge increment to ideological polarization *in the nation as a whole* was automatically generated.

A weaker version of the same effect could then be found in the other longtime incarnation of regional dissidence, among the Northeastern

Republicans (see figure 4.6).[13] In the High New Deal Era, their faction had been a serious part, and sometimes a near majority, of the surviving congressional party. The Republican recovery associated with the Late New Deal Era was to be concentrated more among Regular Republicans: having lost more seats going into the High New Deal, they had more to regain when coming back out. Yet Northeastern Republicans remained a major regional faction within this resurgent national party, enjoying a kind of postwar heyday during the 1950s.

The 1960s then began a long, slow, downward slide for these Northeastern (and comparatively more moderate) dissidents. Their share of the congressional party and hence of Congress as a whole continued to decline during the Era of Divided Government. That decline carried on, unbroken, into the Era of Partisan Volatility, and while the new era brought with it the added insult of seeing their faction outpaced by the Southern Republicans, the latter were not really the root of their practical problem. If Southern Democratic seats were being shed to Southern Republicans, Northeastern Republican seats were of course being shed to Northern *Democrats*. And the same story could be pretty much told by looking at either house of Congress.

The overall result was that the second of the two great dissident party factions from the postwar party system—but really from well before the coming even of the New Deal—was radically diminished in its importance within the American party system. The end of the "solid South" was the bigger and more dramatic expression of this development. But if the story of Northeastern Republicans was both smaller and ideologically opposite to this Southern story, the two developments nevertheless combined to marginalize the great previously dissident—and more moderate—factions within both of their respective parties.

On the other hand, while the South was rejoining the Union, polarizing both Southern and national politics as it did so, and while the Northeast was recapitulating the same effect in a much more limited but fully consistent fashion, there was a different kind of structural change affecting political parties everywhere, North and South, East and West. This involved the demise of the old intermediary structure of partisan politics, that is, of political parties as formal hierarchies of party officeholders, and its replacement by a new intermediary structure, of parties as social networks among issue activists instead. A major stimulus to this development had been the shift from materialistic to purposive incentives. A major consequence had been ideological polarization among party activists. That latter had been a structural cornerstone of the preceding period.

Yet while the logic of this inherently polarizing development was similar whenever and wherever it occurred, the impact of this logic varied greatly, depending on its interaction with other key elements in the political structure of an electoral period. In the Late New Deal Era, this ultimate change in the nature of political parties had been only just beginning, a side story to the politics of its time. There were reform clubs among Democrats in major urban areas.[14] There were cause groups among Republicans scattered around the country.[15] But those reforms clubs remained essentially "splinters" within the Democratic Party, while those cause groups were largely "fringe" phenomena, not yet integral to Republican Party operations.

In the Era of Divided Government, participatory politics arrived much more broadly, and with a vengeance. There was participatory ideological doctrine, there were participatory social movements, and there were participatory institutional reforms. The combination produced the split-level polarization diagnostic of its era. The internal nature of party organizations was transformed, in the process reconstituting the activist strata of both. Yet this restructuring ran into a kind of firewall when it came up against elected officialdom. From above, these were often incumbent officials, likely to have been elected in a previous period while holding office well into its successor. From below, their constituents were rarely as polarized as their active co-partisans, while their constituencies often mixed policy preferences differently from the preferences of those increasingly polarized activists.

Yet in the successor period, the Era of Partisan Volatility, the ideological dynamic that had captured the activist stratum in both parties broke through this previous firewall, capturing elected officialdom and fostering generalized polarization. That result contributed powerfully to the volatility of outcomes that would denominate the new era, as voters combined and recombined the partisan possibilities of an increasingly polarized world. In its major structural implication, this breakthrough contributed a nationally polarizing trend to go with the regional polarization stemming from the demise of dissident party factions.[16] Presumably, this national trend made political change even more intense in previously dissident regions, since they were experiencing the nationwide trend at the same time. Yet because this shift in the ideological composition of the two parties *was* nationwide, the operative point is that ideological polarization was proceeding apace even in previously orthodox regions.

In the House, this national effect was actually common to all Republicans, Southern and non-Southern alike (figure 4.8A). A handful of Southern Republicans did exist before the 1980s, but serious growth occurred only after that date. By then, the increasing polarization of Republican members was effectively general, that is, affecting Republican congresspersons without regard to region. To say the same thing differently: Southern Republicans as they came into Congress were no more moderate than the non-Southern party colleagues they were joining. Nor did they become more moderate as their numbers increased. Southern Republicans and non-Southern Republicans moved in tandem at every point, and always rightward from the 1980s on.

The story of growing polarization among Democrats did differ by region for a long time, though again not forever. Northern Democrats in the House had been polarizing gradually in a long arc from the 1930s onward. By the 1980s, they had few nonconformists left to surrender. There had been numerous Southern Democrats across this same period, of course, outnumbering their Northern colleagues on rare occasions. Into the 1960s, these regional Democrats had been dissident and moderate as a collectivity, sitting close to the institutional mean. Yet thereafter, in common with Republicans of all stripes, they began to move clearly if gradually away from that mean, ultimately coming to approximate their Northern Democratic brethren and thus eliminating the old Southern Democratic difference—and the largest ideologically centrist faction.

There was one step change, different in kind, within this otherwise evolutionary process among Southern Democrats. Arriving in 1992, at the very beginning of the Era of Partisan Volatility, this change involved creation of so-called majority-minority districts in the House, part and parcel of the reauthorization of the Voting Rights Act in 1985. For the 1990s, this produced a onetime increment of twelve black congresspersons. At the time, race-conscious redistricting was controversial on its own terms. For retrospective purposes, the point is rather that all twelve of these new black members were national, not regional, Democrats.[17] They varied impressively as personalities, but they contained no ideological nonconformists by the measures used here. They were thus the fully polarized equivalent of the nine new Southern Republicans who were created that same year—and who proved to be just the

Figure 4.8. Ideological Polarization: South and Non-South

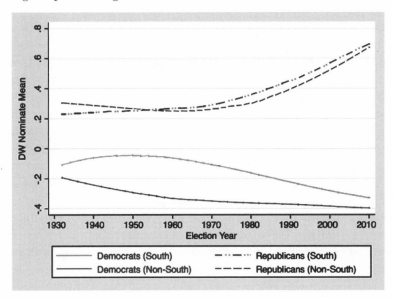

A. The House

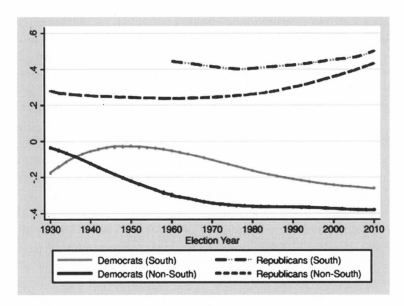

B. The Senate

prologue to an even larger cohort of new Southern Republicans two years later.

The Senate featured the same general story, with adjustments peculiar to a peculiar institution (figure 4.8B). There could be no senatorial counterpart to this onetime change in the ideological composition of the House, since the constitution guaranteed the integrity of Senate districts. Moreover, before 1960, there simply were no Southern Republican senators. After 1960, they were an increasingly important part of their senatorial party and thus of the entire Senate. Yet there was nothing evolutionary about the *ideology* of these new Southern Republicans even then. Arriving as strong conservatives, they just stayed that way. It was their non-Southern brethren who moved increasingly to the right after 1980.

Among Democratic senators, the story was more like that of their House counterparts. Northern Democrats had likewise polarized— moved left—from the 1930s onward, though having begun closer to the institutional mean, they did have farther to move. Southern Democrats remained much closer to this institutional mean into the 1960s as they did in the House, while moving left, toward their Northern Democratic brethren, thereafter. If they still came to rest at a more moderate (though still increasingly ideologized) position than Northern Democratic senators or Republican senators from any region, as in fact they did, this was modest moderation within a much-reduced cohort.

One further product of ideological polarization on this sweeping scale was that it went on to alter the relationship between the elective institutions of national government and the Supreme Court. In the High New Deal Era, open warfare *between* presidency and Court had been, implicitly but powerfully, the real story of ideological conflict. The resolution of that conflict through a fundamental shift in the substantive focus of the Court, from economic rights and liberties to individual rights and liberties, meant that the role of the Court in both successor periods would instead be to pump a largely new set of policy conflicts into American politics, where they eventually but inevitably came back around to confront the elective institutions of national government once again.

In the Late New Deal Era, the most dramatic instance of this confrontation involved civil rights and school desegregation. The Court was thus central to fueling one of the three great policy conflicts of the era: social welfare, foreign affairs, and now—courtesy of *Brown v. Board of Education* and its progeny—civil rights. In the Era of Divided Government, this process of pumping new substantive conflicts into American politics was focused instead on a diverse array of essentially cultural issues. Ranging from criminal justice to school prayer to abortion policy, these reinforced one of the two great issue clusters that gave the era as a whole its substantive focus, an issue cluster that crosscut economic welfare so as to sustain split partisan control of the institutions of American national government.

The propensity of the Court to stand up for the minority side in these cultural disputes was what then interacted with ideological polarization in the Era of Partisan Volatility, thereby reversing the previous relationship between the Supreme Court and the elective institutions of national politics. In this period, the effective partisanship of potential justices themselves did become a major issue for party politics. While this remained largely an activist conflict, breaking through only intermittently into mass politics, it did sometimes go far enough to generate actual campaign ads about what the next presidential election might mean for ideological balance on the Court. By contrast, the effective partisanship of any new justices was a much more constant topic of concern at the activist level, trumping judicial experience and ideological balance as both Democrats and Republicans actively attempted to enmesh the Court in their partisan nets.[18]

Perhaps the implications of this far-reaching polarization for *substantive conflict* should have seemed inevitable, though the operational result would be striking even then. To wit, what had been three major and independent realms of policy combat in the Late New Deal Era, then two major but crosscutting realms in the Era of Divided Government, collapsed into a single dimension encompassing all those previous disputes in the Era of Partisan Volatility. In the process, all of the previous means of characterizing and dividing the two parties on policy grounds were collapsed—aligned—into a single, augmented, dominant division: liberals versus conservatives by way of Democrats versus Republicans.

It was not that the old world of partisan politics had lacked ideological distinctions. Indeed, these had become increasingly clear with regard to economic welfare by the end of the High New Deal Era, at least in the non-South. Economic welfare did owe its primacy to the dominant policy crisis of the High New Deal, the Great Depression, rather than to the simple arrival of a new Democratic majority or the accompanying factional surge by Northern Democrats. Yet the substantive power of the issue was already sufficient to begin organizing party politics around concerns for domestic welfare by the time the approach of international crisis and then of World War II helped bring this earliest version of unidimensionality to a close.

Substantive conflict in the Late New Deal Era became instead multidimensional, adding both foreign affairs and civil rights to the continuing role of economic welfare. If it had been possible for welfare concerns to retain policy predominance, they might have trivialized and suppressed both the Cold War and the civil rights revolution by aligning the bases of their support with the one already characterizing welfare issues. Policy conflict might then have been unchanged, merely recalibrating the balance between welfare liberals and welfare conservatives. Yet the shifts in party balance that reduced the Democratic edge nationwide, in concert with the rebalancing of partisan factions that ended the short dominance of the Northern Democrats, automatically reinvigorated *three* other factions—all with policy priorities that did not align with those on domestic welfare.[19]

Conflicts over economic welfare continued into the Era of Divided Government, more or less unchanged in their underlying alignments and ideological implications. Yet these conflicts were joined this time by era-defining divisions over *cultural values,* with their crosscutting social groups and institutionalized partisan tensions. Indeed, those newly emergent issue divisions were strong enough and sufficiently crosscutting that they managed to generate and sustain split partisan control of American national government. Had new social movements with their largely cultural foci been even more dominating, they might have buried economic welfare and returned to unidimensional policy conflict, around cultural values this time. Had social movements and cultural issues been less intrusive, economic welfare might have resurged as a unilateral focus of policy conflict.

In the event, neither condition was met, so that policy divisions became (and remained for a time) crosscutting in partisan terms. The Era of Partisan Volatility was then actually closest to the High New Deal in one regard: it too featured a single dominating dimension to policy conflict. But this time, it was not the substantive content to this conflict that made politics unidimensional. Rather, the relationship ran the other way around: it was the extremity of ideological polarization that permitted only a single underlying dimension of policy conflict. In effect, this polarization had gone so far that it forced the collapse of previous conflicts into a single continuum. In other words, a polarized two-party system proved sufficiently strong as to bring economic welfare, foreign affairs, civil rights, and cultural values into a single alignment: liberals versus conservatives by way of Democrats versus Republicans.

How could this have happened? That is, how did previously major conflicts collapse and become aligned in one dominant dimension? An answer by way of social movements would note simply that the participatory recruitment of individual activists from these movements into party politics, and the subsequent socialization of these new activists into broader programs than those involving just the specific issues that had originally motivated them, effectively eliminated many potential policy tensions. Party workers generated by issue activism may have come into politics through one or another issue attachment, an intense attachment that directed them more or less automatically to one or the other political party. Yet most such issue-driven activists then had little trouble accommodating the alternative attachments of fellow activists, since these were reliably less important than the key motivating interest of the individual(s) in question.

Social scientists still felt compelled to go looking for the individual-level processes by which new activists could comfortably agglomerate diverse substantive divisions into a unidimensional alignment. After all, it was certainly arguable that higher educational levels or greater political experience should have given these individuals more-varied issue positions along with a greater ability to hold more-varied combinations of these positions in their heads. An absence of variety and a dearth of nuance are not ordinarily championed as products of education and experience. In turn, if party activists had been *offended* by the unidimensional amalgamation of these issues—the formalistically logical response of the better educated or the more experienced—these were simultaneously the individuals who were best equipped to resist the trend.

Yet in a world of increasing ideological polarization, that simply did not happen, and scholars quickly found the necessary, individual-level, aligning mechanisms to explain a unidimensional outcome. Bellwether research here came from Thomas Carsey and Geoffrey Layman. In an opening attack on the puzzle, Carsey and Layman argued that the common debate over whether party identification or issue preferences dominated the drive for ideological polarization was misplaced.[20] The proper question was the level of awareness of difference on a policy issue among party identifiers, along with the degree of salience for the issue(s) in question:

Among individuals who are not aware of partisan differences on the issues, there is no evidence of changes in party identification to fit with policy attitudes or of bringing issue attitudes into line with partisanship. . . . As expected, individuals who are aware that the GOP is more conservative than the Democratic Party on an issue, but who do not find the issue to be particularly important, appear to change their views on the issue to bring them into line with their partisanship and not the reverse. . . . In contrast, individuals who are aware of party differences on an issue and do find the issue to be salient are much more likely to change their party identifications based on their issue attitudes.[21]

With additional colleagues, the two scholars then refocused on the partisan activists who normally played the crucial operative role in institutionalizing these issues, asking the critical question of how these individuals could fit previously diverse substantive concerns—and policy conflicts—into a single party program.[22] Carsey, Layman, and their colleagues, working very much in the framework of Wilson, Ware, and Mayhew, began by confirming the growing polarization on multiple issue dimensions at the very time these were coming into uniform alignment, and they noted the essential role of active partisans in permitting, indeed encouraging, this trend:

In recent years, however, partisans in government and the electorate have grown increasingly polarized on multiple major policy dimensions—not just the newer "cultural" issues such as abortion and gay rights, but also the racial and civil rights issues that emerged in the 1960s and the economic and social welfare issues that originated in the New Deal. Republicans have become more consistently conservative on all these dimensions, whereas Democrats have grown more consistently liberal. . . .

Conflict extension, as theorized in this article, cannot occur unless activists are willing to accommodate one another's most important policy preferences by including them in the party agenda. We have suggested, more strongly, that some activists may even internalize the key positions of candidates and other activists.[23]

Consideration of individual-level dynamics among these activists then led back to questions about the structural and institutional conditions that had to be (and were) present in order for these dynamics to produce parallel, growing, ideological polarization in previously autonomous issue domains:

These activists may push the parties toward extreme stands on multiple issues if two conditions are met. The first is that activists are motivated by policy goals and thus advocate non-centrist positions on the policies that motivate them. The other is that the parties' nomination processes are open to diverse actors other than those currently controlling the party agenda, thus giving issue activists more influence over the selection of party candidates and party issue positions.

In contemporary party politics, both of these conditions are clearly met.[24]

At bottom, this development—growing ideological polarization in multiple issue domains that are nevertheless increasingly aligned—represented nothing less than a blanketing nationalization of American party politics.[25] In the prenationalized world of the Late New Deal Era, there could be a greater difference between Mississippi Democrats and New York Democrats or Mississippi Republicans and New York Republicans than there was between Mississippi Democrats and Mississippi Republicans or New York Democrats and New York Republicans. In the Era of Divided Government, this had already ceased to be true among party activists. Yet the older basic distinction survived—carried on—among Mississippi and New York Democratic and Republican *members of Congress.*

This split-level effect was what was erased in the Era of Partisan Volatility. Once again, Congress, by containing all party factions and all policy divisions, facilitates a measure of the ability of this augmented polarization to extend into the world of elected officials and amalgamate the universe of policy conflicts. One very useful body of evidence for tracking the disappearance in Congress of the old distinctions by party faction and policy realm was generated over time by *National Journal,* the weekly magazine of political analysis. In 1981, the magazine began to isolate major legislative conflicts in the realms of economic welfare (which it labeled "Economics"), foreign affairs (just "Foreign"), and cultural values (dubbed "Social"), giving every member a conservative-to-liberal score that signified agreement with the Republican or Democratic parties for the preceding Congress.[26] Table 4.2 compares the situation in the first five years of this series, all within the Era of Divided Government, with the situation in the most recent five, solidly inside the Era of Partisan Volatility.

The Senate in the Era of Divided Government still attested to the great staying power—the effective resistance—of elected officials in the face of ideological polarization among their own party activists

Table 4.2. Comprehensive Ideological Polarization: The Appearance of a Single Policy Alignment

A. The Era of Divided Government, 1981–1985

	1. The Senate					2. The House				
	Economic	*Foreign*	*Social*	*N*	*%*	*Economic*	*Foreign*	*Social*	*N*	*%*
Northern Democrats	78	75	71	173	35	74	73	71	898	41
Southern Democrats	62	52	48	58	12	52	38	48	375	17
Northeastern Republicans	45	45	60	57	11	34	40	42	220	10
Regular Republicans	22	24	27	212	42	17	21	20	681	31

B. The Era of Partisan Volatility, 2010–2014

	1. The Senate					2. The House				
	Economic	*Foreign*	*Social*	*N*	*%*	*Economic*	*Foreign*	*Social*	*N*	*%*
Northern Democrats	73	62	61	241	48	76	73	74	827	38
Southern Democrats	56	56	55	31	6	71	64	70	212	10
Northeastern Republicans	32	31	34	25	5	38	30	35	139	6
Regular Republicans	20	18	19	203	41	23	26	21	998	46

Note: N is the number of respondents.

(table 4.2A.1). Senate voting behavior on economic welfare did show the neat ideological alignment that one would have expected from the High New Deal onward: Northern Democrats on the left, to Southern Democrats, to Northeastern Republicans, to Regular Republicans on the right, strung out more or less regularly across the ideological spectrum. Yet while Senate voting behavior on foreign affairs was arrayed in the same general fashion, the critical point here was that Southern Democrats and Northeastern Republicans were considerably closer to each other than either faction was to the remainder of its own party. With Senate voting behavior on cultural values, lastly, these dissident factions went all the way over to swapping ideologies, with Southern Democrats closer to Regular Republicans and Northeastern Republicans closer to Northern Democrats.

The House told the same overall story, tickled in its details (table 4.2A.2). The alignment on economic welfare, the substantive core of a New Deal party system, was effectively identical to that of the Senate: left to right among Northern Democrats, Southern Democrats, Northeastern Republicans, and Regular Republicans, at proportionate ideological intervals. Factional alignments on foreign affairs and cultural values were roughly similar to their Senate version, in the sense that Southern Democrats and Northeastern Republicans were closer to each other than to either of the dominant party factions, the Northern Democrats or the Regular Republicans. For the House, however, it was foreign affairs rather than cultural values that reversed distinctions between the two centrist factions, with Northeastern Republicans ever so slightly more *liberal* than Southern Democrats by 1981, though Southern Democrats were in turn modestly more liberal than Northeastern Republicans on cultural values.

In the most recent years of the Era of Partisan Volatility, in a development that should no longer retain any great element of surprise, this variation by party faction and substantive domain had largely disappeared in both bodies. For the Senate, the economic welfare alignment remained familiar. But now, Southern Democrats were closer to Northern Democrats than to any Republican faction, just as Northeastern Republicans were closer to Regular Republicans than to any Democratic faction (table 4.2B.1). The oldest established factional alignment had thus become more ideologically polarized.

More striking were the changes in the other two realms. Foreign affairs offered an alignment parallel to the one characterizing economic welfare, as it had in the earlier era. But now, the strong centrism characterizing major dissident factions had been transformed. Southern Democrats were closer to their Northern brethren, while Northeastern Republicans were closer to their Regular counterparts. Cultural values took the same developments even further, reversing the previous relationship between Southern Democrats and Northeastern Republicans in order to repeat the general alignment characterizing economic welfare and foreign affairs. Here too, Southern Democrats were now closer to Northern Democrats, Northeastern Republicans closer to Regular Republicans.

For the House, the economic welfare alignment, while still in the order that had characterized the Era of Divided Government, had become like the Senate in featuring Southern Democrats closer to Northern Democrats than to any Republican faction, and Northeastern Republicans closer to Regular Republicans than to any Democratic faction (table 4.2B.2). Moreover, the same could now be said of both foreign affairs and cultural values: not just an overall order parallel to the one that characterized economic welfare, but Southern Democrats closer to their Northern brethren and Northeastern Republican closer to their Regular counterparts. In the House, this did require a larger shift in factional preferences on foreign affairs as opposed to cultural values. Yet that shift had obviously been accomplished.

Several further aspects of change stand out in the modern period. First, it was Southern Democrats in both bodies who had undergone the greatest ideological change as a faction. Table 4.3A shows the evolution of the ideological gap between Southern and Northern Democrats on economic welfare, foreign affairs, and cultural values. With the exception of economic welfare, where this gap was little changed in the Senate, every shift in both bodies was major—such that the Southern Democrats lagged their Northern counterparts by a great deal in the earlier period, by little in the most recent years. Table 4.3B then shows the evolution of this same ideological gap between Northeastern and Regular Republicans. On the one hand, there was an even more generalized decrease in this gap among Republicans, for both bodies and in all three domains over time. On the other hand, this Northeastern-Regular gap among Republicans did remain generally larger than the South-North gap among Democrats.

A final way to look at the same story compares the gap across time between Southern Democrats and Northeastern Republicans, the dissident (and centrist) factions (table 4.3C). In earlier years, this gap was

Table 4.3. Comprehensive Ideological Polarization: The Disappearance of the Centrists

A. The Decline of Partisan Factionalism, Northern versus Southern Democrats

	1. The Senate					2. The House				
	Economic	Foreign	Social	N	%	Economic	Foreign	Social	N	%
Divided Government, 1981–1985	16	23	23	231	47	22	35	34	1273	58
Partisan Volatility, 2010–2014	17	6	6	272	54	5	9	4	1039	48

B. The Decline of Partisan Factionalism, Regular versus Northeastern Republicans

	1. The Senate					2. The House				
	Economic	Foreign	Social	N	%	Economic	Foreign	Social	N	%
Divided Government, 1981–1985	23	21	33	269	53	17	19	22	901	42
Partisan Volatility, 2010–2014	12	13	15	228	46	15	4	14	1137	52

C. The Divergence of Centrist Factions, Southern Democrats versus Northeastern Republicans

	1. The Senate					2. The House				
	Economic	Foreign	Social	N	%	Economic	Foreign	Social	N	%
Divided Government, 1981–1985	17	7	12	116	23	18	2	6	595	27
Partisan Volatility, 2010–2014	24	25	21	56	11	33	34	35	351	16

truly modest: largest, as one might expect, on economic welfare, minimal elsewhere. In more recent years, by contrast, this gap had grown everywhere, while both foreign affairs and cultural values had simultaneously *caught up* to economic welfare. This gap among centrist factions—savaging the nonconformists from the Fleisher and Bond analysis—was now large by party in the Senate, very large by party in the House. Accordingly, the Senate might still offer the occasional prospect of expanded majorities on particular issues, while the House looked unlikely to do so at all.

There was a residuum of factional relationships left in both bodies, in the fact that Southern Democrats were always more moderate than Northern Democrats while Northeastern Republicans were always more moderate than Regular Republicans, era after era and domain on domain. Yet that was all that remained of an earlier, larger, and considerably more complex variation. Moreover, and this was the final further development common to both bodies in the Era of Partisan Volatility, all of the preceding still understates the degree of convergence within parties and across policy domains, because the share of both the Senate and the House made up of Southern Democrats plus Northeastern Republicans had itself declined across the same period.

Not only were these dissident factions less nonconformist than they had been in an earlier day. If they remained the home of much of the nonconformity that managed to survive, both dissident factions had nevertheless declined as a share of the total Congress. In the Era of Divided Government, these factions had each constituted about 10 percent of the Senate. In the Era of Partisan Volatility, this was down to about 5 percent (compare tables 4.2A.1 and 4.2B.1). And the House told roughly the same tale: Southern Democrats falling from 17 percent to 10 percent, Northeastern Republicans declining from 10 percent to 6 percent (compare tables 4.2A.2 and 4.2B.2). Dissident groups were not just declining in their ideological deviation, then. They were also declining as a statistical presence for this residual dissidence.

The outside world would continue to contribute to keeping all the old substantive issues alive in the public mind. There were certainly exogenous shocks to keep economic welfare forcefully in the public mind, as with the Great Recession that began in late 2007. There were likewise exogenous shocks to keep foreign affairs at the front of the public brain, as with the terror attacks of what became known as "9/11" in 2001. And the cultural realm continued to produce its multitude of lesser stimuli, from abortion to stem cells to gun rights to gay marriage to climate change to criminal justice, so that the public hardly had the opportunity to ignore them. Yet in a world where there was quite literally no overlap remaining among members of Congress—every Democratic representative or senator was to the left of every Republican representative or senator—there was no room for more than one overall alignment in these issue realms.

This new unidimensionality, so different from the variant that had characterized the High New Deal Era, thus represented a dramatic reordering of the political universe, that is, of the relationship among party balance, ideological polarization, and substantive conflict during the Era of Partisan Volatility. But how could such a reordering stabilize—indeed, institutionalize—itself? Which is to say: What were the ongoing operational dynamics to carry this summary realignment? A serious attempt to get at this question is Seth Masket, *No Middle Ground*.[27] Beginning with the generalized ideological polarization of the modern world, Masket attempted to work backward to the recurrent elements of partisan politics that produced it.

Like Alan Ware and David Mayhew before him, Masket began with a lament about the unavailability of systematic data, which would establish his argument definitively, even in his chosen mega-case of California. Like Ware,[28] he nevertheless went in search of the intermediary structure that had to provide the first and most proximate answer to his question. Like Mayhew,[29] he needed some central concept to organize what he found:

> Nominations are made in primaries that typically have low turnout, little advertising, no rival party labels among which to choose, and virtually no media attention until they are over. For these reasons, nominations are often easily controlled by political insiders, including legislative leaders, interest groups, activists, and others. I call this collection of actors the *informal party organization*, or IPO, and I argue that these IPOs are the heart, soul, and backbone of contemporary political parties. Since activists are a prominent and energetic component of these organizations, IPOs tend to seek the most ideologically extreme candidate they feel they can get elected in a general election. And, since most general elections are not seriously contested today, winning at that stage is often not much of a constraint.
>
> My claim, then, is that the parties control the public behavior of their office-holders by acting as gatekeepers to public office. Just as it is nearly

impossible to win office without the nomination of a major political party, so it is nearly impossible to win the nomination of a major political party without the backing of a local IPO.[30]

In search of lasting but informal coalitions among his main players—always some mix of legislative leaders, ideological activists, benefit seekers, career staffers, and aspiring candidates—Masket turned to a detailed study of major incarnations in the state of California. The resulting California "case" was both productive and provocative. Looking backward, Mayhew had given California the lowest score on his scale of traditional party organizations (TPOs).[31] Yet looking forward, Ware had surfaced the rudiments of what looked something like a modern alternative in his examination of the San Francisco Bay Area.[32] Masket could thus defend his chosen example as suggestive on three separable grounds. First, if his IPOs could be shown to be dominant in this most hostile of environments, they certainly had the potential to triumph elsewhere. Second, the presence of a long reform tradition aimed at minimizing the role of political parties had been dislodged in California by deliberately partisan reforms, producing a kind of "natural experiment" on the impact of such arrangements. And third, California remained the largest of the states, so that it contained a noteworthy share of all American politics within its borders.

Yet Masket also turned to translating—and thus updating—the theoretical framework offered by James Q. Wilson for understanding the transition from political parties that were essentially formal hierarchies of party offices to political parties that were instead social networks among issue activists.[33] Here, what needed to be done was to demonstrate that the incentive system set out and distinguished by Wilson could explain not just the demise of the old TPOs with their explicitly formal structure but also the rise of an informal but stable structure of IPOs that had largely replaced them:

> One can easily imagine such amateurs getting involved, but what made them into a party? That is, if there was no patronage readily available, what kept these activists in line, pursuing a common partisan agenda across different neighborhoods, legislative districts, and states?
>
> The answer is ideology. Ideology creates coalitions of people who believe in particular policies, even among those personally unaffected by those policies. It binds people across geographical distances and allows them to coordinate actions without a formal central coordinator. The utility of ide-

ology as a binding agent for party groups was somewhat compromised in the mid-twentieth century since ideology was only moderately coordinated with party—both parties contained significant liberal and conservative elements. In recent decades, however, the parties have sorted themselves out along ideological lines, making it easier to guide a party organization on ideology alone.[34]

In the end, Masket found his new IPOs to be concerned not just with managing politics in their particular bailiwicks. He discovered that they were reliably concerned with coordinating activities across multiple levels of government, a concern shared by all his major players. Seen one way, this restored the importance of localized organizations. Partisan activists were being driven by shared values as much at the local as at the national level. Yet in the modern world and unlike the world of the old TPOs, this localization was disciplined by ideology, and relatively extreme ideology at that, so that it no longer gave rise to factional variation:

> Although the shape of the modern party is more of a network than a machine hierarchy, the function is essentially the same: a small group of people operating only barely within the law manages to control elections and thereby the government. The major difference between these modern informal party organizations (IPOs) and their machine forebears is the existence of ideological activists. Machines distrusted ideologues; IPOs rely on them. The result is extreme candidates and highly polarized politics.[35]

That picture imparts a certain inevitably—more than usual—to the policy-making process associated with this mix of party balance, ideological polarization, and substantive conflict, the mix characterizing the Era of Partisan Volatility. At the very least, if the two parties were increasingly organized by a coherent ideological core, if more and more substantive issues were being pulled into alignment with this core, and if the cores themselves were moving farther apart, certain characteristics of any resulting process of policy-making appear to follow. Most centrally, policy proposals that emerged from (or became attached to) the ideological cores of one or the other party seemed destined to acquire augmented support from that party, augmented opposition from the other. Beyond that, more and more policies that were not obviously derivative of those programmatic cores on their face seemed likely nevertheless to become infused by them.

Accordingly, there should have been, as indeed there was, a sharp increase in policies drawing nearly uniform lines of partisan support and opposition. In point of fact, Congress began immediately to generate policy votes with a partisan purity rarely seen in either the Late New Deal or the Era of Divided Government. The first major legislation of the new Clinton presidency, his Omnibus Deficit Reduction Act of 1993, introduced the pattern: a final tally of 218–216 in the House that covered a Democratic division of 217–41 and a heretofore remarkable Republican division of 0–175, coupled with a final tally in the Senate of 51–50 that covered a Democratic division of 50–6, a Republican division of 0–44, plus a casting vote by (Democratic) Vice President Al Gore.[36] But in fact, four of the first five major laws in the new Clinton administration produced this pattern, reliably in the House though in a more moderated fashion in the Senate.[37] The next three were as follows:

Family and Medical Leave Act:
House 247–152, with Democrats 210–29 and Republicans 36–123
Senate 71–27, from Democrats 55–2 and Republicans 16–25

Motor Voter Act:
House 259–164, with Democrats 238–14 and Republicans 20–150
Senate 62–36, from Democrats 56–0 and Republicans 6–36

National Service Act:
House 275–152, with Democrats 248–6 and Republicans 26–146
Senate 57–40, from Democrats 51–4 and Republicans 6–36

The Bush presidency generated many opportunities to replicate the same overall pattern, which it inevitably did. Thus the Bush tax cuts of 2001 passed by 240–154 in the House, broken down as 211–0 among Republicans but 28–153 among Democrats, with a final tally in the Senate of 58–33, broken down as 46–2 for Republicans but 12–31 for Democrats. The Bush tax cuts of 2003 were to draw those lines even more sharply:

Tax Cut Act of 2003:
House 231–200, with Republicans 224–1 and Democrats 7–198
Senate 51–50, from Republicans 48–3, Democrats 2–46, and
   casting vote by (Republican) Vice President Dick Cheney

Lest this seem somehow to be a pattern of division focused mainly on fiscal matters, the Medicare Reform Act of 2003, the prescription drug plan, President Bush's signature health care initiative, told the same story by way of a major substantive bill:

Medicare Reform Act of 2003:
House 220–215, with Republicans 204–25 and Democrats 16–189
Senate 54–44, from Republicans 42–9 and Democrats 11–35

Yet the truly amazing incarnations of an exaggerated partisan outline had to await the presidency of Barack Obama. His first Congress, the 111th, lit up the pattern. Thus the $787 billion stimulus program in 2009 featured an overall vote in the House of 244–188, broken down as 244–11 among Democrats and 0–177 among Republicans, coupled with an overall vote in the Senate of 61–37, broken down as 56–0 for Democrats and 3–37 for Republicans. Remarkably, the next two laws on the list of consequential legislation for the Obama administration told essentially the same story:

Expansion of the State Children's Health Insurance Program of 2009:
House 290–135, with Democrats 250–2 and Republicans 40–133
Senate 66–32, from Democrats 55–0 and Republicans 9–32

Lilly Ledbetter Fair Pay Act of 2009:
House 250–177, with Democrats 247–5 and Republicans 3–172
Senate 61–36, from Democrats 54–0 and Republicans 5–36

Moreover, the signature legislation of the entire Obama presidency, the Affordable Care Act of 2010—"Obamacare"—retold this story yet again, as did the Financial Services Regulation Act of 2010, also known as Dodd-Frank:

Affordable Care Act of 2010:
House 220–207, with Democrats 220–32 and Republicans 0–175
Senate 56–43, from Democrats 54–3 and Republicans 0–40

Financial Services Regulation Act of 2010:
House 237–192, with Democrats 234–19 and Republicans 3–173
Senate 60–39, from Democrats 55–1 and Republicans 3–38

A different twist on this diagnostic pattern to the policy-making process characterizing the Era of Partisan Volatility, rare but always consequential when it occurred, involved presidents joining a majority of the *other* party in order to pass specific pieces of legislation. Party lines in Congress itself were not thereby breached; it was just that the president and the congressional opposition voted together. Inevitably, in a world in which party lines were reliably and tightly drawn, presidents who became convinced that one or another policy response was essential to the national—or their own—interest did on occasion have to secure legislation that meant crossing the aisle and mobilizing the other party in order to produce a policy majority. Bill Clinton generated two major instances, one in his first Congress and one in his second. First was his North American Free Trade Agreement (NAFTA) of 1993. Second was his Welfare Reform Act of 1996. Both were stereotypical in the House, though the Senate proved easier to drag along:

North American Free Trade Act of 1993:
House 234–200, but Democrats 102–156 and Republicans
   132–43
Senate 61–38, still losing Democrats 27–28 but winning
   Republicans 34–10

Welfare Reform Act of 1996:
House 328–111, but Democrats 98–98 and Republicans 230–2
Senate 78–21, with Democrats narrowly 25–21 but Republicans
   53–0

George W. Bush did not produce any such votes until the end of his presidency, when a perceived need to respond to a growing economic crisis was shared by congressional Democrats but not his fellow Republicans. In that environment, both his housing relief program of 2008, rescuing Fannie Mae and Freddie Mac, the federal home insurers, and his $700 billion rescue package for the financial sector acquired this dissident pattern. Once again, the House divided more sharply on partisan lines, while the Senate proved easier to bring along:

Housing Relief Bill of 2008:
House 272–151, with Democrats 227–3 but Republicans 45–149
Senate 72–13, from Democrats 43–0 and Republicans 27–13

Financial Bailout Bill of 2008:
House 263–171, with Democrats 172–63 but Republicans 91–108
Senate 74–25, from Democrats 39–9 and Republicans 34–15

Finally, Barack Obama secured his own version of the same pattern. His debt ceiling deal of 2011, raising the ceiling on the national debt while cutting overall expenditures, required an actual Republican majority. His fiscal cliff deal of 2012 depended just on attracting a sufficiently large Republican minority. In both cases, the House was stereotypical, the Senate more acquiescent:

Debt Ceiling Bill of 2011:
House 269–161, with Republicans 174–66 but Democrats 95–95
Senate 74–26, from Republicans 28–19 and Democrats 45–6

Fiscal Cliff Bill of 2012:
House 257–169, with Republicans 85–151 and Democrats 172–16
Senate 89–8, from Democrats 47–3 and Republicans 40–5

The Bush and Obama examples of this distinctive twist on the policy-making process characterizing the Era of Partisan Volatility were different in their motivations from their Clinton counterparts. By the time George W. Bush and Barack Obama turned to this cross-party pattern, they were doing so in the face of (what they perceived as) some inescapable crisis-of-the-day. By contrast, Bill Clinton was not obviously compelled to do either NAFTA or welfare reform. Both bills were, however, critical to his effort to rebrand himself as a "New Democrat," that is, a moderate who could assert his vision of the public interest against the ideological polarization of his era. On the legislative specifics, Clinton was successful. On the effort to move his *party* counter to the underlying structure of policy-making in his time, he was not: ideological polarization continued apace.

A different testimonial to the power of this diagnostic pattern of partisan division and policy-making came from the way an overarching alignment could infuse substantive realms previously characterized very differently, even by what had once been crosscutting partisan positions. Here, the outstanding example was trade policy. During the Late New Deal, foreign trade had been a substantive domain that reliably cut across party attachments: each party had its protectionist and its free-trade wings.[38] Yet by the Era of Partisan Volatility, the trade issue too had become increasingly aligned—and only more so as time passed—by the ideological polarization leading to a unidimensional alignment of policy preferences overall. Democrats had become protectionists, as Republicans had become free traders.

While the result remained less stark than it did, for example, on matters of welfare policy in its traditional guise, the congressional vote diagnostic of the period reappeared again and again in matters of trade policy, unfailingly so in the House, under both Democratic and Republican presidents. We have already seen this pattern surface in one of the first major policy initiatives of the new Clinton presidency, his North American Free Trade Agreement. Yet it resurfaced in one of the last serious policy initiatives of his (two-term) administration:

> Permanent normal trading relations with China (2000):
> House 237–197, but Democrats 73–138 and Republicans 164–57
> Senate 83–13, with Democrats 37–7 and Republicans 46–8

Because trade policy was increasingly aligned by party, Democratic and Republican presidents did find themselves in a different position when pursuing new trade initiatives. Republicans could count on standing with the majority of their congressional party; Democrats could not. Thus the Bush administration made the president look less of an outlier than the Clinton administration had, though the dominance of the policy-making structure of the Era of Partisan Volatility was still present for all to see:

> Fast-Track Trade Authority (2002):
> House 251–212, with Republicans 190–27 but Democrats 25–183
> Senate 64–34, from Republicans 43–5 and Democrats 20–29
>
> Central America Free Trade Agreement (2005):
> House 217–215, with Republicans 202–27 but Democrats 15–187
> Senate 55–45, from Republicans 43–12 and Democrats 11–33

By contrast, the Obama administration took the president back to the incentives and dilemmas confronting his last Democratic counterpart, Bill Clinton. Regardless, Barack Obama did not flinch, even as he relied heavily on Republican congressional support:

Colombia Trade Agreement (2011):
House 262–167, with Democrats 31–158, Republicans 231–9
Senate 66–33, from Democrats 21–30, Republicans 44–2

Panama Trade Agreement (2011):
House 300–129, with Democrats 66–123, Republicans 234–6
Senate 77–22, from Democrats 30–21, Republicans 46–0

South Korea Trade Agreement (2011):
House 278–151, with Democrats 59–130, Republicans 219–21
Senate 83–15, from Democrats 37–14, Republicans 45–1

Perhaps the first person to recognize a larger pattern to policy-making across these otherwise diverse clusters of legislative outcomes, a pattern that would yield the summary term for the process characterizing the Era of Partisan Volatility—"omnibus legislation"—was Barbara Sinclair in *Unorthodox Lawmaking*.[39] In pursuing a set of case studies concentrated around the time the new era was being born, Sinclair was struck by the way that an older model of the policy-making process, one that had grown up along with the behavioral revolution and was implicitly revered by political scientists, seemed increasingly at variance with policy-making as she observed it. Her perceptions were to widen and deepen as the Era of Partisan Volatility unfolded, becoming increasingly stylized in tandem with the policy-making process she chronicled. As a result, their evolution is nicely mirrored in subsequent editions of *Unorthodox Lawmaking*.[40]

Sinclair began with the classical model, always a bit of an abstraction but an excellent template for understanding legislative productivity. In this, a bill is introduced, is assigned to a committee, and goes on to a subcommittee. The subcommittee holds hearings, considers issues, and marks up a product. The full committee begins with this draft, marks it up again, and moves it toward the floor. The leadership gives it a place on the calendar, interested lawmakers get to debate it, and whatever passes goes to the other house of Congress, to a conference committee, or directly to the president. This template was further nuanced for the two houses of Congress. The House of Representatives needed a more structured incarnation in order to produce anything at all, while senators sought to resist such strictures so as to pursue their individual interests.

What struck Sinclair was that, by what we now know to be the end of the Era of Divided Government, this model was as capable of misleading as of informing analyses of the actual process of policy-making. Thus without major interventions from the leadership, bills increasingly went to multiple committees. When this multiple committee process played out, its products frequently had to be detoured to one or another ad hoc body in order for legislation to move at all. From one side, the leadership of the House then often used its draconian rules in a truly restrictive fashion, purchasing speed at the price of consultation. From the other side, outspoken individuals in the Senate responded increasingly with threats of a filibuster, using associated demands for a supermajority to leverage the delay necessary for individual influence.[41]

Sinclair's first detailed foray into this brave new world featured careful reconstruction of the politicking around the Omnibus Drug Initiative Act of 1988, the National Service Trust Act of 1993, the Omnibus Budget Act of 1993, the Job Creation and Wage Enhancement Act of 1995 (a bill that ultimately died), and the attempt by Republican congressional leadership to force movement toward a balanced budget in 1995–1996 (also ultimately failing). Fresh case studies in subsequent editions included the Patient's Bill of Rights of 2000, the Bush tax cuts of 2001, the prescription drug reforms of 2003, the Bush tax cuts of 2003, the Energy Act of 2005, the Economic Stimulus Package of 2008, the Emergency Economic Stabilization Act, and last but possibly the most complex of all, the Affordable Care Act of 2010.

In the end, however, Sinclair's opening summary of this new policy environment remained a fitting introduction to the omnibus legislation diagnostic of the process of policy-making throughout the Era of Partisan Volatility:

> Legislation that addresses numerous and not necessarily related subjects, issues, and programs, and therefore is usually highly complex and long, is referred to as omnibus legislation. Although there is no consensus technical definition of what constitutes an omnibus bill, every Congress watcher would classify as omnibus the 1988 trade bill that spanned the jurisdiction of thirteen House and nine Senate committees and the antidrug bill passed the same year. It covered drug abuse education and prevention, treatment, punishment of abusers and sellers, big and small, and the interdiction of drugs flowing into the United States from abroad by air, sea, and land. Many of the bills generally labeled omnibus are money bills of some sort. The most common omnibus measures in the contemporary Congress are bud-

get resolutions and reconciliation bills, both of which stem from the budget process.[42]

This model of the modern process of policy-making was utterly unlike the model characterizing previous periods, especially the Late New Deal Era, where these patterns had first been extensively studied. Fortunately, Aaron Wildavsky, a central figure in those early examinations and the scholar who popularized the notion of "incrementalism" as an overarching description of the policy-making process of the time, had continued to work in the budgetary realm. Yet by the time Sinclair was describing the new period in terms of unorthodox lawmaking, Wildavksy had decided that it no longer made sense to provide fresh editions of his classic work, *The Politics of the Budgetary Process*, since he himself could no longer recognize the world that it once described.

Accordingly, what might otherwise have been another new edition became instead a fresh volume, *The New Politics of the Budgetary Process*,[43] itself acquiring multiple editions as time passed. Gathered at the beginning of the fourth edition, the prefaces to these successor editions provide a hugely useful thumbnail sketch of the changes producing a new world of policy-making.[44] Already by the time of the second edition of this new volume, Wildavsky had said good-bye to incrementalism as a summary term for the larger process of policy-making in the United States: "If there is now less consensus and more dissensus, how is the budgetary process affected? There should be more disputes over larger amounts that take longer to resolve. And so there have been. . . . Consensus means that there is agreement on the budgetary base; when that consensus dissipates, so does incrementalism."[45]

Being a student of the historical process and its politics, Wildavsky was also intensely aware of attempts within Congress after the death of incrementalism to restore a semblance of its informal impact through the addition of compensating formal procedures. The grandfather of these efforts had been the Budget and Impoundment Act of 1974, reflecting the structure and incentives of its period, the Era of Divided Government. Here, a reliably Democratic Congress struck back at a regularly Republican presidency by specifying in detail the process by which budgets were to be converted into actual expenditures, so that a president could no longer alter budgetary outcomes by failing to complete expenditures that had been congressionally authorized. Yet the major provision that would come into its own in the successor period, the Era of Partisan Volatility, was creation of a "reconciliation process" featuring new budget committees in Congress and new rules under which their products were entitled to receive automatic votes within the full chambers, so as to circumscribe the possibility of dilatory moves. Wildavsky was never a believer:

> The reliable speeding up of budgetary reform is convincing evidence that a politics of ideological dissensus is on us. From the Budget Act of 1921 to the Budget Act of 1974 took a little over half a century. Then the Act of 1974 was substantially modified as the Gramm-Rudman-Hollings Act in 1986, a bare twelve years later. Now OBRA has come a mere four years after Gramm-Rudman. This speed-up, I think, is due to heroic but failing efforts to replace the classical norms of balance, annualarity, and comprehensiveness with new procedures that provide by legislative stipulation what used to be done by informal understandings. The budget resolutions of the 1974 act, the deficit-reduction targets of the 1986 act, and the stipulated agreements of the 1990 act give legal directions providing overall ceilings, divisions among major programmatic areas, and pathways for adjusting to new circumstances. The more precise these instructions become and the more they straitjacket the budgetary process, however, the more fragile they are. With basic differences over policy left standing, these [differences] surface to weaken and then destroy the most carefully wrought paper plans.[46]

In truth and perhaps inevitably, the Era of Partisan Volatility saw not just the rapid-fire production of formal adjustments to the budgetary process but also saw the intermittent but reliably consequential use of these adjustments to cobble together and force through the omnibus legislation that characterized the policy-making process of the period. A dramatic early incarnation of this alternative use of the reformed budgetary process, and especially of its reconciliation arrangements—a use more or less completely at variance with the face intent of those budgetary reforms—had come with the Economic Recovery Tax Act of 1981 (ERTA), the opening shot in the effort by President Ronald Reagan to address an ongoing stagflation while redirecting the ideological drift of American politics. This largest tax cut in American history relied upon being voted as reconciliation to avoid the possibility of a filibuster in the Senate.

President Bill Clinton then saw the same logic and reaped the same benefit with his Omnibus Deficit Reduction Act of 1993, combining spending cuts, a tax *increase*, and a hike in the Earned Income Tax Credit. Again, reconciliation protected a major bill unlikely to pass without its strictures. But the ultimate innovation in using this reconciliation process—beyond the dreams of either Reagan or Clinton—came from President Barack Obama, who, at the very end, needed reconciliation to pass the Affordable Care Act of 2010.[47] What made this application so additionally remarkable was that Congress had tried to strike back against precisely this use of the reconciliation process through what became known as the Byrd Rule, specifying that reconciliation could be used only on budgetary matters and explicitly not on matters of policy substance. Only when the congressional parliamentarian affirmed that the Byrd Rule was not violated by the Affordable Care Act, because it was indeed a purely budgetary matter without policy consequences, did it pass the Senate and become law.

Accordingly, the propensity toward what Sinclair called unorthodox lawmaking became only more intense as the Era of Partisan Volatility aged, becoming a purer and purer incarnation of itself. Policy-making was thus increasingly characterized by long stretches of intense partisan warfare, interrupted only intermittently by spikes of legislative activity, the product of which was often omnibus legislation, bundling a set of major concerns that could relieve the pressure for action while allocating rewards on all sides. This was the dominant—and diagnostic— pattern of the period, though it could be tweaked by one set of explicitly partisan events and overwhelmed by a second, mercifully rare group of essentially nonpartisan others.

One of these exceptions, the more explicitly political version, arose when short partisan surges produced unified party control of national government. Thus Bill Clinton owed his Omnibus Deficit Reduction Act of 1993 to his capture of the White House while Congress was still in Democratic hands, a contribution that disappeared only two years later. George Bush likewise owed his tax cuts of 2001 to the Republican capture of all three branches of elective national government, though this capture in 2000 was undone even more rapidly, by the defection of Republican senator James Jeffords of Vermont in 2001.[48] And Barack Obama certainly owed the Affordable Care Act of 2010 to his capture of the White House while Congress was already in Democratic hands, though this contribution too disappeared only two years later.

Old-fashioned partisan fluctuations could thus channel a policy-making process otherwise characterized by long stretches of legislative stasis into a sudden but usually short opportunity to make policy with minimal concern for the wishes (and inevitable fulminations) of the opposite party. For both Clinton and Obama, this possibility was nevertheless a two-edged sword, since each was to possess unified control for only two years of an eight-year presidency. Clinton still managed some major legislative successes under those conditions, precisely because he was not a stereotypical—that is, a stereotypically polarized—president. Being just such a president, Obama faced a much more difficult world. On the other hand, genuine national crises, the other development occasionally escaping the operational strictures of the modern process of policy-making, could in principle trump the usual partisan considerations when they occurred, albeit for only a short period even then.

Such crises could actually supply the bipartisan support otherwise so diagnostically absent during the Era of Partisan Volatility. Yet the power of an institutionalized process of policy-making built around ideological polarization and omnibus legislating remained impressive even in the face of such crises. The archetypal example of the bipartisan power of a consensually recognized external crisis can be found in the terrorist attacks of September 11, 2001, producing the Use of Force Resolution of 2001 and the USA Patriot Act of that same year, though there were already Democratic dissenters from the latter. Indeed, even the argument from terrorism could go only so far in suppressing the impact of ideological polarization. A year later, the bipartisan response was gone with the Iraq War Resolution of 2002; it stayed gone with creation of the Department of Homeland Security:

Use of Force Resolution of 2001:
House 401–1, with Republicans 214–0 and Democrats 204–1
Senate 98–0, from Republicans 47–0 and Democrats 50–0

USA Patriot Act of 2001:
House 357–66, with Republicans 211–3 and Democrats 145–62
Senate 98–1, from Republicans 49–0 and Democrats 48–1

Iraq War Resolution of 2002:
House 296–133, with Republicans 215–6 but Democrats 81–126
Senate 77–23, from Republicans 48–2 and Democrats 29–21

Creation of the Department of Homeland Security in 2002:
House 299–121, with Republicans 212–6 but Democrats 87–114
Senate 90–9, from Republicans 48–0 and Democrats 41–8

Those last two are votes that would have been strikingly untypical of the response to much less impressive crises during the Era of Divided Government. Congressional Democrats were the dissenters here, though as we have already seen, President Bush would be unable to generate a consensual response to economic crisis at the end of his term, even in the face of the Great Recession of 2007, where his own Republicans were the dissenters this time. The overall difference with the Era of Divided Government could hardly be more striking. Or at least, it is hard to imagine the policy-making process of that predecessor era responding to either a national concern with homeland security or a national demand for economic rescue with anything short of near unanimity.

Yet the policy-making process characteristic of the Era of Partisan Volatility had no difficulty in either case in generating its diagnostic—polarized—partisan split. More and more as the era aged, then, the process of policy-making came to depend on stereotypical embodiments of what Barbara Sinclair had summarized as omnibus legislation, in order to break through policy stalemates between political parties so ideologically polarized that they could not find agreement on creation of a framework for containing terrorism or responding to the worst economic downturn since the Great Depression. Three examples dealing with fiscal matters late in the Era of Partisan Volatility, to date, are particularly good at making this point: the bipartisan budget deal of 2010, the debt ceiling deal of 2011, and the fiscal cliff deal of 2012.

The bipartisan tax deal of 2011 was caught up in—and thus brought together—the otherwise separate fates of two existing pieces of legislation, one a major tax arrangement, the other a major welfare program.[49] The tax arrangement involved the Bush tax cuts of 2001 and 2003, slated to expire on December 31, 2010. The welfare program involved emergency unemployment benefits from 2009, which actually did expire on November 31, 2010, before a deal could be consummated. The two provisions became joined in the hunt for an omnibus solution, while acquiring a number of add-on provisions not strictly related to either and demonstrating the intensity of partisan divisions before the pressure of time forced an ultimate resolution.

The House of Representatives moved first, only three days after emergency unemployment benefits had expired, with a bill restoring the Bush tax proposals but capping their cuts and allowing the old rates to rise above their cap. That bill passed the House easily, albeit on a sharply partisan division: 234–188, with Democrats 231–20 but Republicans 3–168. Senate Republicans, however, had already blocked cloture on a Senate version of the same proposals, suggesting an obvious willingness to filibuster any bill with that form. So President Obama turned to direct negotiations with the Republican congressional leadership, announcing a compromise bill on December 6.

This compromise was intended to sustain the Bush tax cuts largely as written while extending unemployment benefits for a further thirteen months (backdated to November 31), tossing in a restoration of the estate tax (a Republican priority), a yearlong reduction in the Social Security payroll tax (a Democratic priority), a two-year patch on the alternative minimum tax (a priority for both parties), and numerous further extensions and add-ons, from tax deductions to renewable-energy incentives. House Democrats were not impressed: three days later, they drove through a nonbinding resolution calling on the Speaker to keep this compromise program from ever coming to the House floor.

Yet four days after the House called for no action on the proposed compromise, the Senate actually invoked cloture on the debate over essentially the same proposal, by the decisive (and bipartisan) margin of 83–15. Two further days later, on December 15, the full body adopted the Obama deal by 81–19. Before adoption, it turned down both a conservative amendment to trim the deficit and a liberal amendment to allow the top tax rate to rise. Senate convergence on the Obama proposal thus seemed secure. The House then made a last-ditch effort to amend that proposal, focusing on the estate tax and increasing it for the wealthiest individual estates, an amendment that was defeated 194–233 (Democrats 194–60, Republicans 0–173).

At that point, the House too apparently saw the outlines of an inescapable resolution. Two days later, on December 17, it passed the compromise bill by 277–148, a bipartisan tally featuring Democrats 139–112 and Republicans 138–36. President Obama signed that legislation later the same day. Two major acts whose target deadlines had long been known thus became the joint vehicle for an omnibus bill adding numerous other "ornaments" to its particular Christmas tree, through a bipartisan vote that masked sharp partisan disagreement until the final forty-eight hours.

The debt ceiling deal of 2011, one session of Congress later, took the same logic to new substance in a changed context.[50] Once again, there was a December 31 deadline, long known to all the players, this time for an increase in the ceiling on the national debt. Once again, the need for intermittent reauthorization fell afoul of the ideological polarization that increasingly characterized politics in the Era of Partisan Volatility. Neither party opposed raising the debt ceiling per se, but Republicans strongly opposed raising the actual debt, while Democrats militantly opposed spending cuts that would prevent a debt increase. What was different was the partisan context. The Democrats had lost their majority in the House of Representatives, courtesy of the midterm election of 2010. Moreover, newly elected Republicans were disproportionately associated with the Republican "Tea Party" faction, a grassroots movement focused on fiscal responsibility, balanced budgets, and, if possible, actual shrinkage of the federal government.

Four serious rounds of cross-institutional and cross-partisan negotiations were to follow. Yet unlike such negotiations in the Era of Divided Government, the first three were to be largely fruitless, while the fourth was rescued only by the impending trigger of default on basic governmental obligations. The first round of discussions began with a bipartisan group of senators, the "Gang of Six" who sought to produce a major deficit-reduction plan. Their project eventually fell apart, mainly through lack of support from either party leader in the Senate. Vice President Joseph Biden then began several months of intense discussions with six other legislative players, the six top leadership figures of the House and the Senate. These talks collapsed in late June.

Negotiations next shifted to private discussions between President Obama and the Speaker of the House, John Boehner (R-OH). The president, however, was unwilling even to offer a detailed proposal of his own, while the Speaker could not be sure that he could deliver House Republicans behind any compromise deal. So these discussions broke down, were restarted, then broke down again. Late in the year, Mitch McConnell (R-KY), minority leader in the Senate, became the key broker for a resolution. McConnell reached out to the vice president, and their joint proposal became the ultimate legislation.

In a remarkably jerry-built omnibus bill, there was an immediate $900 billion increase to the debt ceiling, coupled with $917 billion of spending cuts over ten years; a promise of $1.2 to $1.5 trillion of subsequent increase in the debt ceiling, coupled with the same amount of deficit reduction, with details to be developed by a new joint committee; creation of this bipartisan and bicameral committee; a new process—"sequestration"—that would trigger across-the-board spending cuts in that same amount if the committee could not (as ultimately it did not) develop these specifics; and assorted immediate caps on discretionary spending for fiscal 2012 onward.

The bill containing all of that went to the House first, the Senate being thought to be on board but unwilling to vote if the House could not deliver a majority. This bill did pass the House 269–161, with Republicans 174–66 but Democrats only 95–95. As predicted, the Senate had an easier time, 74–26, with Republicans 45–6 and Democrats 28–19. Accordingly, the debt crisis had been avoided, spending reductions had been proposed, and a new procedure had been created. In the process, the president had guaranteed that the issue would not recur until after the 2012 election. The Speaker of the House had prevented Republicans from being publicly blamed for default. Democrats had prevented any entitlement reform. And Republicans had prevented any tax increases.

Ironically, the resolution of both fiscal efforts, the bipartisan tax deal of 2010 and the debt ceiling deal of 2011, came together to create the next triggering crisis—and a new omnibus effort—through what became known as the fiscal cliff deal of 2012–2013.[51] By the beginning of 2012, all sides knew that the original Bush tax cuts, salvaged through the bipartisan tax deal of 2010, would again expire on December 31. Absent congressional action by that date, the sequestration provisions of the debt ceiling deal of 2011 would kick in, imposing mechanical spending cuts across the board, a result that almost no one wanted. The combination—a "fiscal cliff"—was widely argued to be sufficient to push the economy back into recession, though that perception, general as it was, proved insufficient to get Republicans to consider tax increases or Democrats to consider spending cuts.

Both parties staked out their tax-cut positions during the month of July. The Senate passed the preferred Democratic bill on July 25, allowing top-bracket cuts to expire and revert, 51–48 (Democrats 50–1, Republicans 0–46). The House passed the preferred Republican bill on August 1, extending all Bush tax cuts in their existing form, 256–171 (Republicans 237–1, Democrats 19–170). The Senate refused to take up the House bill, and Congress got no further before recessing for the summer and then the fall election campaign. In November, the president was solidly reelected, Democrats picked up two seats in the Senate, while the House retained its Republican majority in reduced form.

Returning to Washington in the election aftermath, President Obama and Speaker Boehner opened private talks. Those collapsed, and the Speaker turned to a sequester replacement plan that squeaked through the House on December 20 by 215–209. This produced a fresh set of discussions between Harry Reid (D-NV), Senate majority leader, and Mitch McConnell, minority leader. Their discussions broke down on December 29, and McConnell turned to his old negotiating partner from the debt ceiling deal, Vice President Biden. The two hammered out final details on an absolutely classic omnibus deal, which did the following:

- Allowed income taxes on families making over $450,000 to increase
- Put off the sequester until March 1 and reduced its amount, offsetting this reduction with spending cuts split equally between domestic and defense, plus expanding taxes on Roth IRA accounts
- Extended emergency unemployment benefits, with no cost offset
- Extended numerous business tax breaks, with no revenue offset
- Made reduced tax rates on capital gains and dividends permanent below a threshold, while increasing them above
- Provided a permanent patch for the alternative minimum tax
- Did the "doc fix," postponing for two years the cuts in reimbursement rates under Medicare that were part of the Affordable Care Act
- Exempted estates under $5 million from the federal estate tax, while increasing rates above that level
- Extended the 2008 farm law through the end of fiscal 2013, averting a sharp rise in milk prices

Confident of the response, Biden and McConnell took this deal directly to the Senate, which passed the omnibus proposal on New Year's Day by a vote of 89–8. Speaker Boehner, aware that he could not bring a majority of his own party with him, nevertheless brought this bill to the House floor, where it passed by a vote of 257–167, losing the Republican majority by 85–151 but salvaged by the Democratic minority at 172–16. Of the three major omnibus fiscal bills—the bipartisan tax deal, the debt ceiling deal, and the fiscal cliff deal—this was thus the most heavily "ornamented," with diverse taxing, spending, and substantive provisions. It was also the one with the sharpest partisan divisions on the way there, achieved on the day that prior tax reforms would have expired and one day before the sequester would have become operational.

In general, such major packages, along with many lesser counterparts during the Era of Partisan Volatility, in effect required a preliminary and extended period of apparent gridlock in order to force the president to act and/or to convince the two congressional parties that their parts of an incipient deal were worth harvesting:

- In the Late New Deal Era, the inclination for a president and both congressional parties to work across the aisle on major legislation was actually decried by many outside analysts as symptomatic of political failings. Yet the underlying necessity was familiar to all the major players and caused them little evident stress.
- In the Era of Divided Government, with a split partisan control that worried outside analysts in a new way, the construction of supermajorities became a normal characteristic of the policy-making process, again recognized by the main players as integral to keeping the policy machinery in action.
- The increasingly polarized process in the Era of Partisan Volatility then provided yet another stimulus for analysts to fret, while omnibus lawmaking—extended partisan deadlock, broken by deals rolling both sides together, often across multiple substantive areas—became the critical exception that kept the machinery running this time.

In the end, though, such omnibus legislation and the strategic use of reconciliation as a means to reach it were only the most direct and dramatic further products of the policy-making process characterizing an entire period. As in any era, many other aspects of American politics were drawn into the maw of—and reflected—the structure of politics characterizing the Era of Partisan Volatility, perhaps more visibly than in more complicated or conditional periods. Thus even ostensibly basic and unchanging aspects of constitutional structure could work differently as the era aged. The separation of powers, that institutional bedrock of American government, looked about as separate as it ever did. Yet a party holding Congress but not the presidency tended increasingly to "legislate" on its own, passing bills designed to signal current or potential supporters in the electorate, in full knowledge that the bills themselves were going nowhere.

From the other side, a party holding the presidency rather than Congress increasingly tried to maximize the policy grounds over which the president could act unilaterally, through varieties of executive action.[52] If this cheered major players in the party of the president, it simultaneously infuriated members of the opposition in Congress. In part as a result, the other great institutional principle of the US Constitution, federalism, likewise came to work distinctively during the Era of Partisan Volatility. Or at least, federalism increasingly encouraged state-level counterparts of the party holding Congress but not the presidency to attempt complete (and not just symbolic) countervailing legislation at the state level, again as both counterweight and signal.[53]

And all the while, the onward march of ideological polarization continued apace. Already in the previous period, this march had largely encompassed partisan activists, both Democratic and Republican, in more or less all the states. Now in the successor period, it encompassed not just party operatives but public officials, in the presidency as well as Congress, in the states and not just at the national level.[54] Moreover, this continuing polarization came to infuse the diverse substantive domains that had previously distinguished policy-making, amalgamating them into a single dominant dimension of policy conflict, while the ideological centers of those polarized parties nevertheless continued to move farther apart.[55]

Figure 4.9 presents the DW-Nominate scores summarizing party midpoints for the years 1930–2010 in both houses of Congress. These are in some sense merely the obverse of the measures in figure 4.5, the ones that capture the share of nonconforming members for much of this same period.[56] By focusing on the norm and not the exceptions, figure 4.9 underscores the result even more strongly. There were some visible differences between the two houses. Democratic senators in the earliest days of this series were especially centrist; Republican members of Congress in the most recent years were additionally distant from the ideological middle. But the overwhelming point of both series remained the same: an increasing distance between the two party midpoints from 1980 onward, one that only expanded as time passed.[57]

In the process, the old centripetal forces had been greatly weakened, though this weakening did unfold across two distinct political periods. Thus it was no longer necessary, as it had been in the Late New Deal Era, for the Democratic Party in Congress to concentrate first and foremost on policy options moderate enough to hold their Southern faction in line. Similarly, it was no longer necessary, as it had been in that same prior period, for Republican candidates for president to cater to their

Figure 4.9. Partisan Polarization in the Longest Run

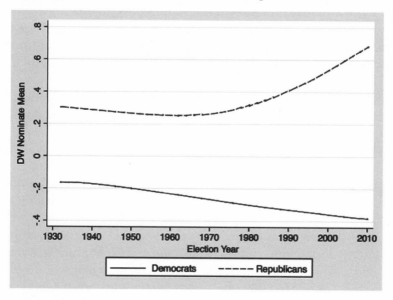

A. The House

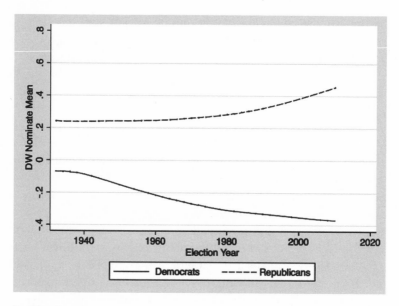

B. The Senate

more moderate Northeastern faction as the only way to draw Northern Democratic voters across the partisan line in a world—now gone— where Democratic presidential candidates would always begin with a secure (and large) Southern base.

By themselves, all those incentives were already in decline in the Era of Divided Government, courtesy of the ideological polarization that increasingly characterized the active parties. Yet what distinguished the Era of Partisan Volatility from this immediate predecessor was not further polarization per se, as it moved beyond party activists to capture public officeholders. Rather, what distinguished the two eras was the power of *electoral volatility* in this later period, and its effective absence in the predecessor. That was what mattered crucially to their respective policy-making processes. The Era of Divided Government had been remarkably stable in partisan terms. Republicans could rely on holding the presidency. Democrats could rely on holding Congress. In such a world, neither had much incentive to temporize, especially when faced with public demands for action. There was no point stalling for time in the belief that one more election would yield a different partisan balance. It would not.

In the Era of Partisan Volatility, by contrast, it might well—and it often did. There was a kaleidoscopic succession of partisan outcomes, unified and split, with either party holding Congress and either party holding the presidency. But what was an era-defining measure for the analyst was a structural fact of politics for the main players, in the same (but opposite) way that stable partisan control had been a structural fact of the preceding period. Now, a system configured in this new and more volatile way meant that it could indeed seem more attractive— even more reasonable—for the leadership of two polarized parties to block current legislation and wait at least for the next midterm and perhaps the next presidential election.

A crucial element of this electoral volatility had to lie in the change of party balance that characterized the new era, a change captured by some measures but obscured by others. Almost all such measures could be read backward to suggest a period of close partisan balance nationwide. Not all of them might have led analysts to describe the period in this way prospectively, that is, if things had not in fact turned out as they did. Nevertheless, the outcomes bespeaking a closer party balance were everywhere. They could be decried, but they could not be escaped. It was not just that every possible combination of partisan outcomes was now conceivable. It was that every possible combination was *realized*, and realized within a remarkably short stretch of political time.

Figures 4.3 and 4.4 are just two graphic representations of that collective outcome. Presumably, enough of the voting public still resided *between* the newly coherent but ever-more-polarized party cores to make all this possible. Obviously, the relevant share of this public was large enough to produce an environment where it made sense to public officeholders, themselves now very much elements of this polarized dynamic, to block and delay in the hopes that one more election might produce a more satisfying environment for policy-making. What ensued at the operational end of politics was a policy-making process characterized by extended stretches of stiff partisan conflict, with almost no elected Republicans or Democrats joining the other side.

This structural logjam was broken intermittently by crisis, by occasional (and always short-run) electoral surges, or just by a buildup of policy pressures so extreme that they required some sort of omnibus legislation to bundle them together and push them through. A close party balance, infused with galloping ideological polarization, sufficient to reduce substantive conflict to a single dimension of alignment: that was what contributed a policy-making process characterized by stretches of stasis broken by these spikes of omnibus policy-making. The result was the fourth distinguishable period in American politics since the Great Depression. If it too was unloved by commentators in its time, it was not self-evidently less productive, a possibility that the conclusion will have to address.

Conclusion

Stability and Change in American Politics, 1932–2016

That is eighty-plus years of party balance, ideological polarization, and substantive conflict. But where does it leave the analysis? Some things are simply summarized. There were four political periods between 1932 and 2016: the High New Deal Era, the Late New Deal Era, the Era of Divided Government, and the Era of Partisan Volatility (figure 5.1). These periods could be demarcated by characteristic electoral outcomes: smothering Democratic preponderance, simple Democratic dominance, split partisan control, and kaleidoscopic variation. Those outcomes were accompanied by processes of policy-making peculiar to their time: presidential, factional, agglomerative, and polarized. These processes, finally, could be linked back to the original demarcating outcomes by way of three great organizing influences: party balance, ideological polarization, and substantive conflict.

A tour of the interactions among these three elements in those four periods produces what is in effect the *intermediary structure of American politics*. Linking the social base for politics with the institutions of government, this structure becomes the central means of transmitting societal wishes into public policy, though it always partially transforms that transmission. A tour of this intermediary structure also confirms that it was the *interaction* of three key influences, and not the evolution of any one, that shaped change in the policy-making process. So, a concluding chapter needs to return to this structure and move through it toward a set of nearly inescapable closing responsibilities:

- A conclusion needs to bring the four eras back in condensed form, asking not only how each worked as a composite but also what caused each to arrive, become institutionalized, yet eventually depart. From there, it is but a short step to asking whether the evolution of these arrivals and departures can say anything further and larger about how political change occurred.

Figure 5.1. Eighty Years of Party Balance, Ideological Polarization, and Substantive Conflict

	High New Deal Era	Late New Deal Era	Era of Divided Government	Era of Partisan Volatility
Time Period	1932–1938	1939–1968	1969–1992	1993–2016
Electoral Outcomes	Democratic Preponderance	Democratic Dominance	Split Partisan Control	Kaleidoscopic Variation
Policy-making Process	Presidential	Factional	Agglomerative	Polarized

- Along the way, each era featured a dominant school of criticism of these same workings. Refusing to think in terms of political structure—what it is, where it came from, what might cause it to go—critics risked irrelevance in their own time, plus the prospect of contributing to the very conditions they decried, should their proposals be realized in a different period. They deserve a nod (but no more) in closing.

- On the other hand, any conclusion must go on to attend to some major factors external to the policy-making process that have intruded repeatedly in the analysis of political eras. These contribute, in effect, some of the major inputs processed through an intermediary structure. Three such factors—an enduring constitutional framework, ever-shifting public demands, and intermittent partisan surges—deserve special attention even as they render conclusions about political change all the more conditional.

- And in the end, after all that, it is necessary to return to current American politics with two further questions in mind. First, how much of this politics should be understood as a logical response to the main structural factors of its own time, in the way that previous periods can best be understood? Second and regardless of that answer, how should the character of politics in the current period be judged by comparison to those earlier eras—worse than, the same as, better than, or just different from them?

So in closing let us try to bring back the four eras in highly condensed form, to seek relationships that appear to run across them, but to remind ourselves of the conditional contexts within which any such further relationships arose. In that light, the opening period of this entire analysis, the High New Deal Era, was most directly a product of public demand for policy responses to a cataclysmic event, the Great Depression. Herbert Hoover had actually begun to respond, traveling an impressive distance for a Republican of his time. Yet his program was judged inadequate by a voting public that brought in not just a new president willing to experiment additionally but what also became a new and enduring partisan majority when the basic outlines of his experiment were publicly endorsed.

The High New Deal Era began with a huge if still contingent change of party balance, from Republican to Democratic. While this new Democratic predominance was not self-actualizing—it would need to be institutionalized by way of the New Deal program—it did contribute a fresh partisan advantage that was to decline but not disappear across all the years to follow. As such, it constitutes a remarkable partisan break point. Yet the relationship between this new party (im)balance and its associated ideological polarization, along with the relationship of both to the substance of policy conflict, is not straightforward, and certainly not definitional.

Registered conventionally, as the ideological distance between the two major parties, polarization declined toward effective irrelevance in the High New Deal Era. There were individual representatives and senators, mostly Democrats, who would have liked to go much farther than the New Deal. There were individual representatives and senators, mostly Republicans, who did not want to go there at all. But what distinguished the practical politics of the period was the fact that Northern Democrats, one of four major factions in American politics and otherwise always a minority across American political history, became a majority of both houses of Congress during these years. Partisan polarization in the conventional sense was thus operationally irrelevant. American politics was, in that sense and for a short period, *unipolar*.

Yet as soon as the analysis moves out to a wider compass, the same politics can be seen to be deeply polarized, more than it would be for another fifty years, and maybe longer. From one side, the main elective institutions of American government, Congress and the presidency, were working on a fundamental change in the nature of public policy, one that would define the Democratic Party for a long time to come. From the other side, the main appointive institution of that politics, the Supreme Court, was committed to sustaining an older vision of the proper—in their view, the "constitutional"—nature of public policy, one that had defined the Republican Party for a long time. Policy conflict became inevitable.

Franklin Roosevelt ultimately attempted to resolve it by restructuring—effectively neutering—the Court. In the meantime, the substantive focus of policy conflict on both sides of this institutional divide was the same. American politics would never again be as monolithically focused on economic welfare, at least as this is written. While the two sides struggled for precedence, the effective process of policy-making was likewise about as simple as it would be at any point during that same period. It was effectively presidential. Had the Supreme Court managed both to fend off this president, which it did, and to sustain its own policy preferences, which it did not, the High New Deal, the Late New Deal, and who knows how much afterward would have been very different.

Instead, the president was ultimately to lose this battle but win the war. Court packing failed, but the Court acceded to the constitutionality of the New Deal. Yet if that particular result was ironic, so was the larger fate of the entire High New Deal. For in very short order, this unipolar ideological structure, its monolithic substantive focus, and the institutional dominance of the presidency, now apparently secured, would all be destroyed—at the polls. In its place would arrive a multipolar factional world with a multidimensional substantive focus and an incremental system of policy-making characterized by constant negotiation and renegotiation of policy coalitions and constant adjustment and readjustment of public policies.

Programmatic initiatives from the High New Deal Era did bring a vastly expanded welfare state to the United States. Many of these initiatives remain in effect a full eighty years later. Yet the High New Deal as defined by its partisan outcomes and policy-making process was also impressively short. Any number of single individuals would serve longer as president than this entire "era." When the period was further characterized by intense demands for public policy, by a huge partisan surge, and by a central role for constitutional structure, it becomes possible to salute the lasting policy impact of the High New Deal while recognizing the difficulty in saying much conclusive about the way that its politics reflected grand relationships among party balance, ideological polarization, and substantive conflict.

Fortunately, the same was to be much less true of its successor period, the long Late New Deal Era. If the High New Deal was over by 1939, the Late New Deal would run through 1968. This new period would see a modest reduction in the party imbalance characterizing the High New Deal, though a pronounced imbalance would remain. The Democratic Party would lose Congress only twice during this period, each time for only one election, while it would lose the presidency to only one man, Dwight Eisenhower. Moreover, the arrival of survey research in general and of the National Election Study in particular guaranteed that aggregate-level impressions could now be backed by individual-level evidence. The NES suggested that unified partisan control of American national government in Democratic hands should have been the expected electoral outcome for this period. Presidential and congressional elections from 1938 through 1967 confirm that this expectation was richly realized.

On the other hand and in striking contrast to the High New Deal, the Late New Deal was to combine substantial party imbalance with a multipolar variant of ideological polarization, resulting in the most effectively *depolarized* stretch in all the years after 1932. The explanation would be rooted in the factional character of the two major parties and in the policy preferences associated with their factions. Said the other way around, one of the things that the Late New Deal confirmed in passing was how much the political structure of the High New Deal had been a simple epiphenomenon of the predominance of Northern Democrats. Take away their majority status, return them to their familiar minority role, and the comprehensive factional structure that had preceded the unipolar world of the High New Deal was instantly restored.

So, for the entire length of the Late New Deal Era, there were to be four stable and consequential party factions: Northern Democrats, Southern Democrats, Regular Republicans, and Northeastern Republicans. These factions would constitute the building blocks of majority coalitions. Their associated preferences would contribute the substance of policy conflict. These policy preferences, however, had been altered by the New Deal program. For Democrats, an older populism that once found its base among Southern Democrats was displaced by a welfare liberalism that found its reliable home among Northern Democrats instead. For Republicans, an older populism that previously found its recurrent home among Regular Republicans was likewise displaced by a welfare liberalism that was more comparatively attractive to Northeastern Republicans. Still, the geographic bases of these factional divisions continued on, so that the coalitional building blocks behind these amended policy preferences remained intact.

One result was probably automatic: majority formation became instantly more complex. In the realm of economic welfare, the formation of majorities became a process of negotiation among four factions, with the substantive details of public policy as coin of the realm for these negotiations. Yet there was a second implication, more directly substantive, to exaggerate this complexity. For the new world of policy conflict quickly added two further policy domains to economic welfare as major dimensions of substantive conflict. Foreign affairs came to seem unavoidable, as propelled by World War II and sustained by the Cold War. Civil rights, emerging from the bottom up rather than the outside in, acquired a fresh but similar urgency. Once these grand alternative issues were loose on the political landscape, the revitalized party factions brought stable programmatic preferences to them too, thereby institutionalizing an expanded policy conflict for the new era.

Economic welfare remained central to this conflict, though conflict over welfare policy was now multifactional. By itself, this multifactionalism would have constrained ideological polarization between the two parties. Where once policy-making could be a matter of ensuring consensus among Northern Democrats, it became instead a matter of judging what these Northern Democrats had to cede in order to hold Southern Democrats in their policy orbit or draw Northeastern Republicans to it if they could not, while extracting as much welfare liberalism as they could without allowing their preferences to take them to positions sufficient to alienate both moderate factions—and thereby build a policy majority on the conservative side.

Yet there was more. For the other key policy realms were not even aligned in the same fashion as economic welfare, effectively depolarizing partisan conflict additionally. In foreign affairs, the battle between internationalism and isolationism pitted Southern Democrats against Regular Republicans at the extremes, converting Northern Democrats and Northeastern Republicans into pivotal factions. In civil rights, the battle between integrationists and segregationists pitted Northern Democrats against Southern Democrats at the extremes, while featuring both Republican factions, the Northeasterners and the Regulars, in the decisive center. The result was a second level of strategic complexity. Because there were now three major dimensions to substantive conflict, aligning the four main factions differently, policy-making in any one domain had to proceed with a simultaneous and careful eye on what a given maneuver in that domain implied about the possibilities of policy-making in each of the other two.

That was a multipolar system for policy-making, built on multiple party factions and multiple policy domains, with multiple but shifting factional coalitions across them. It was in all those regards about as far away from the unipolarity of the High New Deal Era as one could get. It was also a highly centripetal and not centrifugal system, focused on holding or losing the more moderate factions in the middle of whichever policy domain was the focus of the day. Divisions within the majority party, the Democrats, were most fundamental to this system in Congress. Yet the presidency buttressed the resulting centrifugal influences by pulling the minority party, the Republicans, toward the center too, since their prospects for gaining this presidency hinged on pulling *Northern* Democratic voters out of the national Democratic coalition.

All this strikes the contemporary analyst as an extended period of policy-making that had to be stereotypically incremental, being built, as it was, on constant but lesser adjustments and readjustments to national policy in major substantive realms. In its time, this incremental*ism* was hailed as the great discovery of social scientists who studied policy-making generically. In their research, these scholars encountered a world of shared norms coupled with shared expectations about the resulting behavior of all the major players. With hindsight, a world of interlocking behaviors appears as the logical result of an extended period structured by politicking among multiple factions in multiple realms aligned in multiple fashions, thereby widening and deepening an inherent incrementalism.

In elucidating the structure and strategy that accompanied this incremental process of policy-making, however, scholars at the time thought that they were unpacking the larger nature of American politics—its true genius or its insistent curse. So they were to be as seriously disabused by the passage of time and the coming of a new era as were their predecessors who had thought that the High New Deal was the emergent model of an American politics to come. The Era of Divided Government, 1969–1992, would confirm instead that what Late New Deal scholars had actually been doing was isolating in rich detail the nature of the policy-making process characterizing yet another specific and extended but ultimately limited political period. For the Era of Divided Government was to be different in more or less every regard from the Late New Deal Era.

This difference began with a clear but only modest further decline in the Democratic edge nationwide. Survey measures of party identification confirmed both the decline and its modesty. Yet what distinguished the era in electoral terms was something entirely different: a recurrent pattern of split partisan control of the elective institutions of national government. Moreover, this split was neither wavering nor idiosyncratic in its composition. Rather, it was always the same, with Republican presidents stapled onto Democratic Congresses. The High New Deal had featured unified partisan control, always in Democratic hands. The Late New Deal had featured unified partisan control mostly in Democratic hands, with occasional Republican victories in Congress and with Republicans entitled to the same unified control when they finally broke the Democratic hold on the presidency. What the Era of Divided Government inaugurated was the notion of *split* control as a settled outcome rather than a transitional characteristic.

Party identification as a concept could not provide much help in understanding this settled outcome, for party identification was anathema to the idea that your partisanship should be causing you to vote for the other party on a regular basis. Even in the abstract, then, something more was required. A narrowed empirical balance of party identifications, albeit considerably narrower than was actually the case in this period, might have conduced toward a wavering range of outcomes, in which the major parties gained control of one office while losing another. Yet that was most definitely not what happened. Rather, a reduced Democratic edge went hand in hand with congressional results largely unchanged from the Late New Deal Era, while the same balance produced a nearly complete blowout in presidential elections, with only the post-Watergate debacle failing to produce a Republican presidency.

As a result, the key difference between eras proved once again to revolve around ideological polarization, albeit in another era-specific fashion. Polarization in the High New Deal Era had been between governmental institutions. Polarization in the Late New Deal Era had instead been among geographic factions. Polarization in the Era of Divided Government was to be across *levels of participation* within political parties. Beneath the surface of election outcomes, both parties had continued to shift away from an old model of partisan structure based on a long-serving hierarchy of party officeholders and toward a new model based on social networks among issue activists. Devastated by the Great Depression, the Republicans had actually gotten there first. By the Era of Divided Government, the Democrats had effectively arrived as well. The result was increasing ideological polarization among those who did the active work of these political parties.

The new model of party organization, shifting away from an established hierarchy of party offices and toward social networks among issue activists, reflected general elements of social change, including a growing white-collar population and the rise of new media of information. This new model likewise reflected specific social movements, springing up outside of politics but inevitably drawn into it. First came the antiwar, environmental, and feminist movements for the Democrats. Then came, especially, the remobilization of evangelical Protestants for the Republicans. These general and specific contributions to a changing party structure were cemented into place through participatory institutional reforms that catered broadly to a burgeoning white-collar population and more pointedly to the typical memberships of new social movements.

What resulted were two bodies of increasingly polarized party activists, stapled onto a mass base of party identifiers who shared neither their overall polarization nor, even more consequentially, the alignment of major issues that increasingly characterized elite politics. Newly consequential activists in both political parties were powerfully cathected by a cluster of mobilizing issues that could be gathered under the rubric of "cultural values." If the old issues of economic welfare had been about the proper distribution of material goods in American society, these new issues were instead about the proper distribution of behavioral norms. Perhaps inevitably, the newly consequential issue activists sought to construct an ideological alignment that *they* judged to be appropriate for the integration of new issues with the old, while at the same time shifting the midpoint of the resulting alignments away from the ideological center.

Yet this new ideological polarization—centered on party activists, exaggerated from previous activist divisions, while pulling familiar issues into a new pattern—bumped up against a general public that had been much less affected by all of its contributory developments. Substantively and not just geographically, these partisan rank and files continued to live where they had previously lived. Which is to say: they had unaligned preferences across the two grand policy realms of the era, while simultaneously holding more moderate positions within each. The result was an immediate and then an institutionalized tension between party activists and their own (putative) rank and files. It was this *split-level polarization* that really generated both divided government and the policy-making process distinctive to it.

The first product of this tension was ideologically opposite and socially crosscutting majorities within the voting public. Crosscutting majorities were what allowed a stable pattern of electoral outcomes featuring Republican control of the presidency and Democratic control of Congress. The further result was a curious process of policy-making, unexpected by early analysts of split partisan control but fully consistent with—again logically derivative of—the mix of party balance, ideological polarization, and substantive conflict that produced it. Early on, as commentators and analysts began to believe (and/or fear) that split control was becoming a regular and not a deviant outcome, the policy-making process that had seemed most likely to result was summarized as "gridlock," with each party capable of preventing the other from legislating but neither capable of legislating by itself.

What resulted instead was a kind of recurrent "grand coalition" involving constant negotiations across parties and across institutions. Both major aspects of partisan change in this period—a changing party structure and split-level polarization—made contributions to this superficially anomalous result. The coming of a more participatory politics, along with the simultaneous weakening of party organizations as brakes on public pressure, meant that elected officeholders, especially in Congress but even as it turned out in the presidency, felt less buffered against issues of the moment and more strongly pressed to respond to them. This is the world, after all, where Republican Richard Nixon could be the great environmentalist and Democrat Jimmy Carter, the lone exception to the lockstep electoral outcomes of the period, could be the great deregulator.

At the same time, a reduced Democratic edge in overall party identifications coupled with increased polarization among active partisans but *not* their rank and files generated the split public majorities producing a stable pattern of partisan outcomes. Public policy thus had to be made through negotiations that were both cross-partisan and cross-institutional, if it were to be made at all. Moreover, there was no point in stalling for one more congressional session in the belief that the Republicans would then control Congress, much less of stalling for one more presidential term in confidence that the Democrats would retake that office and unify government. Add to this the established desire of incumbent members of Congress to produce benefits for their constituents, plus the increased permeability of party politics to the main social movements of the moment, and you had an increased impetus to seek the coalitions necessary to make policy now.

In contrast to the Late New Deal Era, Republicans had to be dealt into all such negotiations, courtesy of their ongoing control of the presidency. Yet Democrats continued to control Congress, so they could never be dealt out. New social movements generating some of the key policy issues for this period—environmentalism was the outstanding example here—were in realms where the major organizations leaned Democratic. So Republican presidents needed to shape policy in areas where they might have preferred not to legislate at all. Yet all the while, the stagflation that dogged much of the era produced constant policy demands of its own, through direct economic problems in society and indirect budgetary crises in government. Democratic Congresses might try to pull the details of a response in their preferred direction, but they were hardly going to take the rap for inaction on problems that the public regarded as fundamental. Because there was little hope that delay would produce a different partisan mix through which to address these problems, both sides were implicitly driven toward cross-partisan and cross-institutional negotiations.

Even more than with the transition into the Era of Divided Government, the transition out of that period required a choice among measures of party balance before it was possible to begin considering the structure of what became the Era of Partisan Volatility. Measured by self-identification in opinion surveys, party balance was unchanged as between the two eras. Measured by partisan outcomes, however, that balance had been transformed. The two parties were as close to parity as they had been since well before the modern world began. Moreover, this latter fact accorded much more strongly with the electoral outcomes characterizing the period, a kaleidoscopic sequence of all possible combinations in rapid succession: unified Democratic control, split control with the presidency Democratic and Congress Republican, unified Republican control, split control with the presidency Republican and Congress Democratic, along with occasional intervals of split control inside Congress for added variety.

Far less open to alternative interpretations was the level of ideological polarization within this electoral kaleidoscope. Year in and year out, through unified or divided control of government, with Democratic or Republican majorities in Congress or the presidency, ideological polarization proceeded apace. The Era of Partisan Volatility was clearly the most polarized of any since the High New Deal. It was more polarized even than the High New Deal if the focus was ideological differences between the political parties rather than ideological tensions between elective and appointive institutions of government. Either way, what had happened in the transition from an Era of Divided Government to the Era of Partisan Volatility was that the growing ideological polarization that had characterized party activists in the former period had gone on to capture public officeholders as well in the latter. Two further changes, one explicitly partisan and one only implicitly so, appeared central to this capture.

First was the disappearance of the long-standing one-party South and its transformation into a major element of the national two-party system. By itself, this added a major increment of ideological polarization to the nation as a whole. A third of the country had long been more or less completely depolarized. When it clicked into the national pattern, the whole country was half again as polarized just by virtue of change in the South. The specific hallmark of this regional change was the appearance of a serious bloc of Southern Republican senators and representatives, growing in number until both were actually a regional majority. Yet these new Republican officeholders arrived not as moderates within a conservative party. Rather, they were every bit as conservative from the start as their non-Southern colleagues. Simultaneously, the remaining Southern Democrats, while retaining a trace of traditional moderation, became largely indistinguishable from their non-Southern counterparts.

Yet while this was occurring, a second, more indirectly polarizing change was occurring throughout the country. In this, the ideological polarization at the activist level that had accompanied changing party structure, new social movements, and institutional reform during the Era of Divided Government moved on to capture public officeholders as well in the Era of Partisan Volatility. This was true in the North and the South, the East and the West. It was true even of Congress, usually a lagging indicator given its strong record of successful incumbency. Where sitting members of Congress had been a kind of firewall against ideological polarization during the preceding period, then, they ingested it during the successor era, becoming full-fledged reflectors thereof. The South might be experiencing both developments simultaneously—hence those new Southern Republicans who were instantly indistinguishable from their older co-partisans—but this second major contribution to ideological polarization was indeed happening everywhere.

In turn, the pattern of substantive conflict that resulted from a close party balance coupled with galloping ideological polarization had two major elements. First, political parties saw the ideological preferences of their officeholders move out from the center, leftward for the Democrats and rightward for the Republicans. At the same time, the main bearers of nonconformity, those cross-pressured representatives who were closer to the midpoint of the other party and those moderate members who were closer to the midpoint of society than to that of their own party, went into precipitous decline. Moreover, in the ultimate testimony to ideological extremism, incumbents of one party who were defeated for reelection tended to be replaced by candidates of the other party who were equally far from the national midpoint *in the opposite direction.*[1]

The second major change in the nature of substantive conflict resulting from close party balance coupled with galloping ideological polarization was also straightforward. Superficially, what happened was that all the great policy domains of the modern world—economic welfare, foreign affairs, civil rights, and cultural values—collapsed into one dimension, liberals versus conservatives by way of Democrats versus Republicans. Yet while that was not a false generalization, it actually stated the relationship the wrong way around. For what had happened operationally was that party activists had been so successful in imposing their view of which issue positions belonged together, at the same time as their public officeholders were becoming internally coherent but ideologically distant, that all four great policy domains had been effectively hammered into one.

This blanketing polarization, now largely untroubled by regional party factions or alternative substantive domains, meant that major policy disputes generated remarkably pure votes: all Republicans against almost all Democrats, over and over. Coupled with close party balance, however, this reliable partisan unity meant that it now *was* worth trying to hold the party together while refusing to negotiate with a similarly unified opposition, in the reasonable belief that one further election might produce a thoroughly different mix of partisan outcomes. This was a striking change from the Era of Divided Government, when confidence that the Republicans would hold the presidency and Democrats would hold Congress in effect created diametrically opposed incentives. Now, increasingly polarized officeholders not only had a stronger *preference* for not compromising with what were increasingly distant partisan opponents but also had greater reason to believe that ideological intransigence would be rewarded with improved party prospects.

The result was a pattern of substantive conflict derided by many analysts as, in effect, legislative gridlock coupled with policy brinkmanship. The vocabulary was alarmist, but a comparison with the nature of policy-making in the two preceding eras offered a less heated analysis that ran roughly in the same direction. During the Late New Deal Era, factionalized parties conduced toward policy production that was constant but incremental. During the Era of Divided Government, static electoral prospects counseled increasingly unified parties to seek policy gains whenever possible. Yet during the Era of Partisan Volatility, fully unified parties reliably favored blocking the opposition as a central strategy, unless and until external forces intervened.

Critics again, in this as in every era, wanted more (and usually different) policy products. Yet policy was still being made. It was just that the main elements driving a policy-making process had changed. Neither the factional deals of the Late New Deal Era nor the agglomerative pressures of the Era of Divided Government were available to drive policy-making. Instead, for the Era of Partisan Volatility, some external action-forcing development was increasingly required. Consensual crises could still force policy responses, with 9/11 and the Great Recession being the obvious examples here. The reauthorization of legislation that was consensually viewed as major could likewise force action, though not without some cliff-hanging moments before the ultimate deal. Tax cuts, budgetary allocations, and the debt limit all performed this function. Finally and most commonly, stalled legislation that continued to have powerful organized champions tended eventually to surmount partisan roadblocks by rolling many policy demands into one collective bill, the diagnostic "omnibus" solution. Agricultural policy was a favorite for this role, with Social Security and Medicare as obvious candidates going forward.

Overall, then, the Era of Partisan Volatility was characterized by long stretches of policy stasis, broken by major spikes of legislative activity. The programmatic specifics of these spikes were certainly colored by the partisan balance within major institutions of American national government at the time they erupted. On the other hand, such spikes tended to feature grand compromises *across* the two parties, encompassing the central concerns of each at the point when critical developments appeared to force action. As ever, this followed more or less naturally from the underlying structure of the era. Because party balance had indeed gotten closer but the two parties had nevertheless moved farther apart, they more or less naturally made policy on a less regular basis but one encompassing the central demands of each side when they did ultimately act. Omnibus policy-making, in some sense the opposite of incrementalism, was the obvious result—as well as being the relevant summary notion.

So, there were four recognizable political periods in the years between 1932 and the current moment. Each could be introduced—isolated—by means of a continuing pattern of electoral outcomes. Those outcomes were in turn produced by interactions among party balance, ideological polarization, and substantive conflict that were themselves distinctive to their period. From these interactions, each era generated a policy-making process that coincided with, and gave practical meaning to, the original pattern of electoral outcomes. Finally, each featured a small further set of structural characteristics, back behind the three main organizing concepts, that helped to explain both the appearance and the continuation of the era, for an extended period but not forever. As a result, it should be possible to talk about political change in a more than idiosyncratic—more than just a happenstance—fashion.

Thus the electoral reinvigoration of a set of established party factions, forced to address an expanded array of substantive issues, brought the High New Deal Era to an end and inaugurated the Late New Deal Era. In turn, a fundamental shift in the nature of American political parties, coupled with the rise of new substantive issues and new social movements, put an end to the Late New Deal Era and underpinned an Era of Divided Government. When the growing ideological polarization of the party activists of that era began to reach into most further aspects of politics, including the stratum of public officeholders, the effect was sufficient to collapse substantive conflicts into one dominant dimension, terminate the Era of Divided Government, and bring on the current Era of Partisan Volatility.

But is it possible to go further? Which is to say: Is it possible to go on and look for political change that runs not just from one era to another but across this entire eighty-year span? The four eras are certainly an attractive lure for larger theorizing. Moreover, if such a search requires a conceptual framework that can be applied over an extended period, one that separates the impact of the major factors continuing to shape politics from the effectively contextual factors that are idiosyncratic to a particular time, then one such framework for organizing the study of American political evolution—and thus searching for larger political patterns—has been provided here.

Alas, what its four eras collectively contribute is mainly disconfirmation of some familiar attempts at overtheorizing, along with a reemphasis on the need to consider the changing *interactions* of long-running political influences. These interactions not only distinguish their eras but actually make continuing influences operate differently in the context of a (different) particular time. At one and the same time, then, a focus on the interaction of party balance, ideological polarization, and substantive conflict, along with the policy-making process they generate, provides a way to talk systematically about political change while emphasizing the limits—by way of the inherently conditional relationship of these interactions—on all such talk.

For example, the four political eras will not sustain an argument, otherwise surprisingly common, that party *imbalance* fosters ideological polarization, that is, movement toward the ideological extremes, while party balance produces depolarization, that is, competition across the ideological middle. This is sometimes summarized as "median voter theory."[2] The ostensible logic is that close balance leads to battles for the crucial median (and hence moderate) voter. Very little in an analysis of American politics across the last eighty years is consistent with that view. If anything—if we have to generalize—an analytic progression across four political periods suggests the opposite.

After the initial explosion of the High New Deal, the partisan imbalance of the Late New Deal was part of a world where both electoral competition and policy competition were depolarized, becoming multifactional within substantive domains and multipolar across them. Increasing party balance in the Era of Divided Government then went hand in hand with increasing polarization among active partisans but not their rank and files, where the latter continued to put policy preferences together in the old way. Only during the Era of Partisan Volatility, with its additionally close party balance, did ideological polarization capture elected officials as well as party activists—and that, of course, meant that electoral and policy competition moved farther from the ideological center.

Such an evolution might be made into a grand alternative relationship between party balance and ideological polarization, in which greater imbalance is associated with lesser polarization while lesser imbalance is associated with greater polarization. Yet the caveat to this alternative argument is likewise a major one. Indeed, even the causal direction within this putative relationship is not obvious. Thus a declining Democratic edge in the Era of Divided Government may have been partially *driven* by increasing polarization among party activists, rather than being a contributor to it. Which suggests that the proper conclusion may once again be that it is the interaction of party balance, ideological polarization, and substantive conflict, as colored in a major way by issues of the day, that determines this association—at a particular point in time but not across time.

On the other hand, working with electoral eras does make it relatively easy to address the relationship between these interactions and the policy-making process. Thus the depolarized party politics of the Late New Deal Era was associated with a policy process that was constantly productive but reliably incremental in its (constant) products. The split-level polarization of the Era of Divided Government was instead associated with a policy-making process of repeated grand bargains, where cross-partisan and cross-institutional negotiations could overcome ideological differences. And the thoroughly polarized politics of the Era of Partisan Volatility was associated with a policy-making process that was highly intermittent, featuring extended stretches of policy stasis broken by occasional but reliably major spikes of legislative activity.

Again, however, the caveat about associations and causality is a major one. At the start, a depolarized party system in the Late New Deal Era might seem inevitably associated with factional deals within and across party lines. Yet the increasingly polarized party system of the middle period, the Era of Divided Government, likewise conduced toward frequent cross-party resolutions, in fact on a larger scale. And in the Era of Partisan Volatility, an exaggerated and all-encompassing ideological polarization has often meant that policy-making *still* requires cross-party action, in some sense more than ever, just rolling ever-larger policies or ever-greater agglomerations thereof into omnibus solutions.

Critics along the way would have tolerated none of this. Period after period, they found the existing process of policy-making to be insufficiently productive. That was the basic critique in the Late New Deal Era, with its incremental policy-making. It was the basic critique in the Era of Divided Government, with its grand coalitions. It remained the basic critique in the Era of Partisan Volatility, with its stasis and spikes. Yet despite their discontent, these critics were uninterested in arguments deriving from the sources of change in the policy-making process to which they objected, and by extension to the forces already working during their era to shape the politics that would characterize its successor. It was not that they ignored the forces that had created the world being criticized. Rather, they almost reflexively viewed these forces as integral to the problem. In response, these critics preferred a simple, direct, and mechanical solution, an institutional fix. Its focus still varied: fix the parties in the Late New Deal Era; fix the Constitution in the Era of Divided Government; fix an institutional matrix in the Era of Partisan Volatility. But always, politics was the problem, not the solution.

Thus James MacGregor Burns, a central critic of the policy-making process of the Late New Deal Era, chafed against the constraints of factional politics. In *The Deadlock of Democracy*,[3] what Burns saw from his subtitle onward—*Four-Party Politics in America*—was essentially the four factions crucial to the structure of the Late New Deal. He preferred to call them Presidential and Congressional Democrats and Republicans. Yet it was our Southern (aka Congressional) Democrats and Northeastern (aka Presidential) Republicans who denied the party system of his time the clarity that might alert the general public to the need for a change in public demands, so as to unleash the modernizing policies that struck this particular critic as so sadly lacking.

Burns traced the roots of this factional politics all the way back to "The Splintering of the Parties" in the Era of Good Feeling, when the Democrats annihilated the Federalists.[4] He saw it reified in disastrous fashion at the election of 1860, with four major candidates for president leading to "The Pulverization of Party" and, not incidentally, the Civil War. Factional politics was restored—institutionalized—by the turn of the twentieth century, among both Republicans and Democrats: "Roosevelt and Taft: Which Republican Party?" and "Woodrow Wilson and the New Democracy." It saw a momentary break in the High New Deal, through "Roosevelt: The Art of the Possible," only to be rubbed out in and around the election of 1938, whence it remained the central problem of the Late New Deal Era:

> The consequence of the four-party system is that American political leaders, in order to govern, must manage multi-party coalitions just as heads of coalition parliamentary regimes in Europe have traditionally done—as the French did, for example, before De Gaulle. But the task of governing in a sense is harder in the Untied States, for the leaders' job is not simply to

pick up enough parliamentary votes to form a cabinet, or even to pass a bill. They must bring together the right combination of presidential party and congressional party strength to accomplish a great variety of tasks day after day and year after year.[5]

What was to be done? The central fix involved a new structure for American political parties. This eschewed the coalition politics dominating the era, which would have had to produce change by way of intra-party negotiations toward policy agreement among established factions. Rather, it simply imposed the desired outcome, in a somewhat mystical fashion, on the theory that subsequent politics would then conform to the desired—two-party, bifactional—structure "naturally," courtesy of a revised framework. With the gift of hindsight, we know that the passage of time was itself going to destroy the factions central to his four-party system. Burns preferred not to wait:

> We need a new kind of bipartisanship. The two presidential parties should join forces in Congress and elsewhere just long enough to work out the rules for the game for a fair, orderly, and competitive battle between the two national parties for the decades to come. . . . state and local parties are so different in outlook and doctrine that the presidential party must disentangle itself from them and set up its own separate independent party, at least in the states and congressional districts, with its own officers, finances, and communication channels. . . . As far as possible the President and his party majorities in Congress should be elected by substantially the same electoral groupings, for the sake of clarity of policy, unity in government, and responsibility to the majority. To do this the parties must pay a price: they cannot be allowed to be all things to all men.[6]

There was to be a key secondary support to his new party system, through amendment of the Constitution itself. Again, the fix was not political, negotiating among factions by way of policies. Rather, it was even more profoundly institutional:

> Still, as a capstone to these reforms, certain constitutional amendments would be extremely helpful and might achieve enough support to pass.
>
> One of these is a four-year term for Representatives, to coincide with presidential terms. . . .
>
> A second needed constitutional amendment is to repeal the 22nd Amendment, but this would doubtless be more controversial than the proposal for a four-year term for Representatives . . .

A final desirable constitutional amendment concerns the Electoral College . . . The presidential candidate with a plurality in a state would receive two electoral votes (equivalent to its two Senators). The remaining 435 electoral votes would then be divided between the presidential candidates in proportion to the national vote for each.[7]

When the Late New Deal Era gave way to the Era of Divided Government, the focus of political criticism inevitably shifted. James Sundquist, leading critic of the policy-making process in this new era, did acknowledge some evolution in the party system and did see ways in which reformed parties could contribute to active and appropriate policy-making. Unlike other analysts of the time, however, who kept waiting for split partisan control to vanish, Sundquist saw the permanence of Republican presidencies coupled with Democratic Congresses as the essence of a continuing problem, one that ultimately resided in the formal structure of government itself, especially in the central role of the separation of powers:

> Since 1981, then, it has not been party weakness as such but divided government and the pressures of electoral politics that have rendered the government impotent to cope with such problems as the mounting deficit. To equip the governmental system to avert this partisan division of the government, to lessen the pressures of too-frequent elections, and to cope with governmental breakdown when and if it occurs, one must look to the constitutional remedies suggested in the preceding chapters. Strengthening political party organizations, even if that could readily be done, as well as adopting any of the suggestions discussed above for formal institutional linkages between the branches, would have only a tardy, indirect, and limited effect.[8]

Accordingly, in *Constitutional Reform and Effective Government*, Sundquist moved comprehensively against the basic institutional framework of American government itself. His tour of possible alterations was extensive, to the point of occasional tensions within its own recommendations. But in the end, the author did not shrink from ranking his proposed reforms in order of need. The first three contributed a more or less complete scuttling of the old constitutional order. Within these, pride of place went to forced straight-ticket voting:

> 1. *The team ticket.* The separation of powers is far more likely to lead to debilitating governmental deadlock when the organs of government are divided between the parties. Several measures give promise of discouraging

the ticket splitting that produces divided government, but only one would prohibit it outright. That is the team ticket, which would combine each party's candidates for president, vice president, Senate, and House into a slate that would be voted as a unit.[9]

Next came a reduction in appeals to the electorate, so as to insulate officeholders from the otherwise implacable pressures of public politicking:

> 2. *Four-year House terms and eight-year Senate terms.* Even a united government is constantly distracted by the imminence of the next election, which is never more than two years away. The two-year life of the Congress—shortest of any national legislature in the world—normally limits an incoming president to barely a year as his "window of opportunity" to lead his party in enacting the program for which it sought its victory. To eliminate the midterm election and thereby lengthen the period of relative freedom from election pressure would require four-year House terms and either four-year or eight-year Senate terms.[10]

Having eliminated ticket-splitting at the grass roots and having synchronized presidential and congressional elections, a reformed institutional structure could then guarantee that the popular vote winner from one of the two major parties would go on and win a presidency now linked inextricably to Congress:

> An ingenious compromise that would virtually assure the election of the popular choice while still discouraging a proliferation of candidates was proposed in 1978 by a task force created by the Twentieth Century Fund. This group . . . recommended that electoral votes be cast as they are now (although automatically, to eliminate the faithless elector), but that a national bonus of 102 votes be awarded the candidate with the most popular ballots.[11]

Burns and Sundquist shared a basic complaint, about insufficient productivity in policy-making, too often accompanied by wrong policies when something was produced. Yet differing political periods caused them to differ in the perceived locus of the problem. The Late New Deal Era, characterized by factional politics and incremental policy-making, led to a focus on party structure as the root dysfunction. The Era of Divided Government, characterized by growing ideological polarization but split partisan control, led to a focus on institutional structure instead. Where the two critics reunited was in their insistence that an increasingly dominant presidency was the main way forward—at the center of the political parties in the Late New Deal Era, at the center of the governmental institutions in the Era of Divided Government.[12]

Only a fractured version of the same approach survived to unite critics in the Era of Partisan Volatility. If anything, a policy-making process characterized by stasis and punctuated by spikes of omnibus activity caused their numbers to grow. Yet the diversity accompanying this growth meant that there was no archetypal representative for these critics—at least to date—and hence no synoptic work that could stand in for them. At bottom, the political structure of a new era, in the form of the pervasiveness of the ideological polarization distinguishing the period, may be what kept them from being unified on either a diagnosis or a response. Instead, they split roughly into camps of generalists and particularists, each with their own way of grappling with the current political era and their own formulation for a contemporary critique.

In the Late New Deal Era, generalist critics, while their collective preferences aligned mainly with New Dealers, had nevertheless asserted the desirability of *two* programmatic parties.[13] In the Era of Divided Government, such critics had instead asserted the desirability of unified partisan control of American national government, thereby accepting the concomitant risk that unity would favor the wrong programmatic party. In the Era of Partisan Volatility, however, their critical descendants had such great difficulty separating themselves from the (polarized) program of their chosen party that they often retreated to the complaint that the other party was so disproportionately advantaged in institutional terms that this advantage in itself defined what needed to be fixed.[14]

More numerous were the particularist critics, focusing upon one or another distortion that ostensibly and especially fueled the ideological polarization of the contemporary era. Particularists did face some of the same problems as generalists, in the risk that an institutional arrangement that pushed politics in one direction at the current moment, but had pushed it in a different direction at some earlier point, would push it differently again when it was embedded in a new mix of party balance, ideological polarization, and substantive conflict at some future date. Still, the particularists were at least able to focus on the policy-making process in a manner less automatically partisan, even if the roster of possible targets for this focus remained large and diverse.

A favorite was the Senate filibuster, an old bête noire reinvigorated for the new era.[15] In principle, the filibuster was neutral as between the two parties, benefiting whichever was the minority in the Senate at the moment. Accordingly, its contribution to a polarized politics was open to the question of whether the filibuster was inherently polarizing or depolarizing. Another frequent particularist target was campaign finance—the role of money in politics—surging back to sustained criticism in the contemporary period.[16] Again, analysis could in principle be neutral as between the parties, since both were frequently awash in cash. So the question was again its contribution to polarization: Was big money ideologically extreme or ideologically indifferent? Even gerrymandering, the oldest bugbear of all, acquired renewed criticism.[17] Redistricting for partisan ends could in principle benefit whichever party got to draw lines at the state level; in that limited sense, it was party-neutral. So it still seemed possible to ask whether the partisan drawing of electoral boundaries tended inherently toward moderation or extremism.

Each critical cluster could be used to criticize the others. Yet in a very different way, the four preceding chapters are themselves an implicit criticism of the critics. Part of this is simply and inherently normative. Complaints about the substantive content of policy output are classically antidemocratic if they become complaints about the policy wishes of the general public rather than about the shaping force of the intermediary structure of American politics.[18] A larger part of this criticism-of-the-critics is intensely practical. Institutional change does *not* appear easier to achieve in practice than coalitional adjustments or policy compromises. Moreover, the elements of actual change between political periods, many of them informal rather than formal, suggest that the practical impact of institutional reforms is reliably unpredictable.

Even more of the implicit counterargument embedded in the preceding chapters involves the disinclination of all too many of the critics to worry much about the intermediary structure of politics, that is, about its roots in party balance, ideological polarization, and substantive conflict, and about the way these elements interact to create an actual process of policy-making.[19] In refusing, critics effectively dismiss the possibility that politics itself, in the conventional sense of structured and recurrent efforts to shape public policy, can have much to do with systemic outcomes. Seen that way, the preceding chapters contain their own, barely implicit, countertheory of political reform. Put colloquially: if you are unhappy with the nature of current American politics in whatever era you reside, then work to adjust the party balance that prevails, work to alter the ideological polarization that you encounter, or work to shift the substantive focus of organized politicking. Said more analytically, political change is most likely to occur *through* politics, not by circumventing it.

One way to address this politics analytically—the way used here—is through three of its recurrently major elements. One result has been a small set of political eras, recognized through patterned electoral outcomes and through an ongoing process of policy-making. More to the point for a concluding chapter, this way of proceeding provides a conceptual tool for talking about the internal dynamics of these comparatively stable periods while simultaneously addressing political *change*. And change there has been: the previous eighty-plus years have proved far from invariant. Party balance has shifted constantly, while the nature of the parties themselves has been transformed. Ideological polarization has changed not only in degree, ebbing and flowing, but also in the very nature of the phenomenon itself. Substantive conflict has shifted, both in its specific foci and in the complexity of the resulting mix. And the accompanying process of policy-making has been nearly unrecognizable from era to era.

So the aim of the approach used here has been to allow the analyst to talk about stability and change without implying either that periods of stability are static—hermetically sealed, somehow repressing variety to the political behavior within them—or that major changes have not been percolating well before they broke through and altered an apparently stable operating arrangement. Sometimes, as with the Great Depression and the New Deal, political change did arrive abruptly. Mostly, however, change can be seen retrospectively to have been building within a superficially stable period before its key elements came together at a particular point—usually a particular election—and then became institutionalized as the operating structure of the ensuing period, before coming apart again, as ever, in the face of other elements that had themselves been slowly building during this successor period.

On the one hand, these results, an analytic way to get a handle on stability and change, still concern the *intermediary* structure of politics. They are not the inputs to that politics, the questions that have to be addressed. They are not the outputs of that politics, the policies that result. On the other hand, they *are* the means by which inputs are shaped on the way to becoming outputs. As such, they ought to be crucial to understanding both the political process at a particular point and its evolution across time. Yet because they can never be the totality of that process, it is perhaps time, in a penultimate part of this concluding chapter, to address two other critical and generic elements of the political process that have remained integral to the preceding story of stability and change. So far, both have been addressed only in passing. One involves the changing specifics of policy inputs. The other involves some enduring influences on the outputs that result. Both need to be addressed explicitly now.

In the matter of policy inputs, there can be a great deal of genuine autonomy to the substantive conflicts that arise in a given political period—autonomy, that is, from the intermediary structure of politics. Sometimes these policy concerns are truly external to that structure. Thus there are moments when events of the day, along with the external demands that they generate, simply overwhelm political structure. The Great Depression and the High New Deal are the inescapable example. An essentially presidential process of policy-making, built on a huge shift in party balance, on a unipolar character to ideological polarization, and on a programmatic concentration on economic welfare, could still shape the policy responses that became the New Deal. Yet "shaping" was all that this intermediary structure could do, and sometimes it could not even do that. President Franklin Roosevelt aggressively opposed two major bonus programs for veterans, arguing that they were counterproductive to the rest of his New Deal program and investing significant resources in derailing them. Public demand simply overwhelmed him.

More common and thus more diagnostic are the less comprehensive and less insistent combinations of events of the day, plus the public demands that go with them. Likewise not obviously a direct product of the structure of politics, these leave more room for structure to play a policy-shaping role. Some mix of such influences does surface in every period, and its elements retain significant autonomy. For example, the fact that the Era of Divided Government produced a policy-making process requiring (and receiving) a recurrent pattern of cross-party and cross-institutional negotiations is *not* what made environmentalism or stagflation into major substantive foci of the period. This policy-making process did powerfully condition the manner in which both of these substantive foci were handled. Yet the Era of Divided Government did not call forth the rise of environmentalism, just as the political structure of this era cannot conceivably have produced either the long postwar boom or the nagging economic slowdown that preceded its own arrival.

A certain reciprocal character is thus ordinarily present. From one side, each political period after the Great Depression was affected by incipient policy substance and associated substantive conflict. Yet from the other side, the structure of each period simultaneously shaped this conflict, coloring the specifics of lawmaking:

- In an example where substance shaped structure, the fact of three major and insistent programmatic foci during the Late New Deal Era, rather than just the one that had characterized the High New Deal, surely exaggerated the partisan depolarization characterizing this period. Moreover, the need to attend to all these multifactional alignments with their distinctive policy preferences in the process of pursuing any one of them was additionally depolarizing.
- In a more balanced example of the interaction of substance and structure, the Era of Divided Government derived crucially from the rise of cultural values as a grand policy alternative to economic welfare. The period was thus characterized by two—not one, not three—great policy divisions. Yet the ability of cultural values to play this role was heavily facilitated by—centrally connected to— the changing structure of political parties that was so central to the coming (and character) of the era.
- And for an example running clearly in the other direction, where structure shaped substance, the ideological polarization of the Era of Partisan Volatility certainly disciplined the substantive conflicts that occurred within its policy-making process, altering their alignment. Though in truth, polarization reached such a state that it was really the *explanation* for how economic welfare, foreign affairs, civil rights, and even cultural values could be amalgamated into a single dominant policy dimension.

One further observation, available only with an extended span of time plus the presence of four distinguishable eras, involves the apparently inherent variety of these substantive foci. Political analyses that focus tightly on substantive conflict are often driven to seek some dominant policy domain, an underlying substance ostensibly fundamental to all of politics. The holy grail becomes a summary statement of the sort whereby "American politics is ultimately and recurrently about economics/culture/race/wars/personalities/shoe size/etc." The preceding chapters implicitly argue that this is a bootless endeavor. In the same way that the intermediary structure of American politics must be teased out by way of the *interaction* of three main political elements—and a changing interaction at that—the substantive focus of this politics has to be teased out through attention to the political eras that constitute this politics, varied and shifting as these eras reliably are.

Economic welfare during the High New Deal; economic welfare, foreign affairs, and civil rights during the Late New Deal; economic welfare and cultural values during the Era of Divided Government; all—and hence none—during the Era of Partisan Volatility: at a minimum these suggest that no single substantive *pattern* dominates American politics. Economic welfare does provide a kind of continuing "spine" to such a focus, but even it is more an organizing device than an operationally dominant phenomenon. Not only does this continuing thread interact with different (major) alternatives at most points in time. It is also regularly trumped by one or another of them in the making of public policy. And that still ignores the way that the rest of the intermediary structure of politics affects the policy expression of economic welfare as a concern of its own.

So, the intermediary structure of American politics, while it usually has a shaping influence on the substantive inputs to that politics, is rarely the dominant determinant of those inputs. These are at least powerfully conditioned by events of their time. In the same way, the intermediary structure of politics, while it ordinarily has a shaping influence on the *outputs* of that politics, is not the only such shaping influence. There are continuing background forces that come together around the critical events of their time, and a concluding chapter on the American political pattern in all the years since 1932 should say something about these other grand influences on the outputs of American politics. They are *enduring* in the sense of being both grand and recurrent. Yet they operate differently depending on the specific issues of the day and on the intermediary structure through which these issues are addressed.

Three generic examples have in fact surfaced repeatedly in an analysis organized around party balance, ideological polarization, and substantive conflict. First are some further institutional influences on the intermediary structure that is the focus here. In the United States, basic *constitutional arrangements* are critical to these, especially in the form of the separation of powers, an influence that has been peeking through most of the preceding analysis.[20] Second are some further implications from the nature and level of *public demand* for policy-making, an ever-changing external influence with an arguable ability to drive that same intermediary structure.[21] These can range from era-shaking to what appear in hindsight to have been little more than fads and fashions. And in between those two grand background influences, there are always short-term *electoral surges.* The proximate goal of most active participants most of the time, these surges stand out far less than the elections marking an overall shift of political eras. Yet they remain capable of changing particular policy products when they occur—and they occur more often than the era-shifters.[22]

Accordingly, the rest of the penultimate task in any such analysis involves taking a quick look at major examples of these "missing ingredients," the ongoing background contributions to a changing American politics.[23] One leading hallmark of the constitutional structure of that politics, the separation of powers, has been ever-present, indeed intrinsically entangled, in the analysis of each successive era since 1932. The most commonly acknowledged embodiment of this separation, the tension between elective institutions of policy-making, that is, between Congress and the presidency, has been so omnipresent as to risk being taken for granted. But a second embodiment, the tension between these elective institutions and an appointive counterpart, the Supreme Court, has hardly ever been absent from this story, being sometimes at its center.

Institutional differences between Congress and the president—in constituencies, in terms of office, and in policy-making approaches—have been intrinsic to questions about party balance. For these, the two institutions always tell partially discordant stories and sometimes sharply dissident ones. Institutional differences have then resurfaced in questions about ideological polarization. The main way to assess the two national parties as collectivities has always been by way of Congress, where some sample of the full range of party factions and their policy preferences is ordinarily present, though the lack of a parallel structure to the presidency has meant that it has had to be worked back into the story in a self-conscious (and often very different) way. Institutional distinctions have recurred yet again in questions about substantive conflict. The two institutional sides, Congress and the presidency, have rarely had the same collective preferences on the specifics of policy, and sometimes their differences have reached the point of featuring different overall priorities for policy-making.

At the extreme, one of these political periods, the Era of Divided Government, is hard to imagine in the absence of the separation of powers as a basic framework for government. Which is to say: split partisan control appears to require separate institutions. In their absence—in the counterfactual presence of a unified institutional structure to American national government—the other diagnostic characteristics of the Era of Divided Government would presumably have worked themselves out in one of two (very different) alternative ways. Either they would have ratcheted up pressure on the general public to choose between its economic and its cultural prejudices, or they would have allowed a single party to control government on the basis of one policy majority, then impose its preferences in the other main policy realm as well.

Yet it was this same separation of powers that helped impel the diagnostic shifts of the Late New Deal Era toward ideological depolarization, by allowing established party factions to find institutional homes in places that required that they be "bargained into" policy-making—just as it was the same institutional separation that had to be captured by the diagnostic features of the Era of Partisan Volatility, namely, its exaggerated ideological polarization, before crucially facilitating its kaleidoscopic mix of partisan outcomes. The point in all these examples is neither that the basic structure of American government changes with the tide, which it does not, nor that this basic structure always conduces in the same direction. Instead and once again, basic institutional arrangements rather clearly *interact* with party balance, ideological polarization, and substantive conflict. So the point is just that these basic arrangements are rarely absent as a major influence on the shifting constellation of factors that define one electoral era and then help replace it with another.

On the other hand, the less stereotypical incarnation of the separation of powers, the one between the elective institutions of American national government and an appointive judicial branch, has been everpresent as well. In the High New Deal Era, this grand institutional divide produced the dominant embodiment of ideological polarization and the dominant theater for policy conflict, such that the resolution of fundamental differences between institutions effectively determined the lasting character of an era. Elective and appointive institutions did show the same concentrated focus on social welfare. That was not the difference between them, as it would sometimes subsequently be. Yet the resolution of their different *preferences* saw the Court leave an old era of economic liberty and shift to a new era of individual rights and liberties, thereby sustaining the separation of powers but changing the substantive content of American politics.

Accordingly, during the Late New Deal and the Era of Divided Government, the judiciary instead became influential by pumping up *one set* of the substantive concerns that helped determine the overall essence of policy conflict in its time. Major cases in the domain of civil rights produced this outcome in the first of these two periods. Diverse cases in the domain of cultural values produced this outcome in the second. Those civil rights cases helped to sustain the multifactional character of the Late New Deal Era by emphasizing a domain that was aligned differently from either economic welfare or foreign affairs. Those cultural values cases went even further, helping to propel the crosscutting policy domains that *produced* an Era of Divided Government.

The Era of Partisan Volatility was different yet again. Really for the first time in this entire eighty-year period, the judiciary became integral to the explicit partisanship—now ideologically polarized—that characterized the American politics of its time. Outside the Court, congressional votes on judicial appointments increasingly followed party lines. Inside the Court, the partisanship of the justices themselves became an increasingly reliable guide to their subsequent decisions. On the one hand, then, the contribution of the court system to the political structure of all four periods was reliably consequential. On the other hand, this contribution was still registered through the particular interactions of party balance, ideological polarization, and substantive conflict that characterized each individual era, as well as through the policy-making process that this interaction produced.

Different in every regard are the *public demands* that well up at every point in time and always drive this policy-making process to some degree. Where constitutional arrangements are essentially stable, drawing a variable impact from their interaction with the rest of American politics, public demands are ever-changing. What makes them an ongoing background influence is just that they are always present in some form and to some degree, even as they vary wildly in generality and composition. There are temporal stretches—even entire eras—when the public demands action on one or more policy matters, defining them as a problem and turning to government for a solution, though even these periods can have numerous other policy realms where the general public has some apparent views, less general and less intense, while organized segments of that public make demands that are even less general but clearly more intense. Seen from the opposite end of the process, policy-making in any particular area is surely advantaged by widespread public demands for legislative action. Though the actual production of specific policies can hardly be used as the measure of demand for same: there are too many other contributors, ranging from events of the day to the behavior of organized intermediaries, with contributions that are at least somewhat autonomous.[24]

Some public demands are so self-evidently powerful as to cause changes in party balance, ideological polarization, and/or substantive conflict more or less on their own. The period from 1932 to 2016 was kicked off—inaugurated—by an obvious example. The Great Depression of 1929 may not have determined the comprehensive specifics of a policy response to societal crisis, but it did generate a demand for policy that was neither a direct product of the predecessor era nor inherent in the political structure of its own time. Yet that is only the extreme case. The full historical period under consideration here offers other instances where the general public clearly demanded governmental action. The civil rights revolution of the early 1960s, the terrorist attacks of 9/11, and even the Great Recession of 2007 surely qualify as lesser but still major stimuli toward the same, largely autonomous, external demand for policy.

That said, the reciprocal character of public demands for policy output and the ongoing structure of a political era should not be lost along the way. For there were policy outputs in this extended period—major policy outputs—that were not obviously a product of widespread demand from the mass public for even a broad and general policy response. The outstanding example is probably the creation of the international institutions of the Cold War in the years immediately after World War II. This was certainly major policy-making by governmental institutions. Yet it was not clear, at least in its time, that the public "demanded" this—certainly not clear until Harry Truman had been reelected to solidify Cold War policy among Democrats and not really clear until Dwight Eisenhower had brought Republicans into the same overall policy coalition.

On the other hand, the interaction between even obvious public demands and an established intermediary structure can be tangled, and the Great Recession of 2007 is a particularly good example.[25] A sitting Republican majority in Congress was actually dislodged *before* the event, at the midterm election of 2006, a familiar point of public discontent with any sitting administration but in this case one well in advance of the economic downturn to follow. Then, when that downturn began in late 2007 and intensified in late 2008, public demand for a policy response was undeniable but produced impressively similar responses from first a Republican and then a Democratic administration.

The Republican minority in Congress was still not enthusiastic about major governmental expenditures in response. But a sitting Republican president, George W. Bush, was. His approach was then replicated and expanded by an incoming Democratic president, Barack Obama. Thus it was the Bush administration that produced a $300 billion housing relief program in July 2008 and a $700 billion bailout of the financial sector in October, all after an initial $168 billion economic stimulus effort in February of that same year. The Obama administration followed in its earliest days with a further $787 billion economic stimulus program.[26] There would be much partisan finger-pointing about all these programs, and their specifics were always in part a product of diagnostic party preferences and internal party negotiations. Yet it would be hard to argue that they were not simultaneously a direct response to intense and widespread public demands.

In short order, however, the Obama administration would also drive through, by the narrowest of partisan margins, the largest increment to the American welfare state since the Great Society under Lyndon Johnson. This was the $1 trillion Affordable Care Act, and it was the culmination of a long-running commitment by the dominant Democratic faction to national health insurance. Active Democratic partisans certainly wanted this program. Yet it always struggled for support within the general public, so that it was ultimately best viewed as the product not of focused public demands for universal health care coverage but of capitalizing on demands for a general response to the Great Recession to implement a long-standing partisan goal. Generalized public demand for new policy in one substantive area, namely, the economy, was thus pushed through an intermediary political structure to produce new policy in a related but different realm, namely, health care.

Lesser programs in less-troubled times were even more difficult to attach directly to public demands. Demand for public policy was rarely absent; most programs could evidence some sort of public constituency. Moreover, such programs were advantaged if this constituency was well organized. They were even more advantaged if they attained general public support once they had become serious options for public policy. Yet there could be extended periods where there was intense policy demand but little or no further preference within the general public about specific policies. The governmental responses to environmental degradation or to persistent stagflation that characterized the Era of Divided Government—and facilitated so much legislation—are good examples, made all the neater by the fact that they drove in such opposite directions, toward governmental regulation in the case of the environment, toward governmental *de*regulation in the case of stagflation.

The lasting partisan impact of even the major and evident instances of public demands for a policy response also varied enormously. If there were four indisputable instances of such demands during this eighty-year period—the Great Depression, the civil rights revolution, the terrorist attacks of 9/11, and the Great Recession—only the first was associated with a direct and substantial change in party balance. The scale of the partisan shift that accompanied it is part of what makes the High New Deal hard to treat as anything other than a massive anomaly—too important in its policy legacy to be ignored, almost too short in temporal duration to deserve being treated as a separate era. Everywhere else, evident public demand was met by major policy response, yet changes in party balance were uneven and equivocal.

Still, there were numerous lesser *partisan surges* during the long period from the Great Depression to the presidential election of 2016. These generated a much more direct and (pre)organized potential for policy-making, even if the realization of that potential still varied widely. Indeed, seen the other way around, all such surges are in some sense the *goal* of those who are active in partisan politics: if many elections do not produce partisan change in the large, that fact hardly prevents the main players from doing whatever they can to seek it. Moreover, lesser swings not only occur; they can produce real policy results. Most clear but lesser surges did not change party balance for the nation as a whole, just as most were not automatically connected to widespread and focused substantive demands. Yet they often (though not always) underpinned specific policy initiatives. So in the absence of inescapable public demand for a particular policy response, lesser partisan surges could still allow one party or the other to capitalize on the surge itself and make policy anyway.

Even one-off surges, exploding in one congressional election only to be neutralized in the next, could generate policy outcomes of lasting consequence. The short-lived Republican surge of 1946, for example—worth one Congress, then snuffed out by the Truman reelection—did not begin to alter the intermediary structure of the Late New Deal Era (table 5.1). But this particular one-term surge, responding in part to public concern over the impact of labor unrest on economic reconversion, did produce the Taft-Hartley Act during its one Congress, still a major element of the national framework for labor-management relations in the United States as this is written, some seventy years later. Ergo, very temporary surge, lasting policy contribution.

Conversely, it was possible for one-off surges to have only a mixed impact on the production of public policy, yet contribute to a larger shift in party balance that had substantial policy consequences later. Thus the Republican surge of 1942 in some sense merely completed the rebalancing of party loyalties begun in 1938, the rebalancing that marked the end of the High New Deal Era. In policy terms, that prior election, the midterm of 1938, had signaled that there would be no third wave of economic welfare programs to go with the waves from 1933 and 1935. But that was largely all it did. The second-wave surge of 1942, however—with substantial assistance from the "full employment" being produced by World War II—resulted in the elimination of the Works Projects Administration, the Civilian Conservation Corps, and the National Youth Administration, along with the effective defunding of other New Deal agencies. Ergo, ongoing partisan change, coupled with substantial but still only retrospective policy impact.

More extreme in this regard was the surge at the midterm election of 1958, swelling the ranks of Northern Democrats at the especial expense of Northeastern Republicans, then sustaining the lion's share of these gains. As a result, this particular shift proved to be important to the overall reworking of the factional balance in American politics, though that reworking would not really come home to roost as a key structural factor until the Era of Partisan Volatility. In the interim, this shift did contribute toward structurally democratizing reforms in Congress during the Era of Divided Government, the subsequent period. Yet it secured little direct policy product from the lame-duck Republican administration under Dwight Eisenhower after 1958, or indeed from the successor Democratic administration under John Kennedy. Ergo, major ramifications for political structure across time, little direct policy impact.[27]

Another major surge that was harvested only indirectly came at the midterm of 1994, bringing an equally large batch of new congresspersons to the Republican Party while ending a Republican drought in Congress that stretched all the way back to 1930. Those gains would confirm the rebalanced character of the Era of Partisan Volatility and the ideological polarization that went with it. Yet while this particular surge attracted a great deal of policy attention as well, thanks to the "Contract with America" that united many of the new Republican congresspersons around a central program, there was much less legislative product than contemporary hand-wringing or hand-clapping would have suggested.[28] Indeed, the policy impact that did result was due more to the encouragement that this 1994 surge offered to a continuing Democratic president, to do welfare reform and then deficit reform, neither of which had been on his active agenda in 1993–1994.

On the other hand, a surge could sometimes lead to major policy change without producing even a temporary partisan majority. Thus while Ronald Reagan did pick up the Senate in 1980, the House eluded him both then and subsequently. Yet a short-term narrowing of the Democratic edge in the House did bring changed coalitional possibilities: both the Reagan tax cut of 1981 (ETRA) and his budget-balancing effort of 1982 (TEFRA) were testimony to the reality of this adjustment, owing their existence in large part to those newly implicit possibilities. Ergo, temporary shift in party balance, still far short of a new majority, coupled with unforeseen but substantial impacts on policy output. Indeed, these latter possibilities were not fully eliminated until a major Democratic surge in the Senate elections of 1986 restored the full, stereotypical, and ongoing partisan character of the Era of Divided Government.

Different yet again, and finally, was the Democratic surge of 2006. From one side, this was sufficient to transfer both houses of Congress back into Democratic hands. From the other side, this particular surge was to be undone far more rapidly than its Republican counterpart of 1994, being rubbed out in striking fashion in the House only two elections later. In that limited sense—that is, ignoring policy impacts—the Republican surge of 2010 would look every bit as impressive. Yet policy impacts should most definitely not be ignored this time: the very temporary midterm result of 2006, when reinforced by the presidential outcome of 2008, would be sufficient to produce the Affordable Care Act, landmark social welfare legislation that was inconceivable in the absence of this short-lived surge. Ergo, temporary change in party balance, major impact on public policy.

Table 5.1. Partisan Surges, 1928–2014

A. The House

Year	Democrats	Republicans	Others	Change in Democrats	Change in Republicans	Change of Control	Margin (%)
1928	164	270	1	−30	+32		45
1930	216	218	1	+ 52	−52		0
1932	313	117	5	+97	−101	x	45
1934	322	103	10	+9	−14		50
1936	334	88	13	+12	−15		57
1938	262	169	4	−72	+81		21
1940	267	162	6	+5	−7		24
1942	222	209	4	−45	+47		3
1944	244	189	2	+22	−20		13
1946	188	246	1	−56	+57	x	13
1948	263	171	1	+75	−75	x	21
1950	235	199	1	−28	+28		8
1952	213	221	1	−22	+22	x	2
1954	232	203	0	+19	−18	x	7
1956	232	203	0	0	0		7
1958	282	153	1	+50	−50		30
1960	264	173	0	−20	+20		21
1962	260	175	0	−4	+2		20
1964	295	140	0	+35	−35		36
1966	248	187	0	−47	+47		14
1968	243	192	0	−5	+5		12
1970	255	180	0	+12	−12		17
1972	243	192	0	−12	+12		12
1974	291	144	0	+48	−48		34
1976	292	143	0	+1	−1		34
1978	279	156	0	−13	+13		28
1980	243	192	0	−36	+36		12
1982	269	166	0	+26	−26		24
1984	255	180	0	−14	+14		17
1986	258	177	0	+3	−3		19
1988	262	173	0	+4	−4		21
1990	267	167	1	+5	−6		23
1992	258	176	1	−9	+9		19
1994	206	228	1	−52	+52	x	5
1996	207	226	2	+1	−2		4
1998	211	223	1	+4	−3		3
2000	213	220	2	+2	−3		2
2002	205	229	1	−8	+9		6
2004	201	233	1	−4	+4		7
2006	233	202	0	+32	−31	x	7
2008	257	178	0	+24	−24		18
2010	193	242	0	−64	+64	x	11
2012	201	234	0	+8	−8		8
2014	188	247	0	−13	+13		14

B. The Senate

Year	Democrats	Republicans	Others	Change in Democrats	Change in Republicans	Change of Control	Margin (%)
1928	39	56	1	−7	+8		18
1930	47	48	1	+8	−8		1
1932	59	36	1	+12	−12	x	24
1934	69	25	2	+10	−11		46
1936	76	16	4	+7	−9		63
1938	69	23	4	−7	+7		48
1940	66	28	2	−3	+5		40
1942	57	38	1	−9	+10		20
1944	57	38	1	0	0		20
1946	45	51	0	−12	+13	x	6
1948	54	42	0	+9	−9	x	13
1950	49	47	0	−5	+5		2
1952	47	48	1	−2	+1	x	1
1954	48	47	1	+1	−1	x	1
1956	49	47	0	+1	0		2
1958	65	35	0	+16	−12		30
1960	64	36	0	−1	+1		28
1962	66	34	0	+2	−2		32
1964	68	32	0	+2	−2		36
1966	64	36	0	−4	+4		28
1968	57	43	0	−7	+7		14
1970	54	44	2	−3	+1		10
1972	56	42	2	+2	−2		14
1974	61	37	2	+5	−5		24
1976	61	38	1	0	+1		23
1978	58	41	1	−3	+3		17
1980	46	53	1	−12	+12	x	7
1982	45	55	0	−1	+2		10
1984	47	53	0	+2	−2		6
1986	55	45	0	+8	−8	x	10
1988	55	45	0	0	0		10
1990	56	44	0	+1	−1		12
1992	57	43	0	+1	−1		14
1994	48	52	0	−9	+9	x	4
1996	45	55	0	−3	+3		10
1998	45	55	0	0	0		10
2000	50	50	0	+5	−5		0
2002	48	51	1	−2	+1		3
2004	44	55	1	−4	+4		11
2006	49	49	2	+5	−4		0
2008	57	41	2	+8	−8	x	16
2010	51	47	2	−6	+6		4
2012	53	45	2	+2	−2		8
2014	44	54	2	−9	+9	x	10

In any case, there is one further point about all these policy products from partisan surges, divergent as they truly are. To wit: much of the preceding analysis has suggested that shifts in party balance and ideological polarization are usually responses to external events or crystallizations of societal trends, rather than anything principally under the direct control of the political parties. On the other hand, the policy emerging from these intermittent but lesser partisan surges often allowed one or the other of the two parties to capitalize on a development that did not obviously call for the policy they were nevertheless going to produce.

In other words, parties cannot bring fresh political eras into existence by deciding—wishing, even strategizing—to do so. Even the High New Deal Era, the most dramatic partisan break in this eighty-year sequence and one ultimately accompanied by a redefinition of both party programs, was not produced by Democratic strategic moves following the 1928 election. Yet changes in the structural character of these political parties can and do shape the intermediary structure of American politics that goes with a change of political era. This is one reason why the policy-making process of each successive period was so different. More to the point here, political parties can also capitalize on lesser partisan surges to extract particular policies that are integral to the party program of their time—that is, to the policy wishes of party activists—and few examples can be more dramatic than the Affordable Care Act, hardly an associated "legislative detail."

In the end, though, it is important to note that the final link in this chain, between four processes of policy-making and the scope and content of the resulting public policy, is perhaps the weakest link of all. Or at least, a comparative summary of the further relationship between the process of policy-making diagnostic of its era and the policy *output* of that era is the most difficult of all to produce. And this is before we reintroduce idiosyncratic and confounding influences like an enduring constitutional structure, shifting public demands, or short-run partisan surges. Scholars who write about public policy tend to prefer constant production, probably because it shows that problems are being addressed, possibly also because it gives them more to study. Yet it is not at all clear—it is certainly not definitional—that, for example, the constant adjustments and readjustments to public policy of the Late New Deal Era were inherently superior to the cross-party and cross-institutional coalitions that characterized policy in the Era of Divided

Government, or even to the infrequent but larger alterations of the Era of Partisan Volatility.

Much contemporary hand-wringing about policy conflict in the contemporary era—the hand-wringing behind a summary view of this era as "gridlock coupled with brinkmanship"—is implicitly premised on treating the long Late New Deal Era, where things were indeed different, as normal. At a minimum, the study of four distinct periods between 1932 and 2016 confirms that this particular comparative premise is empirically false. In the aggregate, that particular era contributed thirty of those eighty-plus years, and that is all. More pointedly, using the Late New Deal Era as a standard effectively requires treating not just the Era of Divided Government but also the Era of Partisan Volatility as anomalous, when they are in fact the most recent forty-eight years and counting—the clear majority of the modern period. If the modern political world begins in 1932, then, incrementalism is the deviant and not the normal state of policy-making for this modern world.

That said, there are important reasons, both empirical and interpretive, for not privileging *any* of these political periods as the natural standard. Empirically, judged purely by the scope of their policy contributions, the High New Deal Era probably retains pride of place, certainly when economic welfare is the focus. If this focus was somewhere other than economic welfare, however, even this answer would be different: probably the Late New Deal Era for foreign affairs, certainly that period for civil rights. Further policy foci would produce additionally different answers, as with the Era of Divided Government for environmentalism or the Era of Partisan Volatility for domestic security. In any case, once the High New Deal Era had met its ever-so-early end, the record of legislative accomplishment in the aggregate becomes even less obvious.

We have been using the Mayhew categorization of historically significant legislative acts to help in getting at the policy-making process in each of the four periods of modern American politics, and it is simple enough to comment on this balance by converting this list to tabular form. To that end, table 5.2 arrays, first, the total of all major legislative acts in the Mayhew canon and, second, the total just of historically significant acts, for the three political periods succeeding the High New Deal. The resulting record of legislative productivity is at best ambiguous. Overall and in the aggregate, the Era of Divided Government finishes first. With a focus on historically significant acts only, the Era of Partisan Volatility—our time—takes the prize instead. The Late New

Table 5.2. Policy Productivity by Political Era

	Major Legislation	Historic Legislation
Late New Deal Era, 1947–1968	123	14
Era of Divided Government, 1969–1992	149	9
Era of Partisan Volatility, 1993–2016	118	19

Deal Era falls in between on both measures, but with a major fillip: (1) the most productive period overall, the Era of Divided Government, comes last in the derby of historical consequence, while (2) the winner for historical consequence, the Era of Partisan Volatility, comes last for overall legislative acts.

Critics of this particular list have complained about the lack of a "denominator," that is, the absence of some measure of major legislative acts that did not pass.[29] Indeed, debate over the specifics of such a measure became a cottage industry for a short period. Here, however, the main takeaways from this debate are different. First, the debate itself only emphasizes the difficulty in generating proof of the overall productivity of the different processes of policy-making characterizing different periods. Surely, to take only one example, the omnibus products of the Era of Partisan Volatility cannot be compared on a one-to-one basis with single legislative acts from earlier periods.

But second, the goal here is to isolate a policy-making process diagnostic of its extended era. For this, a catalog of policies that were not made is hugely problematic.[30] Put gently, once actual policies cease to be the measure, proof of greater productivity (much less "better" productivity) becomes powerfully dependent on imposed principles of counting. Again, the point is that convincing proof for the aggregate supremacy of one policy-making process over another *in the long run* is very hard to produce. Moreover, all this still suppresses an important further interpretive point.

To wit: for the denizens of each electoral era in turn, including the one that will ultimately succeed the contemporary version, the benchmark task is to isolate the handful of fundamentals that have shaped and continue to sustain the process of policy-making as it actually occurred in their time. It makes little sense to talk about the roots or fortunes of this policy-making process, much less its theoretical policy alternatives, in the absence of this prior understanding. We have used the interaction of party balance, ideological polarization, and substantive conflict to provide this benchmark. Other approaches are easily possible, though this one does have the further advantages that its key elements can be isolated in all periods; that their interaction is different in every period; and that the resulting process of policy-making is impelled not by human perversity but by its opposite—an attempt to respond to the structural incentives generated by this process.

At a minimum, there is no reason to believe that our period is different from each of the preceding periods in this final and fundamental regard: the sense that political actors seek public policy within the structural constraints of their own (and not some other) period. For the contemporary period, we have derived an Era of Partisan Volatility from a distinctive mix—our distinctive mix—of party balance, ideological polarization, and substantive conflict. So in closing and as a reprise, what does contemporary American politics look like in this light?

- The balance between the two parties within the general public is closer than in the High New Deal Era, the Late New Deal Era, or the Era of Divided Government. This is true even when party identification is the measure. It is truer—and more realistic—when voting behavior is the focus, though a Democratic edge remains.
- The political parties as organizations are just as clearly farther apart than in the High New Deal Era, the Late New Deal Era, or the Era of Divided Government. It would have been theoretically possible for the two to move closer together as they became more closely balanced. That is not what happened.
- The electoral upshot has been ironic. Voters have an easier time choosing between parties that are ideologically distant. But this comes at the price of public disappointment, as winners prove more committed to the programs of their (nonoverlapping) political parties than to the preferences of a voting public, the bulk of which inevitably lives in between.
- Though if this public is constantly disappointed, it is easier than ever to respond by shifting partisan control of governmental institutions, any or all of them. A close party balance requires relatively little change among voters—a small net shift at the polls, just differential turnout—in order to change partisan control and

produce the electoral kaleidoscope characterizing the contemporary era.

All this leaves us in a peculiar but familiar position, for a social scientist or perhaps for anybody. We do have sufficient information and analysis to put the lie to some familiar arguments about the structure of modern American politics. Yet the same material cannot be made sufficiently constraining that we can talk with confidence about where the critical factors within that politics more or less must go next. Is that because we have just not thought deeply enough or reached back far enough? Or is it because politics—as, indeed, all of social life—even when reduced to three key elements thereof, is just far more contingent than we ordinarily admit? Perhaps that is all that a realistic analysis can ask?

Notes

Chapter 1. Birth Pangs of the Modern World

1. For a view of this break point that makes it only one among a series of critical and parallel others, see James L. Sundquist, *Dynamics of the Party System: Alignment and Realignment of the Political Parties in the United States* (Washington, DC: Brookings Institution, 1973). For a view that acknowledges the consequence of this particular break but denies the parallels and emphasizes its distinctiveness, see David R. Mayhew, *Electoral Realignments: A Critique of an American Genre* (New Haven, CT: Yale University Press, 2002).

2. For the earlier argument over the dynamics of this change, compare Robert S. Erikson and Kent L. Tedin, "The 1928–1936 Partisan Realignment: The Case for the Conversion Hypothesis," *American Political Science Review* 75 (1981): 951–962, with Kristi L. Andersen, *The Creation of a Democratic Majority, 1928–1936* (Chicago: University of Chicago Press, 1979).

3. For the later argument that this was an evolving process rather than a clear break, see especially Helmut Norpoth, Andrew H. Sidman, and Clara H. Suong, "Polls and Elections: The New Deal Realignment in Real Time," *Presidential Studies Quarterly* 43 (2013): 146–166. See also Eric Schickler and Devin Caughey, "Public Opinion, Organized Labor, and the Limits of New Deal Liberalism, 1936–1945," *Studies in American Political Development* 25 (2011): 162–189.

4. Many useful perspectives on the contributions of these various programs are collected in Randall E. Parker, ed., *The Economics of the Great Depression: A Twenty-First Century Look Back at the Economics of the Interwar Years* (Northampton, MA: Edward Elgar, 2007).

5. Powerfully helpful in aligning the High New Deal Era within the analytic framework used here were Michael Barone, *Our Country: The Shaping of America from Roosevelt to Reagan* (New York: Free Press, 1990), esp. chapters 6–14; Alonzo L. Hamby, *For the Survival of Democracy: Franklin Roosevelt and the World Crisis of the 1930s* (New York: Free Press, 2004), in its American chapters; and David M. Kennedy, *Freedom from Fear: The American People in Depression and War* (New York: Oxford University Press, 1999), chaps. 1–12.

6. Marriner S. Eccles, *Beckoning Frontiers* (New York: Knopf, 1951), 95. Walter Lippmann, perhaps the leading political commentator of his time, made the same point less kindly: "Franklin D. Roosevelt is no crusader. He is no tribune of the people. He is no enemy of entrenched privilege. He is a pleasant man who, without any important qualifications for the office, would very much like to be President" (*New York Times*, September 4, 1932, quoted in Hamby, *For the Survival of Democracy*, 100).

7. Lewis L. Gould, *The Grand Old Party: A History of the Republicans* (New York: Random House, 2003), esp. chaps. 7 and 8; John Gerring, *Party Ideologies in America, 1828–1996* (Cambridge: Cambridge University Press, 1998), pts. 2 and 3.

8. Regionally, "Southern Democrats" here represent the eleven states of the original Confederacy, hence Alabama, Arkansas, Florida, Georgia, Louisiana, Mississippi, North Carolina, South Carolina, Tennessee, Texas, and Virginia. "Northern Democrats" represent all other states. "Northeastern Republicans" represent the New England and Middle Atlantic states, hence Connecticut, Delaware, Massachusetts, Maine, Maryland, New Hampshire, New Jersey, New York, Pennsylvania, Rhode Island, Vermont, and West Virginia. "Regular Republicans" represent all others.

9. For a concentrated overview, see Henry J. Abraham, *Justices and Presidents: A Political History of Appointments to the Supreme Court* (New York: Oxford University Press, 1974), chap. 7, "Into the Twentieth Century: From Theodore Roosevelt to Franklin Roosevelt, 1901–1933."

10. On the abortive World Economic Conference, see Kenneth S. Davis, *FDR: The New Deal Years, 1933–1937* (New York: Random House, 1979), chap. 5, "The Wrecking of the London Conference."

11. Susan Estabrook Kennedy, *The Banking Crisis of 1933* (Lexington: University Press of Kentucky, 1973), chap. 7, "Enter Roosevelt."

12. Quoted in Anthony J. Badger, *FDR: The First Hundred Days* (New York: Hill & Wang, 2008), 40–41.

13. A helpful and concise assembly is Hamby, *For the Survival of Democracy*, 127–129. A fuller survey is Badger, *FDR.*

14. The full and extended story is found in Stephen R. Ortiz, *Beyond the Bonus March and the GI Bill: How Veterans Politics Shaped the New Deal Era* (New York: New York University Press, 2010).

15. Ortiz argues that the bill was not only democratically responsive but economically *and politically* successful: "The passing of the Bonus in 1936 may well have been the most successful piece of 'Second' New Deal legislation, even if FDR did veto it. When veterans began receiving payments in June, nearly $2 billion flowed into the national economy, making 1936 the best economic year since the Crash. This fiscal stimulus boosted the economy in time for the 1936 election" (*Beyond the Bonus March and the GI Bill,* 11).

16. The reactive, hurried, and jerry-built character of this otherwise operational keystone to the New Deal comes through in most major accounts: Kennedy, *Freedom from Fear,* 149–153; Barone, *Our Country,* 67–68; as well as William E. Leuchtenburg, *Franklin D. Roosevelt and the New Deal, 1932–1940* (New York: Harper & Row, 1963), 55–58.

17. Kennedy, *Freedom from Fear,* 257–278; Hamby, *For the Survival of Democracy,* 298–306.

18. Edwin Amenta, *Bold Relief: The Institutional Origins of American Social Policy* (Princeton, NJ: Princeton University Press, 1998), 4–5. For an analysis of the last eighty years of American politics, it is worth quoting the larger paradox within which Amenta frames this development: "And so this historical episode

suggests two paradoxes. The far-reaching policy of work and relief challenged the conventional wisdom about American social policy. The United States became a world leader in public social spending during the Depression and did so on the basis of work and relief, not social insurance. Also, the failure to complete a work and relief state confounds standard social science arguments about the impact of crises, political regimes, and state bureaucrats and revenues on social policy" (7).

19. For the full running story, see Kennedy *Freedom from Fear*, 324–338; Hamby, *For the Survival of Democracy*, 288–291, 335–338, 346–352; and William E. Leuchtenburg, *The Supreme Court Reborn: The Constitutional Revolution in the Age of Roosevelt* (New York: Oxford University Press, 1995), esp. chap. 4, "The Origins of Franklin D. Roosevelt's 'Court-Packing' Plan," and chap. 5, "FDR's 'Court-Packing' Plan."

20. 295 U.S. 495 (1935), argued May 2–3, 1935; decided May 27, 1935, by a vote of 9–0.

21. U.S. 1 (1936), argued December 9–10, 1935; decided January 6, 1936, by a vote of 6–3.

22. U.S. 587 (1936), argued April 28–29, 1936; decided June 1, 1936, by a vote of 5–4.

23. The famous wisecrack from James A. Farley, manager of the Roosevelt campaign—"As Maine goes, so goes Vermont"—was saluted at the time as testament to the scale of the apparent affirmation of the Roosevelt presidency. The old saw that gave this wisecrack its pungency, "As Maine goes, so goes the nation," was thereby transformed into a laughingstock, though Maine had never been an especially distinctive bellwether, beyond being a Republican state in a Republican era before 1932. Even its hypothetical priority was due to the fact that bad weather and bad communication had long caused the state to hold its general election in September rather than the November favored by everyone else. In any case, in hindsight, the new version—the Farley wisecrack—now serves every bit as much as a symbolic tribute to the confidence, afterward treated as hubris by many historians, with which Roosevelt undertook his Court-packing effort.

24. 300 U.S. 379 (1936), argued December 16–17, 1936; decided March 29, 1937, by a vote of 5–4.

25. What had been a 5–4 vote against an effectively identical law in New York became a 5–4 vote in favor of such a law in Washington, with Justice Owen Roberts generating the shift. In its time, this was widely viewed as Roberts responding to the Court-packing efforts of Roosevelt, but subsequent research would show that Roberts had already revealed his change of position to judicial colleagues in the late fall.

26. 301 U.S. 1 (1937), argued February 10–11, 1937; decided April 12, 1937, by a vote of 5–4.

27. The comprehensive story in full sweep is Peri E. Arnold, *Making the Managerial Presidency: Comprehensive Reorganization Planning, 1905–1980* (Princeton, NJ: Princeton University Press, 1986), esp. chap. 4, "Managing the New Deal." Of the policy-making process of the time, with regard to governmental reorga-

nization as with so much else, Arnold notes: "But what distinguished the use of executive reorganization planning in the New Deal was that it was thoroughly a presidential tool. For the first time in the history of reorganization planning, its goals were those imposed by a president" (81).

Chapter 2. The Long Arm of the New Deal

1. Among many on 1946 and 1948, see Alonzo L. Hamby, *Man of the People: The Life of Harry S. Truman* (New York: Oxford University Press, 1995). Among many on 1952 and 1954, see Stephen E. Ambrose, *Eisenhower the President*, vol. 2, *1952–1969* (London: George Allen and Unwin, 1984).

2. Herbert H. Hyman, *Taking Society's Measure: A Personal History of Survey Research* (New York: Russell Sage Foundation, 1991).

3. The measure was introduced in canonical form in Angus Campbell, Philip E. Converse, Warren E. Miller, and Donald E. Stokes, *The American Voter* (New York: Wiley, 1960), 122. The authors trace the concept itself back to George Belknap and Angus Campbell, "Political Party Identification and Attitudes toward Foreign Policy," *Public Opinion Quarterly* 15 (1952): 601–623.

4. A. James Reichley, *The Life of the Parties: A History of American Political Parties* (New York: Free Press, 1992); Alan Ware, *The Democratic Party Heads North, 1877–1962* (Cambridge: Cambridge University Press, 2006); Richard L. Rubin, *Party Dynamics: The Democratic Coalition and the Politics of Change* (New York: Oxford University Press, 1976).

5. For an early preview, see James Q. Wilson, *The Amateur Democrat: Club Politics in Three Cities* (Chicago: University of Chicago Press, 1966).

6. V. O. Key Jr., *Southern Politics in State and Nation* (New York: Knopf, 1949); Nicol C. Rae, *Southern Democrats* (New York: Oxford University Press, 1994); Stanley P. Berard, *Southern Democrats in the U.S. House Of Representatives* (Norman: University of Oklahoma Press, 2001).

7. Lewis L. Gould, *The Grand Old Party: A History of the Republicans* (New York: Random House, 2003), esp. chaps. 8 and 9; Robert Mason, *The Republican Party and American Politics from Hoover to Reagan* (Cambridge: Cambridge University Press, 2012), esp. chaps. 1–4; Charles O. Jones, *The Republican Party in American Politics* (New York: Macmillan, 1965). For generic problems of the minority party, which the Republicans clearly were during the Late New Deal Era, see Jones, *The Minority Party in Congress* (Boston: Little, Brown, 1970), and Matthew N. Green, *Underdog Politics: The Minority Party in the U.S. House of Representatives* (New Haven, CT: Yale University Press, 2015).

8. Ronald L. Feinman, *Twilight of Progressivism: The Western Republican Senators and the New Deal* (Baltimore: Johns Hopkins University Press, 1981); John Gerring, *Party Ideologies in America, 1828–1996* (Cambridge: Cambridge University Press, 1998); Daniel DiSalvo, *Agents of Change: Party Factions in American Politics, 1868–2012* (New York: Oxford University Press, 2012).

9. Michael Barone, *Our Country: The Shaping of America from Roosevelt to Reagan* (New York: Free Press, 1990), tells this story well in chaps. 9, 11, and 13.

10. The following were helpful in aligning the Late New Deal Era with the analytic framework used here: Barone, *Our Country*, chaps. 15–41; John Morton Blum, *Years of Discord: American Politics and Society, 1961–1974* (New York: Norton, 1991), chaps. 1–10; and James T. Patterson, *Grand Expectations: The United States, 1945–1974* (New York: Oxford University Press, 1996), chaps. 1–21.

11. See, among many, James L. Sundquist, *Politics and Policy: The Eisenhower, Kennedy, and Johnson Years* (Washington, DC: Brookings Institution, 1968), pt. 1; Robert X. Browning, *Politics and Social Welfare Policy in the United States* (Knoxville: University of Tennessee Press, 1986); James T. Patterson, *America's Struggle against Poverty, 1900–1985* (Cambridge, MA: Harvard University Press, 1986); and John F. Witte, *The Politics and Development of the Income Tax* (Madison: University of Wisconsin Press, 1985).

12. James T. Patterson, *Congressional Conservatism and the New Deal* (Lexington: University Press of Kentucky, 1967); John F. Manley, "The Conservative Coalition in Congress," *American Behavioral Scientist* 17 (1973): 223–247; David W. Brady and Charles S. Bullock III, "Is There a Conservative Coalition in the House?," *Journal of Politics* 42 (1980): 549–559; Mack C. Shelley II, *The Permanent Majority: The Conservative Coalition in the United States Congress* (University: University of Alabama Press, 1983).

13. David M. Kennedy, *Freedom from Fear: The American People in Depression and War* (New York: Oxford University Press, 1999); John Lewis Gaddis, *The Cold War* (London: Penguin, 2007); Robert A. Pastor, *Congress and the Politics of U.S. Foreign Economic Policy, 1929–1976* (Berkeley: University of California Press, 1980); Alonzo L. Hamby, *The Imperial Years: The United States since 1939* (New York: Weybright and Talley, 1976).

14. John Lewis Gaddis, *The United States and the Origins of the Cold War, 1941–1947* (New York: Columbia University Press, 1972).

15. The internationalism of the Southern Democrats as a faction comes through clearly in Ira Katznelson, *Fear Itself: The New Deal and the Origins of Our Time* (New York: Norton, 2013). For World War II, see chap. 8, "The First Crusade"; for the Cold War, see chap. 12, "Armed and Loyal."

16. Wayne S. Cole, *Roosevelt and the Isolationists, 1932–1945* (Lincoln: University of Nebraska Press, 1983); Justus D. Doenecke, *Not to the Swift: The Old Isolationists in the Cold War Era* (Lewisburg, PA: Bucknell University Press, 1979).

17. That foundational work on party identification in the United States, Campbell et al., *American Voter*, already contained the story in chap. 3, "Perceptions of the Parties and Candidates."

18. Alonzo L. Hamby, *For the Survival of Democracy: Franklin Roosevelt and the World Crisis of the 1930s* (New York: Free Press, 2004), 344–346.

19. Jeffery A. Jenkins and Justin Peck, "Building toward Major Policy Change: Congressional Action on Civil Rights, 1941–1950," *Law and History Review* 31 (2013): 139–198; Michael J. Klarman, *From Jim Crow to Civil Rights: The Supreme Court in the Struggle for Racial Equality* (New York: Oxford University Press, 2004), chaps. 4–7; Richard M. Valelly, *The Two Reconstructions: The Struggle for Black Enfranchisement* (Chicago: University of Chicago Press, 2004), chaps.

7–10; Hugh Davis Graham, *The Civil Rights Era: Origins and Development of National Policy, 1960–1972* (New York: Oxford University Press, 1990), chaps. 1–7.

20. Edward G. Carmines and James A. Stimson, *Issue Evolution: Race and the Transformation of American Politics* (Princeton, NJ: Princeton University Press, 1989), chap. 6, "Mobilizing Change in Mass Identifications," esp. figures 6.4, 6.5, and 6.6.

21. U.S. 649 (1944), argued November 10 & 12, 1943; reargued January 12, 1944; decided April 3, 1944, by a vote of 8–1.

22. U.S. 537 (1896), argued April 13, 1896; decided May 18, 1896, by a vote of 7–1.

23. U.S. 483 (1954), argued December 9, 1952; reargued December 8, 1953; decided May 17, 1954, by a vote of 9–0; and 349 U.S. 294 (1955), reargued April 11–14, 1954, on the question of relief; decided May 31, 1955, by a vote of 9–0.

24. James T. Patterson, *Brown v. Board of Education: A Civil Rights Milestone and Its Troubled Legacy* (New York: Oxford University Press, 2001), chaps. 1–6.

25. A summary overview is Henry J. Abraham, *Justices and Presidents: A Political History of Appointments to the Supreme Court* (New York: Oxford University Press, 1974), chaps. 8 and 9.

26. Hamby, *The Imperial Years*, 192.

27. David R. Mayhew, *Divided We Govern: Party Control, Lawmaking, and Investigations, 1946–1990* (New Haven, CT: Yale University Press, 1991), table 4.1, 52–73, as supplemented by "List of Important Enactments by Congress, 1991–2012," developed by Mayhew and compiled by R. Douglas Arnold, some of which is included in the second edition of *Divided We Govern* (2005), the rest of which can be found on Mayhew's website at Yale University.

28. These are labeled "Sweep One" and "Sweep Two" and are defined prospectively at pages 37–44 and 44–50.

29. The wartime years are covered in Barone, *Our Country*, chaps. 14–17, and Kennedy, *Freedom from Fear*, chaps. 11–14. Additionally helpful is Nancy Beck Young, *Why We Fight: Congress and the Politics of World War II* (Lawrence: University Press of Kansas, 2013).

30. Kennedy, *Freedom from Fear*, 783.

31. R. Alton Lee, *Truman and Taft-Hartley: A Question of Mandate* (Lexington: University Press of Kentucky, 1966).

32. "Housing Act of 1949 S1070—P.L. 171," in *CQ Almanac 1949*, 5th ed. (Washington, DC: Congressional Quarterly, 1950), 273–286.

33. "Congress Enacts Area Redevelopment Bill," in *CQ Almanac 1961*, 17th ed. (Washington, DC: Congressional Quarterly, 1961), 247–256.

34. For the comprehensive story, see Paul Manna, *School's In: Federalism and the National Education Agenda* (Washington, DC: Georgetown University Press, 2006), and Gareth Davies, *See Government Grow: Education Politics from Johnson to Reagan* (Lawrence: University Press of Kansas, 2007).

35. The Senate was once again a policy afterthought, with Northern Democrats 42–0, Southern Democrats 13–3, Northeastern Republicans 9–1, and Regular Republicans 9–13, for a grand total of 73–18.

36. See especially Robert A. Divine, *The Illusion of Neutrality* (Chicago: University of Chicago Press, 1962), chaps. 8 and 9.

37. Hamby, *The Imperial Years*, esp. the section titled "Containment in Europe," 124–130. Even in its time, the Truman Doctrine was viewed by all the major players as a huge turning point in the American role in the world. *Congressional Quarterly* noted that almost every senator and representative spoke to the matter from the floor during the legislative debate. "Aid to Greece and Turkey," in *CQ Almanac 1947*, 3rd ed. (Washington, DC: Congressional Quarterly, 1948), 247–262.

38. Richard E. Neustadt, "Congress and the Fair Deal: A Legislative Assessment," in *Harry S. Truman and the Fair Deal*, ed. Alonzo L. Hamby (Lexington, MA: Heath, 1974), 16–17.

39. This led to the particularistic slogan for campaigning in minority areas in New York at the presidential election of 1956: "A vote for Stevenson is a vote for Eastland." Cited in Sundquist, *Politics and Policy*, 230.

40. "Congress Approves Civil Rights Act of 1957," in *CQ Almanac 1957*, 13th ed. (Washington, DC: Congressional Quarterly, 1958), 553–569; Sundquist, *Politics and Policy*, chap. 6, "For Minority Equal Rights," esp. 222–238.

41. "Civil Rights Act of 1964," in *CQ Almanac 1964*, 20th ed. (Washington, DC: Congressional Quarterly, 1965), 338–353, but especially Graham, *Civil Rights Era*, chap. 5, "The Civil Rights Act of 1964."

42. Smith did introduce an intendedly disruptive gambit with lasting consequences, by adding "sex" to the classes of individuals protected by the act; when the congressional leadership and the White House tried to remove this, a phalanx of older, white, conservative, male, Southern Democrats saved it on the floor.

43. There was more motion inside those two votes than the aggregates might suggest, with two Democrats voting against cloture but for passage; two Republicans voting for cloture but against passage; and two Republicans joining those two switching Democrats, against cloture but for passage.

44. "Congress Enacts Open Housing Legislation," in *CQ Almanac 1968*, 24th ed. (Washington, DC: Congressional Quarterly, 1969), 152–165; Graham, *Civil Rights Era*, chap. 10, "From Ghetto Riots to Open Housing, 1966–1968."

45. Thomas L. Karnes, *Asphalt and Politics: A History of the American Highway System* (Jefferson, NC: McFarland, 2009), esp. 87–93; Mark H. Rose and Raymond A. Mohl, *Interstate: Highway Politics and Policy since 1939* (Knoxville: University of Tennessee Press, 1979), chaps. 6 and 7.

46. An especially rich chronicle is Duane Tananbaum, *The Bricker Amendment Controversy: A Test of Eisenhower's Leadership* (Ithaca, NY: Cornell University Press, 1988).

47. In a combination of monumentality and farce, the deciding vote was cast by Harley Kilgore, Democratic senator from West Virginia, who had to be extracted from a nearby tavern and assisted to the Senate floor, where he may or may not actually have spoken the recorded "nay." Yet opponents knew that his intended vote would be "no" and strongly suspected that the five nonvoters

would make the outcome worse, not better, should the measure be called up again.

48. David B. Truman, *The Congressional Party: A Case Study* (New York: Wiley, 1959).

49. Richard F. Fenno Jr., *The Power of the Purse: Appropriations Politics in Congress* (Boston: Little, Brown, 1966).

50. Aaron Wildavsky, *The Politics of the Budgetary Process* (Boston: Little, Brown, 1964), 62.

51. For the methodology itself, see Truman, *Congressional Party*, 45–48, plus the appendix, "The Analysis Procedure."

52. Truman, *Congressional Party*, 59, 61.

53. Ibid., 80.

54. Fenno, *Power of the Purse*, xiii.

55. Ibid., 410.

56. Wildavsky, *Politics of the Budgetary Process*, 130–131.

57. Otto A. Davis, M. A. H. Dempster, and Aaron Wildavsky, "A Theory of the Budgetary Process," *American Political Science Review* 60 (1966): 529–547.

58. Otto A. Davis, M. A. H. Dempster, and Aaron Wildavsky, "Towards a Predictive Theory of Government Expenditure: U.S. Domestic Appropriations," *British Journal of Political Science* 4 (1974): 419–452.

59. Wildavsky, *Politics of the Budgetary Process*, 131.

Chapter 3. The Rise of Participatory Politics

1. Kevin Phillips claimed to know, in *The Emerging Republican Majority* (New Rochelle, NY: Arlington House, 1969), but he too would ultimately prove to have the story wrong.

2. A retrospective look at an old era coming apart—comprehensive in its focus and almost Shakespearean in its tragic overtones—is Gareth Davies, *From Opportunity to Entitlement: The Transformation and Decline of Great Society Liberalism* (Lawrence: University Press of Kansas, 1996). See also Iwan W. Morgan, *Beyond the Liberal Consensus: A Political History of the United States since 1965* (New York: St. Martin's, 1994), esp. chap. 2, "The Unraveling of the Liberal Consensus, 1965–1968."

3. One of the earliest scholars to recognize the arrival of a new period, with all its associated interpretive problems, was Everett Carll Ladd Jr., most pointedly in "Liberalism Upside Down: The Inversion of the New Deal Order," *Political Science Quarterly* 91 (1976–1977): 577–600.

4. The landmark work for this view is Bruce E. Keith, David B. Magleby, Candice J. Nelson, Elizabeth Orr, Mark C. Westlye, and Raymond E. Wolfinger, *The Myth of the Independent Voter* (Berkeley: University of California Press, 1992).

5. Pär Jason Engle and Byron E. Shafer, "Where Are We in History? 2010 in the Longest Run," *Forum* 8, no. 4 (2010): article 1.

6. To say the same thing in a more methodologically provocative fashion,

for the entire Era of Divided Government, with the lone exception of that one-term "Carter accidency," whichever party had the fewer self-identified adherents always won the major national election in the United States.

7. The story is richly captured in David R. Mayhew, *Placing Parties in American Politics: Organization, Electoral Settings, and Government Activity in the Twentieth Century* (Princeton, NJ: Princeton University Press, 1986), about which much more later.

8. Peter McCaffery, *When Bosses Ruled Philadelphia: The Emergence of the Republican Machine, 1867–1933* (University Park: Pennsylvania State University Press, 1993). For the more general background to organized Republican politics, see A. James Reichley, *The Life of the Parties: A History of American Political Parties* (New York: Free Press, 1992), esp. chap. 7, "Machine Politics: The Gilded Age."

9. The metaphor belongs to Alan Ware in *The Breakdown of Democratic Party Organization, 1940–1980* (Oxford: Clarendon Press, 1985), about which much more later as well.

10. On the theoretical front, see Herbert D. Croly, *Progressive Democracy* (New York: Macmillan, 1915). On the practical point, and very much opposed to Croly and the Progressives, see Henry Jones Ford, *The Rise and Growth of American Politics: A Sketch of Constitutional Development* (New York: Macmillan, 1898).

11. James Q. Wilson, *Political Organizations* (New York: Basic Books, 1973).

12. Ware, *Breakdown of Democratic Party Organization.*

13. Mayhew, *Placing Parties in American Politics.*

14. Peter B. Clark and James Q. Wilson, "Incentive Systems: A Theory of Organizations," *Administrative Science Quarterly* 6 (1961): 129–166.

15. Wilson, *Political Organizations*, 95.

16. Ibid., 97–112.

17. Ibid., 96.

18. Ware, *Breakdown of Democratic Party Organization*, 42.

19. Ibid., 241.

20. Mayhew, *Placing Parties in American Politics*, 5.

21. Ibid., 19–20.

22. Ware, *Breakdown of Democratic Party Organization*, chap. 3, "1940–1960: Indian Summer for the Parties?"; Mayhew, *Placing Parties in American Politics*, 225.

23. Mayhew, *Placing Parties in American Politics*, 22, 199. Note that the minority of states with TPOs at the 1950 census contained a solid majority of the national population and were still only a narrow minority of the total twenty years later.

24. As it turns out, the radical diminution of the TPOs will also be crucial to the character of the Era of Partisan Volatility: hence High New Deal plus Late New Deal versus Divided Government plus Partisan Volatility with regard to party structure.

25. Mayhew, *Placing Parties in American Politics*, 318, 321.

26. For the argument elaborated, see Sidney M. Milkis, *The President and the Parties: The Transformation of the American Party System since the New Deal* (New

York: Oxford University Press, 1993). For its application to this reform surge, see Milkis, *Political Parties and Constitutional Government: Remaking American Democracy* (Baltimore: Johns Hopkins University Press, 1999), chap. 5, "Rewriting American Politics."

27. Among many, William J. Crotty, *Decision for the Democrats: Reforming the Party Structure* (Baltimore: Johns Hopkins University Press, 1978). For the larger philosophical framework within which the reformers operated, see James W. Ceaser, *Presidential Selection: Theory and Development* (Princeton, NJ: Princeton University Press, 1979).

28. The root and branch story can be found in Byron E. Shafer, *Quiet Revolution: The Struggle for the Democratic Party and the Shaping of Post-reform Politics* (New York: Russell Sage Foundation, 1983).

29. Table 3.1 is taken directly from Byron E. Shafer, *Bifurcated Politics: Evolution and Reform in the National Party Convention* (Cambridge, MA: Harvard University Press, 1988), 86, 87, with the later addition of 2008.

30. For a richly detailed snapshot of the situation in 1952, see Paul T. David, Malcolm Moos, and Ralph M. Goldman, *Presidential Nominating Politics in 1952*, 5 vols. (Baltimore: Johns Hopkins University Press, 1954).

31. For a condensed summary, see David W. Rohde, *Parties and Leaders in the Postreform House* (Chicago: University of Chicago Press, 1991), esp. chap. 3, "Reform and Its Consequences: A Closer Look." For the full account, see Leroy N. Rieselbach, *Congressional Reform* (Washington, DC: CQ Press, 1986), and Julian E. Zelizer, *On Capitol Hill: The Struggle to Reform Congress and Its Consequences, 1948–2000* (Cambridge: Cambridge University Press, 2004).

32. A comprehensive overview is William T. Gormley Jr., *Taming the Bureaucracy: Muscles, Prayers, and Other Strategies* (Princeton, NJ: Princeton University Press, 1989), esp. chap. 2, "Institutional Reform."

33. Many analysts at the time did recognize *something* resembling this cluster. One of the earliest and most influential attempts to address it was Richard M. Scammon and Ben J. Wattenberg, *The Real Majority* (New York: Coward-McCann, 1970).

34. One of the most consistent contributors to this way of thinking about American politics—via a two-dimensional framework embodying economics and culture—is Edward Carmines. His review of the potential payoff from doing so is Edward G. Carmines and Michael W. Wagner, "Political Issues and Partisan Alignments: Assessing the Issue Evolution Perspective," *Annual Review of Political Science* 10 (2006): 67–81.

35. Charles DeBenedetti, *An American Ordeal: The Antiwar Movement of the Vietnam Era* (Syracuse, NY: Syracuse University Press, 1990).

36. Ware goes on to underline the fact that the main actors in the antiwar movement were actually *antiparty* in traditional terms: "Nevertheless, there are two important respects in which these issue conflicts did harm the Democratic Party. First, they helped to make issue-oriented activists much more skeptical about the value of party; what occurred in the 1960s was issue-activism that was not party-oriented, as it was in the 1950s, but which was prepared to use party institutions for realizing objectives as, and when, they seemed useful. . . .

Secondly, the issue conflicts actually revived long-standing anti-party sentiments in America, sentiments which were minority ones in the amateur Democratic movement of the 1950s, but which became more apparent in the late 1960s" (Ware, *Breakdown of the Democratic Party*, 246–247).

37. Samuel P. Hays, *Beauty, Health, and Permanence: Environmental Politics in the United States, 1955–1985* (Chicago: University of Chicago Press, 1987), has a focus encompassing the whole environmental movement. In their survey of issue-oriented interest groups, Frank R. Baumgartner and Bryan D. Jones, *Agendas and Instability in American Politics* (Chicago: University of Chicago Press, 1993), find that "the largest, most visible, and fastest growing of the citizens' sector is the environmental movement" (184). For the women's movement, see Anne N. Costain, *Inviting Women's Rebellion: A Political Process Interpretation of the Women's Movement* (Baltimore: Johns Hopkins University Press, 1992).

38. The latter were beginning to reengage seriously by the late 1970s, though it was the later 1980s before they were fully recognized major political players and the early 1990s before they had acquired systematic scholarly attention. By then—the early years of the Era of Partisan Volatility—they were an ideological counterweight to those social movements that had been central to the newly participatory politics of the previous era, especially in the realm of cultural values. Clyde Wilcox, *God's Warriors: The Christian Right in Twentieth-Century America* (Baltimore: Johns Hopkins University Press, 1992); Duane Murray Oldfield, *The Right and the Righteous: The Christian Right Confronts the Republican Party* (Lanham, MD: Rowman & Littlefield, 1996).

39. *Engel v. Vitale*, 370 U.S. 412 (1962); argued April 3, 1962; decided June 25, 1962, by 7–1. *Abington School District v. Schempp* and *Murray v. Curlett*, argued February 27–28, 1963; decided June 17, 1963, 8–1. For poll results on the decision, see *Oxford Companion to the Supreme Court of the United States*, ed. Kermit L. Hall (Oxford: Oxford University Press, 1992), 1.

40. *Gideon v. Wainwright*, 372 U.S. 335 (1963); argued January 15, 1963; decided March 18, 1963, by 9–0. *Miranda v. Arizona*, 384 U.S. 436 (1966); argued February 28, 1966; decided June 13, 1966, by 5–4. The quote about impact is from *Oxford Companion to the Supreme Court of the United* States, 552.

41. *Green v. County School Board of New Kent County*, 391 U.S. 430 (1968); argued April 3, 1968; decided May 27, 1968, by 9–0. *Swann v. Charlotte-Mecklenberg Board of Education*, 401 U.S. 1 (1971); argued October 12, 1970; decided April 30, 1971, by 9–0.

42. *Griswold v. Connecticut*, 381 U.S. 479 (1965); argued March 29, 1965; decided June 7, 1965, by 7–2. *Roe v. Wade*, 410 U.S. 113 (1973); argued December 13, 1971; reargued October 11, 1972; decided January 22, 1972, by 7–2.

43. Jeffrey Berry, the great chronicler of the rise of citizens groups in this period, puts the matter succinctly for the Democrats: "But liberalism is not dead. Indeed, it thrives. Liberalism, however, changed its stripes. Today, American liberalism stresses culture, status, life-style, morality, and rights—post-materialism. Traditional liberalism, concerned with issues of economic equality and promoted primarily by unions and groups sympathetic to the poor,

is in retreat" (*The New Liberalism: The Rising Power of Citizen Groups* [Washington, DC: Brookings Institution, 1999]).

44. Table 3.2 is taken directly from Byron E. Shafer, "The Pure Partisan Institution: National Party Conventions as Research Sites," in *Oxford Handbook of American Political Parties and Interest Groups*, ed. L. Sandy Maisel (New York: Oxford University Press, 2010), 279. The data for 1956 are from Herbert Mc-Closky, Paul J. Hoffman, and Rosemary O'Hara, "Issue Conflict and Consensus among Party Leaders and Followers," *American Political Science Review* 52 (1958): 27–45.

45. Figure 3.4 is taken directly from Byron E. Shafer and William J. M. Claggett, *The Two Majorities: The Issue Context of Modern American Politics* (Baltimore: Johns Hopkins University Press, 1995), 48, 49. Details of the underlying survey can be found in the technical appendix to Gallup Organization Staff, eds., *The People, the Press, and Politics: The Times Mirror Study of the American Electorate* (Reading, MA: Addison-Wesley, 1988).

46. One set of attempts to work with these distinctions and interpret contemporary politics through them is collected in Byron E. Shafer, *The Two Majorities and the Puzzle of Modern American Politics* (Lawrence: University Press of Kansas, 2003).

47. William J. M. Claggett and Byron E. Shafer, *The American Public Mind: The Issue Structure of Mass Politics in the Postwar United States* (New York: Cambridge University Press, 2010), 228–232.

48. The most lasting of these was public order, often referenced as "crime in the streets." For an extended period, the issue proved easy for Republicans, hard for Democrats—and easy for the general public. An early underlining of the *potential* of the issue was James Q. Wilson, "Crime in the Streets," *Public Interest* 5 (1966): 26–35. For its realization, see Michael W. Flamm, *Law and Order: Street Crime, Civil Unrest, and the Crisis of Liberalism in the 1960s* (New York: Columbia University Press, 2005).

49. James L. Sundquist, an early nonadmirer of divided government, continued to articulate this alleged impossibility of policy-making in its era, an argument gathered in his *Constitutional Reform and Effective Government* (Washington, DC: Brookings Institution, 1986). That argument gets a second look in the conclusion to this book.

50. Philip G. Joyce, *The Congressional Budget Office: Honest Numbers, Power, and Policy-making* (Washington, DC: Georgetown University Press, 2011).

51. Robert Mason, *Richard Nixon and the Quest for a New Republican Majority* (Chapel Hill: University of North Carolina Press, 2004).

52. And that one was the Economic Stabilization Act of 1970, when a Democratic House gave a Republican president powers to impose wage and price controls, *powers that he did not want.*

53. David R. Mayhew, *Divided We Govern: Party Control, Lawmaking, and Investigations, 1946–1990* (New Haven, CT: Yale University Press, 1991).

54. Further implicit testimony to the power of these two themes for public policy in the Era of Divided Government lies in the fact that first the environment and then the economy came to require an "impact statement" with the

proposal of any new legislation anywhere, the sole realms where this was true. See Gormley, *Taming the Bureaucracy*, chap. 2, "Institutional Reform."

55. Samuel Hays, in *Beauty, Health, and Permanence*, offers a grudging but impressive tribute to Nixon's environmental productivity: Environmental Protection Agency, 1970; National Highway Traffic Safety Administration, 1970; Occupational Health and Safety Administration, 1971; Consumer Product Safety Commission, 1972; Mining Enforcement and Safety Administration, 1973; Nuclear Regulatory Commission, 1973; Federal Energy Administration, 1973.

56. Martha Derthick and Paul J. Quirk, *The Politics of Deregulation* (Washington, DC: Brookings Institution, 1985), offer a less grudging but equally impressive tribute to Carter's deregulatory productivity: Airline Deregulation Act of 1978; Decontrol of Natural Gas Prices in 1978; Motor Carrier Act of 1980; autonomous actions by the Federal Communications Commission, driven especially by the Second Computer Inquiry in 1980; Depository Institutions and Monetary Control Act of 1980; Trucking Deregulation Act of 1980; and Staggers Rail Act of 1980.

57. Hays, *Beauty, Health, and Permanence*, brings these elements together.

58. Dennis W. Johnson, *The Laws That Shaped America: Fifteen Acts of Congress and Their Lasting Impact* (New York: Routledge, 2009), makes NEPA one of its fifteen laws, at chap. 12, "Protecting the Environment."

59. "Environmental Quality Council," in *CQ Almanac 1969*, 25th ed. (Washington, DC: Congressional Quarterly, 1970), 525–527; Richard A. Liroff, *A National Policy for the Environment: NEPA and Its Aftermath* (Bloomington: Indiana University Press, 1976), esp. chap. 2, "Legislative History of NEPA."

60. John C. Whitaker, *Striking a Balance: Environment and Natural Resource Policy in the Nixon-Ford Years* (Washington, DC: American Enterprise Institute, 1976), 27.

61. Gormley, *Taming the Bureaucracy*, has that story.

62. "Clean Air Bill Cleared with Auto Emission Deadline," in *CQ Almanac 1970*, 26th ed. (Washington, DC: Congressional Quarterly, 1971), 472–486; Charles O. Jones, *Clean Air: The Policies and Politics of Pollution Control* (Pittsburgh: University of Pittsburgh Press, 1975), chap. 7, "Speculative Augmentation in Washington, 1970."

63. Commentators at the time made much of his exclusion from the signing ceremony of Edmund Muskie, Democratic senator from Maine, who had managed the Senate bill but was already the apparent front-runner for the Democratic presidential nomination of 1972.

64. For a comprehensive overview, see Robert M. Collins, *More: The Politics of Economic Growth in Postwar America* (Oxford: Oxford University Press, 2000). For the individual administrations, see Allen J. Matusow, *Nixon's Economy: Booms, Busts, Dollars, and Votes* (Lawrence: University Press of Kansas, 1998); W. Carl Biven, *Jimmy Carter's Economy: Policy in an Age of Limits* (Chapel Hill: University of North Carolina Press, 2002); John W. Sloan, *The Reagan Effect: Economics and Presidential Leadership* (Lawrence: University Press of Kansas, 1999).

65. Indeed, in remarkably short order, public concern with stagflation produced the other great reporting requirement of the era, the economic impact

statement, with a precisely opposite ideological thrust: "In a sense, the economic impact statement was the mirror image of the environmental impact statement. While the latter required non-environmental agencies to take environmental impacts into account, the former required health and safety agencies to take non-environmental impacts into account" (Gormley, *Taming the Bureaucracy*, 52).

66. In a story not untypical of congressional policy-making, Kennedy had leveraged a comparatively obscure subcommittee chairmanship, of the Administrative Practices and Procedures Subcommittee of the Senate Judiciary Committee, into lasting influence over deregulatory policy. This did intermittently put him in tension with Senator Howard Cannon (D-NV), who was chairman of the Aviation Subcommittee of the Senate Commerce Committee, which had formal responsibility for the CAB.

67. "Congress Clears Airline Deregulation Bill," in *CQ Almanac 1978*, 34th ed.(Washington, DC: Congressional Quarterly, 1979), 496–504; Bradley Behrman, "Civil Aeronautics Board," in *The Politics of Regulation*, ed. James Q. Wilson (New York: Basic Books, 1980), 75–120; Anthony E. Brown, *The Politics of Airline Deregulation* (Knoxville: University of Tennessee Press, 1987).

68. If President Ford had secured little legislation toward his deregulatory goals, he had begun appointing sympathetic members of the CAB and ICC, and Jimmy Carter continued that trend.

69. "Congress Clears Trucking Deregulation Bill," in *CQ Almanac 1980*, 36th ed. (Washington, DC: Congressional Quarterly, 1981), 242–248; Derthick and Quirk, *Politics of Deregulation*; Dorothy Robyn, *Braking the Special Interests: Trucking Deregulation and the Politics of Policy Reform* (Chicago: University of Chicago Press, 1987).

70. Monica Prasad, "The Popular Origins of Neoliberalism in the Reagan Tax Cut of 1981," *Journal of Policy History* 24 (2012): 351–383.

71. "Congress Enacts President Reagan's Tax Plan," in *CQ Almanac 1981*, 37th ed. (Washington, DC: Congressional Quarterly, 1982), 91–104; Sloan, *Reagan Effect*, chap. 5, "The First Year: Hit the Ground Running."

72. "Reconciliation Savings: $130 Billion by 1985," in *CQ Almanac 1982*, 38th ed. (Washington, DC: Congressional Quarterly, 1983), 199–204; Sloan, *Reagan Effect*, 157, 228.

Chapter 4. A Political Structure for the Modern World

1. Scholarly analyses of this particular election would include Paul R. Abramson, John H. Aldrich, and David W. Rohde, *Change and Continuity in the 1992 Elections* (Washington, DC: CQ Press, 1994); James W. Ceaser and Andrew Busch, *Upside Down and Inside Out: The 1992 Elections and American Politics* (Lanham, MD: Rowman & Littlefield, 1993); Michael Nelson, ed., *The Elections of 1992* (Washington, DC: CQ Press, 1993); Gerald M. Pomper, ed., *The Election of 1992: Reports and Interpretations* (Chatham, NJ: Chatham House, 1993). One effort to look back at this after the fact is Ronald B. Rapoport and Walter J. Stone,

Three's a Crowd: The Dynamics of Third Parties, Ross Perot, and Republican Resurgence (Ann Arbor: University of Michigan Press, 2011).

2. This still understates electoral variation in the new period, by ignoring the difference between split control where the party of the president lacks only one versus both houses of Congress. It will be necessary to turn to this further distinction later.

3. Indeed, some of the most thoughtful and careful analyses of the Era of Divided Government arrived just as the Era of Partisan Volatility was being born, as with Gary C. Jacobson, *The Electoral Origins of Divided Government: Competition in House Elections, 1946–1988* (Boulder, CO: Westview Press, 1990); Gary W. Cox and Samuel Kernell, eds., *The Politics of Divided Government* (Boulder, CO: Westview Press, 1991); or James A. Thurber, ed., *Divided Democracy: Cooperation and Conflict between the President and Congress* (Washington, DC: CQ Press, 1991).

4. Frances E. Lee, "American Politics Is More Competitive Than Ever, and That Is Making Partisanship Worse," in *Political Polarization in American Politics*, ed. Daniel J. Hopkins and John Sides (New York: Bloomsbury, 2015), 76–79; figure 4.3 appears on page 77 of that piece.

5. Adapted from figure 4.B in Byron E. Shafer, Regina L. Wagner, and Pär Jason Engle, "The 2014 Midterm in the Longest Run: The Puzzle of a Modern Era," *Forum* 12, no. 4 (2014): article 1.

6. Those who like their analysis additionally fine-grained should note that the 2000 elections added another twist, and in that sense one further partisan mix, by offering up a 50/50 balance in the Senate that was subsequently changed to 49/51 by the defection of Senator James Jeffords (R-VT) to formal independence, thereby allowing the other party, the Democrats, to assume chamber control.

7. A diverse introduction to contemporary polarization, its creation and constitution, is Pietro S. Nivola and David W. Brady, eds., *Red and Blue Nation?*, vol. 1, *Characteristics and Consequences of America's Polarized Politics* (Washington, DC: Brookings Institution, 2006), along with Nivola and Brady, eds., *Red and Blue Nation?*, vol. 2, *Consequences and Correction of America's Polarized Politics* (Washington, DC: Brookings Institution, 2008). The Hopkins and Sides collection referenced in note 4 is a condensed but even more diverse introduction.

8. Richard Fleisher and Jon R. Bond, "The Shrinking Middle in the U.S. Congress," *British Journal of Political Science* 34 (2004): 429–451.

9. Scores and category cut-points are defined at ibid., 435. Figure 4.4 is a generous update provided by the authors in 2012.

10. A focused investigation of the specifics and their dynamic is Sean M. Theriault, *Party Polarization in Congress* (Cambridge: Cambridge University Press, 2008). For the more fine-grained politics in and around these grand trends, see James T. Patterson, *Restless Giant: The United States from Watergate to Bush v. Gore* (New York: Oxford University Press, 2005), chaps. 8–12.

11. Compare Earl Black and Merle Black, *The Rise of Southern Republicans* (Cambridge, MA: Harvard University Press, 2002), with Byron E. Shafer and Richard Johnson, *The End of Southern Exceptionalism: Class, Race, and Partisan Change in the Postwar South* (Cambridge, MA: Harvard University Press, 2006).

12. V. O. Key Jr., *Southern Politics in State and Nation* (New York: Knopf, 1949), pt. 3, "The One-Party System—Mechanisms and Procedures."

13. Tracked in Howard L. Reiter and Jeffrey M. Stonecash, *Counter Realignment: Political Change in the Northeastern United States* (New York: Cambridge University Press, 2011).

14. James Q. Wilson, *The Amateur Democrat: Club Politics in Three Cities* (Chicago: University of Chicago Press, 1966).

15. A useful tour is contained in Donald T. Critchlow, *Phyllis Schlafly and Grassroots Conservatism: A Woman's Crusade* (Princeton, NJ: Princeton University Press, 2005).

16. More generally, see Matthew Levendusky, *The Partisan Sort: How Liberals Became Democrats and Conservatives Became Republicans* (Chicago: University of Chicago Press, 2009).

17. For the aggregate details of this change, see Seth C. McKee, "Majority Black Districts, Republican Ascendancy, and Party Competition in the South, 1988–2000," *American Review of Politics* 23 (2002): 123–139. For a careful attempt to disentangle its collective causes, see Kevin A. Hill, "Does the Creation of Majority Black Districts Aid Republicans? An Analysis of the 1992 Congressional Elections in Eight Southern States," *Journal of Politics* 57 (1995): 384–401.

18. As ever, this would prove to be easier said than done, though that story itself has a partisan mottle. Richard Nixon would begin the conscious effort to "rein the Court back in," that is, to bring it more into step with public preferences. From Nixon onward, Republican presidents would get many more opportunities to appoint than their Democratic counterparts: twelve for the Republicans but only four for the Democrats. Yet all the Democratic appointees, chosen to be ideological liberals, pleased their appointers, while a solid minority of the Republican appointees, chosen to be ideological conservatives, proved to be swing voters (Justices Powell, O'Connor, and Kennedy) or even liberals (Justices Blackmun, Stevens, and Souter). And that does not count the intended Nixon nominees (Clement Haynsworth and G. Harold Carswell) and Reagan nominee (Robert Bork) who could not be confirmed.

19. Though it is difficult to imagine this counterfactual even then, which is to say: it is difficult to imagine how foreign policy could have been prevented from intruding into American politics from abroad, or how what became recognized as the civil rights revolution could have been prevented from intruding into that politics at home.

20. Thomas M. Carsey and Geoffrey Layman, "Changing Sides or Changing Minds? Party Identification and Policy Preferences in the American Electorate," *American Journal of Political Science* 50 (2006): 464–477.

21. Ibid., 472, 474.

22. Geoffrey C. Layman, Thomas M. Carsey, John C. Green, Richard Herrara, and Rosalyn Cooperman, "Activists and Conflict Extension in American Party Politics," *American Political Science Review* 104 (2010): 324–346.

23. Ibid., 324, 327.

24. Ibid., 326.

25. For some early thinking about that possibility, see William M. Lunch, *The Nationalization of American Politics* (Berkeley: University of California Press, 1987).

26. For an early presentation and the first full description of the methods behind it, see "Party Unity on Tax, Spending Issues—Less in House, More in Senate," *National Journal*, May 7, 1983, 936–952.

27. Seth E. Masket, *No Middle Ground: How Informal Party Organizations Control Nominations and Polarize Legislatures* (Ann Arbor: University of Michigan Press, 2014).

28. Alan Ware, *The Breakdown of Democratic Party Organization, 1940–1980* (Oxford: Clarendon Press, 1985).

29. David R. Mayhew, *Placing Parties in American Politics: Organization, Electoral Settings, and Government Activity in the Twentieth Century* (Princeton, NJ: Princeton University Press, 1986).

30. Masket, *No Middle Ground*, 9.

31. Mayhew, *Placing Parties in American Politics*, 185–188.

32. Ware, *The Breakdown of Democratic Party Organization*, 51–59.

33. James Q. Wilson, *Political Organizations* (New York: Basic Books, 1973), chap. 6, "Political Parties."

34. Masket, *No Middle Ground*, 193.

35. Ibid., 19.

36. Small vote discrepancies in the aggregate total for these partisan tallies, in this and subsequent examples, are due to the votes of one or two nominal partisan independents.

37. As in previous chapters, the list from David R. Mayhew, *Divided We Govern: Party Control, Lawmaking, and Investigations, 1946–1990* (New Haven, CT: Yale University Press, 1991), provides the standard for distinguishing major legislation here.

38. For the old world, see Raymond A. Bauer, Ithiel de Sola Pool, and Lewis Anthony Dexter, *American Business and Public Policy: The Politics of Foreign Trade* (New York: Atherton Press, 1964).

39. Barbara Sinclair, *Unorthodox Lawmaking: New Legislative Processes in the U.S. Congress* (Washington, DC: CQ Press, 1997).

40. The need for some escape from the conventional model of congressional policy-making—in our terms, already more appropriate to the Late New Deal Era than to the Era of Divided Government—also shines through in Kenneth A. Shepsle, "Congressional Institutions and Behavior: The Changing Textbook Congress," in *American Political Institutions and the Problems of Our Time*, ed. John E. Chubb and Paul E. Peterson (Washington, DC: Brookings Institution, 1989), 238–266.

41. In this regard, see Sarah A. Binder, *Stalemate: Causes and Consequences of Legislative Gridlock* (Washington, DC: Brookings Institution, 2003), and Gregory Koger, *Filibustering: A Political History of Obstruction in the House and the Senate* (Chicago: University of Chicago Press, 2010).

42. Sinclair, *Unorthodox Lawmaking*, 64.

43. Aaron Wildavsky, *The New Politics of the Budgetary Process* (Glenview, IL: Scott, Foresman, 1988).

44. Aaron Wildavsky and Naomi Caiden, *The New Politics of the Budgetary Process*, 4th ed. (New York: Addison-Wesley, 2001), xv–xxxiii.

45. Ibid., xxvi.

46. Ibid., xxiv–xxv.

47. Sinclair, *Unorthodox Lawmaking*, chap. 8, "Making Nonincremental Policy Change through Hyperunorthodox Procedures: Health Care Reform in 2009–2010."

48. Only to be restored by the midterm elections of 2002, which in turn underpinned the Bush tax cuts of 2003.

49. "White House, Lawmakers Agree on Extension of Bush-Era Tax Cuts," in *CQ Almanac 2010*, 66th ed. (Washington, DC: CQ–Roll Call Group, 2011), 143–145.

50. "Default Avoided at Eleventh Hour," in *CQ Almanac 2011*, 67th ed. (Washington, DC: CQ–Roll Call Group, 2012), 311–316.

51. "Last-Minute Deal Averts Fiscal Cliff, Punts Big Issues to New Congress," in *CQ Almanac 2012*, 68th ed. (Washington, DC: CQ–Roll Call Group, 2013), 73–77.

52. As in Kenneth R. Mayer, *With the Stroke of a Pen: Executive Orders and Presidential Power* (Princeton, NJ: Princeton University Press, 2001). Graham G. Dodds, *Take Up Your Pen: Unilateral Presidential Directives in American Politics* (Philadelphia: University of Pennsylvania Press, 2013), provides a tour across all of American history, implicitly reminding the reader that this institutional arrangement, like others large and small, depends heavily for its operation and its impact on its interaction with the other major influences shaping politics in any given period.

53. A development systematically pursued in Jessica Bulman-Pozen, "Partisan Federalism," *Harvard Law Review* 127 (2014): 1078–1146.

54. For arguments over whether this onward march of partisan polarization had overtaken even the mass media that covered American politics, see Matthew Levendusky, *How Partisan Media Polarize America* (Chicago: University of Chicago Press, 2013), and Kevin Arceneaux and Martin Johnson, *Changing Minds or Changing Channels? Partisan News in an Age of Choice* (Chicago: University of Chicago Press, 2013).

55. Landmarks in the inevitable debate over the representational character of all this are Morris P. Fiorina, *Disconnect: The Breakdown of Representation in American Politics* (Norman: University of Oklahoma Press, 2009), and Alan I. Abramowitz, *The Disappearing Center: Engaged Citizens, Polarization, and American Democracy* (New Haven, CT: Yale University Press, 2010).

56. For the derivation of these DW-Nominate scores, see Keith T. Poole and Howard Rosenthal, *Congress: A Political-Economic History of Roll Call Voting* (New York: Oxford University Press, 1997).

57. One could go on and on with the legislative examples of greater partisan coherence coupled with increasingly distant midpoints. Thus even the confirmation votes in the Senate for Supreme Court nominees came to give evidence

of this pattern. Scott Bassinger and Maxwell Mak, "The Changing Politics of Supreme Court Confirmation," *American Politics Research* 40 (2012): 737–763.

Conclusion

1. In the hands of Joseph Bafumi and Michael Herron, this development even acquired a distinctive moniker, "leapfrog representation," whereby congresspersons who were more extreme than their constituents and were defeated for reelection could be expected, in the Era of Partisan Volatility, to be replaced by candidates of the other party who were likewise more extreme than those same constituents. Bafumi and Herron, "Leapfrog Representation and Extremism: A Study of American Voters and Their Members of Congress," *American Political Science Review* 104 (2010): 519–542.

2. A crucial founding text is Anthony Downs, *An Economic Theory of Democracy* (New York: Harper & Row, 1957). An overview of the subsequent intellectual evolution is Roger Congleton, "The Median Voter Model," in *The Encyclopedia of Public Choice*, ed. Charles K. Rowley and Friedrich Schneider (New York: Kluwer Academic, 2004).

3. James MacGregor Burns, *The Deadlock of Democracy: Four-Party Politics in America* (Englewood Cliffs, NJ: Prentice-Hall, 1963).

4. Capitalized quotations in this section are all chapter titles from Burns's book.

5. Burns, *Deadlock of Democracy*, 260. This too was easily recognizable as another rendering of the notion of "incrementalism" that was increasingly used to describe the policy-making process of the era.

6. Ibid., 325–327.

7. Ibid., 330–332.

8. James. L. Sundquist, *Constitutional Reform and Effective Government* (Washington, DC: Brookings Institution, 1986), 276–277.

9. Ibid., 323.

10. Ibid., 323.

11. Ibid., 195. And just in case all of that somehow misfired, the fourth recommendation was that there be a process involving "a method for special elections to reconstitute a failed government" (323), where such failure included "a *systematic deadlock* between the executive and the legislative branches so severe as to cripple the capacity of the government to cope with crisis" (201).

12. Their use of a parliamentary analogy was curious in this regard, since what they really preferred was extreme presidentialism: more or less an elected prime minister who would effectively appoint the Parliament!

13. In retrospect, the available wisecrack was that those critics would finally get exactly what they desired—and deserved—in the Era of Partisan Volatility.

14. Vigorous examples included Jacob S. Hacker and Paul Pierson, *Off Center: The Republican Revolution and the Erosion of American Democracy* (New Haven, CT: Yale University Press, 2005), and Thomas E. Mann and Norman J. Ornstein, *It's Even Worse Than It Looks: How the American Constitutional System Collided with the*

New Politics of Extremism (New York: Basic Books, 2012). See also Paul Pierson and Theda Skocpol, eds., *The Transformation of American Politics: Activist Government and the Rise of Conservatism* (Princeton, NJ: Princeton University Press, 2007).

15. As with Gregory Koger, *Filibustering: A Political History of Obstruction in the House and the Senate* (Chicago: University of Chicago Press, 2010), or Sarah A. Binder, *Minority Rights, Majority Rule: Partisanship and the Development of Congress* (New York: Cambridge University Press, 1997).

16. Raymond La Raja, *Small Change: Money, Political Parties, and Campaign Finance Reform* (Ann Arbor: University of Michigan Press, 2008); Peter L. Francia, *The Financiers of Congressional Elections: Investors, Ideologues, and Intimates* (New York: Columbia University Press, 2003); Eric S. Heberlig, *Congressional Parties, Institutional Ambition, and the Financing of Majority Control* (Ann Arbor: University of Michigan Press, 2012).

17. Erik J. Engstrom, *Partisan Gerrymandering and the Construction of American Democracy* (Ann Arbor: University of Michigan Press, 2013); Mark S. Monmonier, *Bushmanders and Bullwinkles: How Politicians Manipulate Election Maps and Census Data to Win Elections* (Chicago: University of Chicago Press, 2001).

18. A frequent riposte, to the effect that the public *would* agree with the particular critic if only politics encouraged its members to see clearly, merely compounds this antidemocratic drift.

19. Some particularist critics in the current period are an obvious exception, as with Raymond J. LaRaja and Bryon F. Schaffner, *Campaign Finance and Political Polarization: When Purists Prevail* (Ann Arbor: University of Michigan Press, 2015).

20. Serious thinking about the impact of the *framework* for American politics, with an effort to distinguish this framework from "presidentialism" generally, occurs in Charles O. Jones, *The Presidency in a Separated System* (Washington, DC: Brookings Institution, 1994), and Jones, *Separate but Equal Branches: Congress and the Presidency* (Chatham, NJ: Chatham House, 1995).

21. Important pieces of the story can be found in John W. Kingdon, *Agendas, Alternatives, and Public Policy* (Boston: Little, Brown, 1984); Nelson W. Polsby, *Political Innovation in America: The Politics of Policy Initiation* (New Haven, CT: Yale University Press, 1984); Paul Burstein, *American Public Opinion, Advocacy, and Policy in Congress: What the Public Wants and What It Gets* (New York: Cambridge University Press, 2014).

22. Various approaches to thinking about such surges would include, election by election, Paul R. Abramson, John H. Aldrich, and David W. Rohde, *Change and Continuity in the 1980 Elections* (Washington, DC: CQ Press, 1982), along with regular subsequent editions; for midterm elections across the entire period, Andrew W. Busch, *Horses in Midstream: U.S. Midterm Elections and Their Consequences, 1894–1998* (Pittsburgh: University of Pittsburgh Press, 1999); and for presidential and congressional elections as a joint dynamic, James E. Campbell, *The Presidential Pulse of Congressional Elections* (Lexington: University Press of Kentucky, 1993).

23. Farther afield from these explicitly political background factors is another set of grand influences. There is always an economics to this politics.

Indeed, we are used to thinking of economic "cycles" as a continual but changing aspect of political life. There is always a social structure to politics. We are used to thinking of this as changing more slowly and in that sense being less "cyclical," though it too certainly changes over time. There are technological developments that can have major and partially autonomous impacts on economics, on social structure, and, of course, on politics. Other analysts can add other favorites: the point here is that their policy impacts can be teased out and analyzed through the more proximate influences of the intermediary structure of politics.

24. The nature of these demands and the nearly inseparable question of their effective measurement are topics that have bedeviled policy analysts for a long time. Diverse efforts to get at them would include James A. Stimson, *Public Opinion in America: Moods, Cycles, and Swings* (Boulder, CO: Westview, 1991); Robert S. Erikson, Michael B. MacKuen, and James A. Stimson, *The Macropolity* (New York: Cambridge University Press, 2002); E. Scott Adler and John D. Wilkerson, *Congress and the Politics of Problem Solving* (New York: Cambridge University Press, 2012).

25. James W. Ceaser, Andrew E. Busch, and John J. Pitney Jr., *Epic Journey: The 2008 Elections and American Politics* (Lanham, MD: Rowman & Littlefield, 2009); Dan Balz and Haynes Johnson, *The Battle for America: 2008* (New York: Viking, 2009); Michael Nelson, ed., *The Elections of 2008* (Washington, DC: CQ Press, 2010).

26. At the same time, this was also classic omnibus legislation, diagnostic of the Era of Partisan Volatility, offering extended unemployment benefits and augmented food stamps, $288 billion in tax cuts, credits for home ownership and student tuition, incentives for educational reform, plus $70 billion of incentives for the environment and energy, with a special focus on green technologies and upgrading the electricity grid.

27. The 1958 election is a major event in Nelson W. Polsby, *How Congress Evolves: Social Bases of Institutional Change* (New York: Oxford University Press, 2004).

28. Nicol C. Rae, *Conservative Reformers: The Republican Freshmen and the Lessons of the 104th Congress* (Armonk, NY: Sharpe, 1998); Richard F. Fenno Jr., *Learning to Govern: An Institutional View of the 104th Congress* (Washington, DC: Brookings Institution, 1997).

29. Two thoughtful forays into this world of denominators are John J. Coleman, "United Government, Divided Government, and Party Responsiveness," *American Political Science Review* 93 (1999): 821–836, and Sarah A. Binder, *Stalemate: Causes and Consequences of Legislative Gridlock* (Washington, DC: Brookings Institution, 2003).

30. And all this ignores the evident fact that nothing should be allowed into this denominator for any one period whose passage cannot be guaranteed in the others. Making all periods artifactually unproductive is not a step forward in scholarly understanding.

Bibliography

Abington School District v. Schempp. 374 U.S. 203 (1963).

Abraham, Henry J. *Justices and Presidents: A Political History of Appointments to the Supreme Court.* New York: Oxford University Press, 1974.

Abramowitz, Alan I. *The Disappearing Center: Engaged Citizens, Polarization, and American Democracy.* New Haven, CT: Yale University Press, 2010.

Abramson, Paul R., John H. Aldrich, and David W. Rohde. *Change and Continuity in the 1980 Elections.* Washington, DC: CQ Press, 1982.

————. *Change and Continuity in the 1992 Elections.* Washington, DC: CQ Press, 1994.

Adler, E. Scott, and John D. Wilkerson. *Congress and the Politics of Problem Solving.* New York: Cambridge University Press, 2012.

"Aid to Greece and Turkey." In *CQ Almanac 1947*, 247–262. 3rd ed. Washington, DC: Congressional Quarterly, 1948.

Ambrose, Stephen E. *Eisenhower the President.* Vol. 2, *1952–1969.* London: George Allen and Unwin, 1984.

Amenta, Edwin. *Bold Relief: The Institutional Origins of American Social Policy.* Princeton, NJ: Princeton University Press, 1998.

Andersen, Kristi L. *The Creation of a Democratic Majority, 1928–1936.* Chicago: University of Chicago Press, 1979.

Arceneaux, Kevin, and Martin Johnson. *Changing Minds or Changing Channels? Partisan News in an Age of Choice.* Chicago: University of Chicago Press, 2013.

Arnold, Peri E. *Making the Managerial Presidency: Comprehensive Reorganization Planning, 1905–1980.* Princeton, NJ: Princeton University Press, 1986.

Badger, Anthony J. *FDR: The First Hundred Days.* New York: Hill & Wang, 2008.

Bafumi, Joseph, and Michael Herron. "Leapfrog Representation and Extremism: A Study of American Voters and Their Members of Congress." *American Political Science Review* 104 (2010): 519–542.

Balz, Dan, and Haynes Johnson. *The Battle for America: 2008.* New York: Viking, 2009.

Barone, Michael. *Our Country: The Shaping of America from Roosevelt to Reagan.* New York: Free Press, 1990.

Bassinger, Scott, and Maxwell Mak. "The Changing Politics of Supreme Court Confirmation." *American Politics Research* 40 (2012): 737–763.

Bauer, Raymond A., Ithiel de Sola Pool, and Lewis Anthony Dexter. *American Business and Public Policy: The Politics of Foreign Trade.* New York: Atherton Press, 1964.

Baumgartner, Frank R., and Bryan D. Jones. *Agendas and Instability in American Politics.* Chicago: University of Chicago Press, 1993.

Behrman, Bradley. "Civil Aeronautics Board." In *The Politics of Regulation*, edited by James Q. Wilson, 75–120. New York: Basic Books, 1980.

Belknap, George, and Angus Campbell. "Political Party Identification and Attitudes toward Foreign Policy." *Public Opinion Quarterly* 15 (1952): 601–623.

Berard, Stanley P. *Southern Democrats in the U.S. House of Representatives.* Norman: University of Oklahoma Press, 2001.

Berry, Jeffrey M. *The New Liberalism: The Rising Power of Citizen Groups.* Washington, DC: Brookings Institution, 1999.

Binder, Sarah A. *Minority Rights, Majority Rule: Partisanship and the Development of Congress.* New York: Cambridge University Press, 1997.

———. *Stalemate: Causes and Consequences of Legislative Gridlock.* Washington, DC: Brookings Institution, 2003.

Biven, W. Carl. *Jimmy Carter's Economy: Policy in an Age of Limits.* Chapel Hill: University of North Carolina Press, 2002.

Black, Earl, and Merle Black. *The Rise of Southern Republicans.* Cambridge, MA: Harvard University Press, 2002.

Blum, John Morton. *Years of Discord: American Politics and Society, 1961–1974.* New York: Norton, 1991.

Brady, David W., and Charles S. Bullock III. "Is There a Conservative Coalition in the House?" *Journal of Politics* 42 (1980): 549–559.

Brown, Anthony E. *The Politics of Airline Deregulation.* Knoxville: University of Tennessee Press, 1987.

Browning, Robert X. *Politics and Social Welfare Policy in the United States.* Knoxville: University of Tennessee Press, 1986.

Brown v. Board of Education of Topeka. 374 U.S. 483 (1954).

Brown v. Board of Education of Topeka II. 349 U.S. 294 (1955).

Bulman-Pozen, Jessica. "Partisan Federalism." *Harvard Law Review* 127 (2014): 1078–1146.

Burns, James MacGregor. *The Deadlock of Democracy: Four-Party Politics in America.* Englewood Cliffs, NJ: Prentice-Hall, 1963.

Burstein, Paul. *American Public Opinion, Advocacy, and Policy in Congress: What the Public Wants and What It Gets.* New York: Cambridge University Press, 2014.

Busch, Andrew W. *Horses in Midstream: U.S. Midterm Elections and Their Consequences, 1894–1998.* Pittsburgh: University of Pittsburgh Press, 1999.

Campbell, Angus, Philip E. Converse, Warren E. Miller, and Donald E. Stokes. *The American Voter.* New York: Wiley, 1960.

Campbell, James E. *The Presidential Pulse of Congressional Elections.* Lexington: University Press of Kentucky, 1993.

Carmines, Edward G., and James A. Stimson. *Issue Evolution: Race and the Transformation of American Politics.* Princeton, NJ: Princeton University Press, 1989.

Carmines, Edward G., and Michael W. Wagner. "Political Issues and Partisan Alignments: Assessing the Issue Evolution Perspective." *Annual Review of Political Science* 10 (2006): 67–81.

Carsey, Thomas M., and Geoffrey Layman. "Changing Sides or Changing Minds? Party Identification and Policy Preferences in the American Electorate." *American Journal of Political Science* 50 (2006): 464–477.

Ceaser, James W. *Presidential Selection: Theory and Development.* Princeton, NJ: Princeton University Press, 1979.

Ceaser, James W., and Andrew Busch. *Upside Down and Inside Out: The 1992 Elections and American Politics.* Lanham, MD: Rowman & Littlefield, 1993.

Ceaser, James W., Andrew E. Busch, and John J. Pitney Jr. *Epic Journey: The 2008 Elections and American Politics.* Lanham, MD: Rowman & Littlefield, 2009.

"Civil Rights Act of 1964." In *CQ Almanac 1964,* 338–353. 20th ed. Washington, DC: Congressional Quarterly, 1965.

Claggett, William J. M., and Byron E. Shafer. *The American Public Mind: The Issue Structure of Mass Politics in the Postwar United States.* New York: Cambridge University Press, 2010.

Clark, Peter B., and James Q. Wilson. "Incentive Systems: A Theory of Organizations." *Administrative Science Quarterly* 6 (1961): 129–166.

"Clean Air Bill Cleared with Auto Emission Deadline." In *CQ Almanac 1970,* 472–486. 26th ed. Washington, DC: Congressional Quarterly, 1971.

Cole, Wayne S. *Roosevelt and the Isolationists, 1932–1945.* Lincoln: University of Nebraska Press, 1983.

Coleman, John J. "United Government, Divided Government, and Party Responsiveness." *American Political Science Review* 93 (1999): 821–836.

Collins, Robert M. *More: The Politics of Economic Growth in Postwar America.* Oxford: Oxford University Press, 2000.

Congleton, Roger. "The Median Voter Model." In *The Encyclopedia of Public Choice,* edited by Charles K. Rowley and Friedrich Schneider, 382–387. New York: Kluwer Academic, 2004.

"Congress Approves Civil Rights Act of 1957." In *CQ Almanac 1957,* 553–569. 13th ed. Washington, DC: Congressional Quarterly, 1958.

"Congress Clears Airline Deregulation Bill." In *CQ Almanac 1978,* 496–504. 34th ed. Washington, DC: Congressional Quarterly, 1979.

"Congress Clears Trucking Deregulation Bill." In *CQ Almanac 1980,* 242–248. 36th ed. Washington, DC: Congressional Quarterly, 1981.

"Congress Enacts Area Redevelopment Bill." In *CQ Almanac 1961,* 247–256. 17th ed. Washington, DC: Congressional Quarterly, 1962.

"Congress Enacts Open Housing Legislation." In *CQ Almanac 1968,* 152–165. 24th ed. Washington, DC: Congressional Quarterly, 1969.

"Congress Enacts President Reagan's Tax Plan." In *CQ Almanac 1981,* 91–104. 37th ed. Washington, DC: Congressional Quarterly, 1982.

Costain, Anne N. *Inviting Women's Rebellion: A Political Process Interpretation of the Women's Movement.* Baltimore: Johns Hopkins University Press, 1992.

Cox, Gary W., and Samuel Kernell, eds. *The Politics of Divided Government.* Boulder, CO: Westview Press, 1991.

Critchlow, Donald T. *Phyllis Schlafly and Grassroots Conservatism: A Woman's Crusade.* Princeton, NJ: Princeton University Press, 2005.

Croly, Herbert D. *Progressive Democracy.* New York: Macmillan, 1915.

Crotty, William J. *Decision for the Democrats: Reforming the Party Structure.* Baltimore: Johns Hopkins University Press, 1978.

David, Paul T., Malcolm Moos, and Ralph M. Goldman. *Presidential Nominating Politics in 1952*. 5 vols. Baltimore: Johns Hopkins University Press, 1954.

Davies, Gareth. *From Opportunity to Entitlement: The Transformation and Decline of Great Society Liberalism*. Lawrence: University Press of Kansas, 1996.

———. *See Government Grow: Education Politics from Johnson to Reagan*. Lawrence: University Press of Kansas, 2007.

Davis, Kenneth S. *FDR: The New Deal Years, 1933–1937*. New York: Random House, 1979.

Davis, Otto A., M. A. H. Dempster, and Aaron Wildavsky. "A Theory of the Budgetary Process." *American Political Science Review* 60 (1966): 529–547.

———. "Towards a Predictive Theory of Government Expenditure: U.S. Domestic Appropriations." *British Journal of Political Science* 4 (1974): 419–452.

DeBenedetti, Charles. *An American Ordeal: The Antiwar Movement of the Vietnam Era*. Syracuse, NY: Syracuse University Press, 1990.

"Default Avoided at Eleventh Hour." In *CQ Almanac 2011*, 311–316. 67th ed. Washington, DC: CQ–Roll Call Group, 2012.

Derthick, Martha, and Paul J. Quirk, *The Politics of Deregulation*. Washington, DC: Brookings Institution, 1985.

DiSalvo, Daniel. *Agents of Change: Party Factions in American Politics, 1868–2012*. New York: Oxford University Press, 2012.

Divine, Robert A. *The Illusion of Neutrality*. Chicago: University of Chicago Press, 1962.

Dodds, Graham G. *Take Up Your Pen: Unilateral Presidential Directives in American Politics*. Philadelphia: University of Pennsylvania Press, 2013.

Doenecke, Justus D. *Not to the Swift: The Old Isolationists in the Cold War Era*. Lewisburg, PA: Bucknell University Press, 1979.

Downs, Anthony. *An Economic Theory of Democracy*. New York: Harper & Row, 1957.

Eccles, Marriner S. *Beckoning Frontiers*. New York: Knopf, 1951.

Engel v. Vitale. 370 U.S. 412 (1962).

Engle, Pär Jason, and Byron E. Shafer. "Where Are We in History? 2010 in the Longest Run." *Forum* 8, no. 4 (2010): article 1.

Engstrom, Erik J. *Partisan Gerrymandering and the Construction of American Democracy*. Ann Arbor: University of Michigan Press, 2013.

"Environmental Quality Council." In *CQ Almanac 1969*, 525–527. 25th ed. Washington, DC: Congressional Quarterly, 1970.

Erikson, Robert S., Michael B. MacKuen, and James A. Stimson. *The Macropolity*. New York: Cambridge University Press, 2002.

Erikson, Robert S., and Kent L. Tedin. "The 1928–1936 Partisan Realignment: The Case for the Conversion Hypothesis." *American Political Science Review* 75 (1981): 951–962.

Feinman, Ronald L. *Twilight of Progressivism: The Western Republican Senators and the New Deal*. Baltimore: Johns Hopkins University Press, 1981.

Fenno, Richard F., Jr. *Learning to Govern: An Institutional View of the 104th Congress*. Washington, DC: Brookings Institution, 1997.

———. *The Power of the Purse: Appropriations Politics in Congress.* Boston: Little, Brown, 1966.

Fiorina, Morris P. *Disconnect: The Breakdown of Representation in American Politics.* Norman: University of Oklahoma Press, 2009.

Flamm, Michael W. *Law and Order: Street Crime, Civil Unrest, and the Crisis of Liberalism in the 1960s.* New York: Columbia University Press, 2005.

Fleisher, Richard, and Jon R. Bond. "The Shrinking Middle in the U.S. Congress." *British Journal of Political Science* 34 (2004): 429–451.

Ford, Henry Jones. *The Rise and Growth of American Politics: A Sketch of Constitutional Development.* New York: Macmillan, 1898.

Francia, Peter L. *The Financiers of Congressional Elections: Investors, Ideologues, and Intimates.* New York: Columbia University Press, 2003.

Gaddis, John Lewis. *The Cold War.* London: Penguin, 2007.

———. *The United States and the Origins of the Cold War, 1941–1947.* New York: Columbia University Press, 1972.

The Gallup Organization Staff, eds. *The People, the Press, and Politics: The Times Mirror Study of the American Electorate.* Reading, MA: Addison-Wesley, 1988.

Gerring, John. *Party Ideologies in America, 1828–1996.* Cambridge: Cambridge University Press, 1998.

Gideon v. Wainwright. 372 U.S. 335 (1963).

Gormley, William T., Jr. *Taming the Bureaucracy: Muscles, Prayers, and Other Strategies.* Princeton, NJ: Princeton University Press, 1989.

Gould, Lewis L. *The Grand Old Party: A History of the Republicans.* New York: Random House, 2003.

Graham, Hugh Davis. *The Civil Rights Era: Origins and Development of National Policy, 1960–1972.* New York: Oxford University Press, 1990.

Green, Matthew N. *Underdog Politics: The Minority Party in the U.S. House of Representatives.* New Haven, CT: Yale University Press, 2015.

Green v. County School Board of New Kent County. 391 U.S. 430 (1968).

Griswold v. Connecticut. 381 U.S. 479 (1965).

Hacker, Jacob S., and Paul Pierson. *Off Center: The Republican Revolution and the Erosion of American Democracy.* New Haven, CT: Yale University Press, 2005.

Hamby, Alonzo L. *For the Survival of Democracy: Franklin Roosevelt and the World Crisis of the 1930s.* New York: Free Press, 2004.

———. *The Imperial Years: The United States since 1939.* New York: Weybright and Talley, 1976.

———. *Man of the People: The Life of Harry S. Truman.* New York: Oxford University Press, 1995.

Hays, Samuel P. *Beauty, Health, and Permanence: Environmental Politics in the United States, 1955–1985.* Cambridge: Cambridge University Press, 1989.

Heberlig, Eric S. *Congressional Parties, Institutional Ambition, and the Financing of Majority Control.* Ann Arbor: University of Michigan Press, 2012.

Hill, Kevin A. "Does the Creation of Majority Black Districts Aid Republicans? An Analysis of the 1992 Congressional Elections in Eight Southern States." *Journal of Politics* 57 (1995): 384–401.

"Housing Act of 1949 S1070—P.L. 171." In *CQ Almanac 1949*, 273–286. 5th ed. Washington, DC: Congressional Quarterly, 1950.

Hyman, Herbert H. *Taking Society's Measure: A Personal History of Survey Research.* New York: Russell Sage Foundation, 1991.

Jacobson, Gary C. *The Electoral Origins of Divided Government: Competition in House Elections, 1946–1988.* Boulder, CO: Westview Press, 1990.

Jenkins, Jeffery A., and Justin Peck. "Building toward Major Policy Change: Congressional Action on Civil Rights, 1941–1950." *Law and History Review* 31 (2013): 139–198.

Johnson, Dennis W. *The Laws That Shaped America: Fifteen Acts of Congress and Their Lasting Impact.* New York: Routledge, 2009.

Jones, Charles O. *Clean Air: The Policies and Politics of Pollution Control.* Pittsburgh: University of Pittsburgh Press, 1975.

———. *The Minority Party in Congress.* Boston: Little, Brown, 1970.

———. *The Presidency in a Separated System.* Washington, DC: Brookings Institution, 1994.

———. *The Republican Party in American Politics.* New York: Macmillan, 1965.

———. *Separate but Equal Branches: Congress and the Presidency.* Chatham, NJ: Chatham House, 1995.

Joyce, Philip G. *The Congressional Budget Office: Honest Numbers, Power, and Policymaking.* Washington, DC: Georgetown University Press, 2011.

Karnes, Thomas L. *Asphalt and Politics: A History of the American Highway System.* Jefferson, NC: McFarland, 2009.

Katznelson, Ira. *Fear Itself: The New Deal and the Origins of Our Time.* New York: Norton, 2013.

Keith, Bruce E., David B. Magleby, Candice J. Nelson, Elizabeth Orr, Mark C. Westlye, and Raymond E. Wolfinger. *The Myth of the Independent Voter.* Berkeley: University of California Press, 1992.

Kennedy, David M. *Freedom from Fear: The American People in Depression and War.* New York: Oxford University Press, 1999.

Kennedy, Susan Estabrook. *The Banking Crisis of 1933.* Lexington: University Press of Kentucky, 1973.

Key, V. O., Jr. *Southern Politics in State and Nation.* New York: Knopf, 1949.

Kingdon, John W. *Agendas, Alternatives, and Public Policy.* Boston: Little, Brown, 1984.

Klarman, Michael J. *From Jim Crow to Civil Rights: The Supreme Court in the Struggle for Racial Equality.* New York: Oxford University Press, 2004.

Koger, Gregory. *Filibustering: A Political History of Obstruction in the House and the Senate.* Chicago: University of Chicago Press, 2010.

Ladd, Everett Carll, Jr. "Liberalism Upside Down: The Inversion of the New Deal Order." *Political Science Quarterly* 91 (1976–1977): 577–600.

La Raja, Raymond. *Small Change: Money, Political Parties, and Campaign Finance Reform.* Ann Arbor: University of Michigan Press, 2008.

"Last-Minute Deal Averts Fiscal Cliff, Punts Big Issues to New Congress." In *CQ Almanac 2012*, 73–77. 68th ed. Washington, DC: CQ–Roll Call Group, 2013.

Layman, Geoffrey C., Thomas M. Carsey, John C. Green, Richard Herrara, and Rosalyn Cooperman. "Activists and Conflict Extension in American Party Politics." *American Political Science Review* 104 (2010): 324–346.

Lee, Frances E. "American Politics Is More Competitive Than Ever, and That Is Making Partisanship Worse." In *Political Polarization in American Politics*, edited by Daniel J. Hopkins and John Sides, 76–79. New York: Bloomsbury, 2015.

Lee, R. Alton. *Truman and Taft-Hartley: A Question of Mandate*. Lexington: University Press of Kentucky, 1966.

Leuchtenburg, William E. *Franklin D. Roosevelt and the New Deal, 1932–1940*. New York: Harper & Row, 1963.

———. *The Supreme Court Reborn: The Constitutional Revolution in the Age of Roosevelt*. New York: Oxford University Press, 1995.

Levendusky, Matthew. *How Partisan Media Polarize America*. Chicago: University of Chicago Press, 2013.

———. *The Partisan Sort: How Liberals Became Democrats and Conservatives Became Republicans*. Chicago: University of Chicago Press, 2009.

Liroff, Richard A. *A National Policy for the Environment: NEPA and Its Aftermath*. Bloomington: Indiana University Press, 1976.

Lunch, William M. *The Nationalization of American Politics*. Berkeley: University of California Press, 1987.

Manley, John F. "The Conservative Coalition in Congress." *American Behavioral Scientist* 17 (1973): 223–247.

Mann, Thomas E., and Norman J. Ornstein. *It's Even Worse Than It Looks: How the American Constitutional System Collided with the New Politics of Extremism*. New York: Basic Books, 2012.

Manna, Paul. *School's In: Federalism and the National Education Agenda*. Washington, DC: Georgetown University Press, 2006.

Masket, Seth E. *No Middle Ground: How Informal Party Organizations Control Nominations and Polarize Legislatures*. Ann Arbor: University of Michigan Press, 2014.

Mason, Robert. *The Republican Party and American Politics from Hoover to Reagan*. Cambridge: Cambridge University Press, 2012.

———. *Richard Nixon and the Quest for a New Republican Majority*. Chapel Hill: University of North Carolina Press, 2004.

Matusow, Allen J. *Nixon's Economy: Booms, Busts, Dollars, and Votes*. Lawrence: University Press of Kansas, 1998.

Mayer, Kenneth R. *With the Stroke of a Pen: Executive Orders and Presidential Power*. Princeton, NJ: Princeton University Press, 2001.

Mayhew, David R. *Divided We Govern: Party Control, Lawmaking, and Investigations, 1946–1990*. New Haven, CT: Yale University Press, 1991.

———. *Electoral Realignments: A Critique of an American Genre*. New Haven, CT: Yale University Press, 2002.

———. *Placing Parties in American Politics: Organization, Electoral Settings, and Government Activity in the Twentieth Century*. Princeton, NJ: Princeton University Press, 1986.

McCaffery, Peter. *When Bosses Ruled Philadelphia: The Emergence of the Republican Machine, 1867–1933*. University Park: Pennsylvania State University Press, 1993.

McClosky, Herbert, Paul J. Hoffman, and Rosemary O'Hara. "Issue Conflict and Consensus among Party Leaders and Followers." *American Political Science Review* 52 (1958): 27–45.

McKee, Seth C. "Majority Black Districts, Republican Ascendancy, and Party Competition in the South, 1988–2000." *American Review of Politics* 23 (2002): 123–139.

Milkis, Sidney M. *Political Parties and Constitutional Government: Remaking American Democracy*. Baltimore: Johns Hopkins University Press, 1999.

———. *The President and the Parties: The Transformation of the American Party System since the New Deal*. New York: Oxford University Press, 1993.

Miranda v. Arizona. 384 U.S. 436 (1966).

Monmonier, Mark S. *Bushmanders and Bullwinkles: How Politicians Manipulate Election Maps and Census Data to Win Elections*. Chicago: University of Chicago Press, 2001.

Morehead v. New York Ex. Rel. Tipaldo. 298 U.S. 587 (1936).

Morgan, Iwan W. *Beyond the Liberal Consensus: A Political History of the United States since 1965*. New York: St. Martin's, 1994.

Murray v. Curlett. 374 U.S. 203 (1963).

National Labor Relations Board v. Jones & Laughlin Steel Corp. 301 U.S. 1 (1937).

Nelson, Michael, ed. *The Elections of 1992*. Washington, DC: CQ Press, 1993.

———, ed. *The Elections of 2008*. Washington, DC: CQ Press, 2010.

Neustadt, Richard E. "Congress and the Fair Deal: A Legislative Balance Sheet." In *Harry S. Truman and the Fair Deal*, edited by Alonzo L. Hamby, 15–42. Lexington, MA: Heath, 1974.

Nivola, Pietro S., and David W. Brady, eds. *Red and Blue Nation?* Vol. 1, *Characteristics and Consequences of America's Polarized Politics*. Washington, DC: Brookings Institution, 2006.

———, eds. *Red and Blue Nation?* Vol. 2, *Consequences and Correction of America's Polarized Politics*. Washington, DC: Brookings Institution, 2008.

Norpoth, Helmut, Andrew H. Sidman, and Clara H. Suong. "Polls and Elections: The New Deal Realignment in Real Time." *Presidential Studies Quarterly* 43 (2013): 146–166.

Oldfield, Duane Murray. *The Right and the Righteous: The Christian Right Confronts the Republican Party*. Lanham, MD: Rowman & Littlefield, 1996.

Ortiz, Stephen R. *Beyond the Bonus March and the GI Bill: How Veterans Politics Shaped the New Deal Era*. New York: New York University Press, 2010.

Oxford Companion to the Supreme Court of the United States. Edited by Kermit L. Hall. Oxford: Oxford University Press, 1992.

Parker, Randall E., ed. *The Economics of the Great Depression: A Twenty-First Century Look Back at the Economics of the Interwar Years*. Northampton, MA: Edward Elgar, 2007.

"Party Unity on Tax, Spending Issues—Less in House, More in Senate." *National Journal*, May 7, 1983, 936–952.

Pastor, Robert A. *Congress and the Politics of U.S. Foreign Economic Policy, 1929–1976.* Berkeley: University of California Press, 1980.

Patterson, James T. *America's Struggle against Poverty, 1900–1985.* Cambridge, MA: Harvard University Press, 1986.

———. *Brown v. Board of Education: A Civil Rights Milestone and Its Troubled Legacy.* New York: Oxford University Press, 2001.

———. *Congressional Conservatism and the New Deal.* Lexington: University Press of Kentucky, 1967.

———. *Grand Expectations: The United States, 1945–1974.* New York: Oxford University Press, 1996.

———. *Restless Giant: The United States from Watergate to Bush v. Gore.* New York: Oxford University Press, 2005.

Phillips, Kevin. *The Emerging Republican Majority.* New Rochelle, NY: Arlington House, 1969.

Pierson, Paul, and Theda Skocpol, eds. *The Transformation of American Politics: Activist Government and the Rise of Conservatism.* Princeton, NJ: Princeton University Press, 2007.

Plessy v. Ferguson. 163 U.S. 537 (1896).

Polsby, Nelson W. *How Congress Evolves: Social Bases of Institutional Change.* New York: Oxford University Press, 2004.

———. *Political Innovation in America: The Politics of Policy Initiation.* New Haven, CT: Yale University Press, 1984.

Pomper, Gerald M., ed. *The Election of 1992: Reports and Interpretations.* Chatham, NJ: Chatham House, 1993.

Poole, Keith T., and Howard Rosenthal. *Congress: A Political-Economic History of Roll Call Voting.* New York: Oxford University Press, 1997.

Prasad, Monica. "The Popular Origins of Neoliberalism in the Reagan Tax Cut of 1981." *Journal of Policy History* 24 (2012): 351–383.

Rae, Nicol C. *Conservative Reformers: The Republican Freshmen and the Lessons of the 104th Congress.* Armonk, NY: Sharpe, 1998.

———. *Southern Democrats.* New York: Oxford University Press, 1994.

Rapoport, Ronald B., and Walter J. Stone. *Three's a Crowd: The Dynamics of Third Parties, Ross Perot, and Republican Resurgence.* Ann Arbor: University of Michigan Press, 2011.

"Reconciliation Savings: $130 Billion by 1985." In *CQ Almanac 1982*, 199–204. 38th ed. Washington, DC: Congressional Quarterly, 1983.

Reichley, A. James. *The Life of the Parties: A History of American Political Parties.* New York: Free Press, 1992.

Reiter, Howard L., and Jeffrey M. Stonecash. *Counter Realignment: Political Change in the Northeastern United States.* New York: Cambridge University Press, 2011.

Rieselbach, Leroy N. *Congressional Reform.* Washington, DC: CQ Press, 1986.

Robyn, Dorothy. *Braking the Special Interests: Trucking Deregulation and the Politics of Policy Reform.* Chicago: University of Chicago Press, 1987.

Roe v. Wade. 410 U.S. 113 (1973).

Rohde, David W. *Parties and Leaders in the Postreform House.* Chicago: University of Chicago Press, 1991.

Rose, Mark H., and Raymond A. Mohl. *Interstate: Highway Politics and Policy since 1939*. Knoxville: University of Tennessee Press, 1979.

Rubin, Richard L. *Party Dynamics: The Democratic Coalition and the Politics of Change*. New York: Oxford University Press, 1976.

Scammon, Richard M., and Ben J. Wattenberg. *The Real Majority*. New York: Coward-McCann, 1970.

Schechter Poultry Corp. v. United States. 295 U.S. 495 (1935).

Schickler, Eric, and Devin Caughey. "Public Opinion, Organized Labor, and the Limits of New Deal Liberalism, 1936–1945." *Studies in American Political Development* 25 (2011): 162–189.

Shafer, Byron E. *Bifurcated Politics: Evolution and Reform in the National Party Convention*. Cambridge, MA: Harvard University Press, 1988.

———. "The Pure Partisan Institution: National Party Conventions as Research Sites." In *Oxford Handbook of American Political Parties and Interest Groups*, edited by L. Sandy Maisel, 264–284. New York: Oxford University Press, 2010.

———. *Quiet Revolution: The Struggle for the Democratic Party and the Shaping of Post-reform Politics*. New York: Russell Sage Foundation, 1983.

———. *The Two Majorities and the Puzzle of Modern American Politics*. Lawrence: University Press of Kansas, 2003.

Shafer, Byron E., and William J. M. Claggett. *The Two Majorities: The Issue Context of Modern American Politics*. Baltimore: Johns Hopkins University Press, 1995.

Shafer, Byron E., and Richard Johnson. *The End of Southern Exceptionalism: Class, Race, and Partisan Change in the Postwar South*. Cambridge, MA: Harvard University Press, 2006.

Shafer, Byron E., Regina L. Wagner, and Pär Jason Engle. "The 2014 Midterm in the Longest Run: The Puzzle of a Modern Era." *Forum* 12, no. 4 (2014): article 1.

Shelley, Mack C., II. *The Permanent Majority: The Conservative Coalition in the United States Congress*. University: University of Alabama Press, 1983.

Shepsle, Kenneth A. "Congressional Institutions and Behavior: The Changing Textbook Congress." In *American Political Institutions and the Problems of Our Time*, edited by John E. Chubb and Paul E. Peterson, 238–266. Washington, DC: Brookings Institution, 1989.

Sinclair, Barbara. *Unorthodox Lawmaking: New Legislative Processes in the U.S. Congress*. Washington, DC: CQ Press, 1997.

Sloan, John W. *The Reagan Effect: Economics and Presidential Leadership*. Lawrence: University Press of Kansas, 1999.

Smith v. Allwright. 321 U.S. 649 (1944).

Stimson, James A. *Public Opinion in America: Moods, Cycles, and Swings*. Boulder, CO: Westview, 1991.

Sundquist, James L. *Constitutional Reform and Effective Government*. Washington, DC: Brookings Institution, 1986.

———. *Dynamics of the Party System: Alignment and Realignment of the Political Parties in the United States*. Washington, DC: Brookings Institution, 1973.

———. *Politics and Policy: The Eisenhower, Kennedy, and Johnson Years*. Washington, DC: Brookings Institution, 1968.

Swann v. Charlotte-Mecklenberg Board of Education. 401 U.S. 1 (1971).

Tananbaum, Duane. *The Bricker Amendment Controversy: A Test of Eisenhower's Leadership.* Ithaca, NY: Cornell University Press, 1988.

Theriault, Sean M. *Party Polarization in Congress.* Cambridge: Cambridge University Press, 2008.

Thurber, James A., ed. *Divided Democracy: Cooperation and Conflict between the President and Congress.* Washington, DC: CQ Press, 1991.

Truman, David B. *The Congressional Party: A Case Study.* New York: Wiley, 1959.

United States v. Butler. 297 U.S. 1 (1936).

Valelly, Richard M. *The Two Reconstructions: The Struggle for Black Enfranchisement.* Chicago: University of Chicago Press, 2004.

Ware, Alan. *The Breakdown of Democratic Party Organization, 1940–1980.* Oxford: Clarendon Press, 1985.

———. *The Democratic Party Heads North, 1877–1962.* Cambridge: Cambridge University Press, 2006.

West Coast Hotel Co. v. Parrish. 300 U.S. 379 (1936).

Whitaker, John C. *Striking a Balance: Environment and Natural Resource Policy in the Nixon-Ford Years.* Washington, DC: American Enterprise Institute, 1976.

"White House, Lawmakers Agree on Extension of Bush-Era Tax Cuts." In *CQ Almanac 2010,* 143–145. 66th ed. Washington, DC: CQ–Roll Call Group, 2011.

Wilcox, Clyde. *God's Warriors: The Christian Right in Twentieth-Century America.* Baltimore: Johns Hopkins University Press, 1992.

Wildavsky, Aaron. *The New Politics of the Budgetary Process.* Glenview, IL: Scott, Foresman, 1988.

———. *The Politics of the Budgetary Process.* Boston: Little, Brown, 1964.

Wildavsky, Aaron, and Naomi Caiden. *The New Process of the Budgetary Process.* 4th ed. New York: Addison-Wesley, 2001.

Wilson, James Q. *The Amateur Democrat: Club Politics in Three Cities.* Chicago: University of Chicago Press, 1966.

———. "Crime in the Streets." *Public Interest* 5 (1966): 26–35.

———. *Political Organizations.* New York: Basic Books, 1973.

Witte, John F. *The Politics and Development of the Income Tax.* Madison: University of Wisconsin Press, 1985.

Young, Nancy Beck. *Why We Fight: Congress and the Politics of World War II.* Lawrence: University Press of Kansas, 2013.

Zelizer, Julian E. *On Capitol Hill: The Struggle to Reform Congress and Its Consequences, 1948–2000.* Cambridge: Cambridge University Press, 2004.

Index